Missions of Fire and Mercy

Until Death Do Us Part

By
William E. Peterson

Cover photo by Eddie Hoklotubbe/William Peterson:
Waiting out the fog over the mountains prior to the initial assault on
the Ashau Valley. We were mortared just after this photo was taken,
with no losses. Note bomb craters on mountainside.

MISSIONS OF FIRE AND MERCY
Until Death Do Us Part

Published by: William E. Peterson

Formatting and book cover design by Jeremy Peterson

All biblical quotes taken from the NIV.

Please visit my website at: **www.MissionsOfFireAndMercy.com**

Printing by Booksurge
7390 B
Charleston, SC 29418

Second Edition

Printed in the United States of America

COMMENTS ABOUT MISSIONS OF FIRE AND MERCY

"The Vietnam War is best seen through the memories of a UH-1 Huey door gunner. Peterson captures the feeling of what it was like to fly and fight and in the end be a survivor!"

—George J. Marrett, author of *"Cheating Death: Combat Air Rescues in Vietnam and Laos."*

"The door gunner has no equal when it comes to gallantry and just plain grit. Every "Rice Warrior" who has flown into a hot LZ (landing zone), has watched the door gunner at work, laying down blazing fire on the enemy, keeping his head down, while offloading and prepping for the next assault. The men who went into battle while riding the UH-1 Huey will remember the smell of JP-4, cordite, and napalm. They will always remember the wop-wop-wop sound of the chopper blades. After the war, the UH-1 and actions of the Door gunner were just fleeting memories. The author has brought them back to life in MISSIONS OF FIRE AND MERCY. This is a pinnacle in Bill Peterson's life."

—J.N. McFadden, *CWO Aviation Ret.*

"This is a well written story about a crew member on a Huey helicopter, standing in the doorway, shooting it out with a skillful and determined enemy hidden in the jungles of Vietnam. Intermingled is a story about four pillars of inner mental peace; i.e. love of God, love of country, love of family and love of sweetheart. Some, or all of these pillars are of great help to military personnel as they face the strong possibility of injury or death. This is a very introspective read."

—Gunnar F. Wilster, *Captain, USN (Retired)*

"Get ready to climb into a Huey and ride the skies with the Ghost Riders, a place where very few have gone. MISSIONS OF FIRE AND MERCY is more than a war story; it is the true experience of a warrior recounted in a tasteful manner that everyone can appreciate. You won't want to miss this tour of duty."

—SP5 Eddie G. Hoklotubbe, Ghost Riders Door gunner, '67-68

"Since his days as one of my flight students, I have pestered Bill about his experiences in Vietnam. Although a VMI graduate, I was never under fire. The author's stories, some humorous, others horrific, have always piqued my interest in the concept of the citizen soldier. I'm honored to have heard many of the episodes herein and to learn of the experiences of a crew chief/gunner in Vietnam."

—Dean Armstrong, Jr., Pilot NWA

Table of Contents

ACKNOWLEDGEMENTS

Before you read this book, I would like you to know that the facts and dates here were taken from letters saved by my father that I sent to my family during my Vietnam tour. Though my memory is poor at best on a day to day basis, I have very good recall on the majority of missions. They have been profoundly engraved into my long-term memory. Wherever possible, actual names have been used. However, on the rare occasions where actual names are not easily recalled, others have been inserted.

Missions of Fire and Mercy has been in the mill for several years. When I first began writing, I went at it with a passion. One of my sisters, Mary Jane Worden (MJ), also an author, was my mentor, and a great editor. When she met an untimely death due to cancer, my desire to write took a back seat...I lost all interest. Through family encouragement, I finally picked up my laptop again and spent several more years documenting my experiences.

My entire family has been very supportive and several helped me with opinions and editing. My Mom and Dad relived my tour by reading rough drafts of chapters one at a time. It brought back a lot of memories for them, and opened their eyes to things they had never been privy to. They wrote a LOT of letters to me, helping me to stay sane. Though Dad did most of the writing, Mom did all of the typing, mailing and filing of their letters, and typed copies of all my letters to send to all my siblings. She deserves an award of meritorious service. My oldest sister and her husband, Fran and Ed Lambeth were instrumental in helping out where MJ was forced to discontinue. The red ink flowed, but for good reason...the manuscript was in great need. My daughter, Jennifer who is a fourth grade teacher, is always looking for papers to correct and was a great help. Without my computer guru son, Jeremy, assisting me through all my computer and brain glitches, I would still be on page one. I was astounded by his patience.

Several friends also had a hand in reading parts or all of the manuscript in its raw form. Eddie Hoklotubbe, my main gunner in Vietnam and his wife Sara, also an author, were great encouragers and editors. Allan Ney, another crew chief, kept hammering on me to get this project completed. Dean Armstrong, my former flight instructor and good friend, was a great encourager and editor. Another good friend, Joy Smelser also owns a now empty red pen. Her help was tremendous. Then there is my daughter-in-law, Kristin. Just when I thought I was finished writing, she read it while grasping a red ink pen, using it vigorously.

Cindi supported me during my tour of duty in so many ways. She has been my wife for forty one years, and has stood by me and been a terrific encouragement to me through thick and thin. My best friend has always supported me in all my ventures. Without her, this book would still be sitting in my computer file folder, begging attention.

GLOSSARY

9+2 Gaggle: Nine slicks with a two ship gunship escort.
AAA: Anti aircraft fire.
AC: Aircraft Commander.
AIT: Advanced infantry training.
AK: AK47 communist semi-auto rifle.
AO: Area of operations.
ARA: Aerial rocket artillery.
AR15: Modified M15.
Arc Light: Code name for a B-52 bomb strike.
Arty: Ground based artillery.
ARVN: Army of the Republic of South Vietnam.
Autorotation: Helicopter emergency procedure for landing without power, such as engine out, loss of tail rotor, or serious mechanical problems.
BDA: Bomb damage assesment.
Big Eye: Infrared scope mounted on jeep.
Bird Dog: Cessna O-1. Tandem aircraft flown by a single pilot and observer in the rear seat.
C&C: Command and control. The commander of an operation often flew above the battlefield where he was able to assess the situation and give orders to the ground forces.
CA: Combat assault.
Charlie, Charles or Mr. Charles: Nickname for the enemy.
Charlie-Charlie: See C&C above.

Chicken Plate: Fifty pound Kevlar chest protector worn by crew chief and gunner. In addition, sliding bullet proof shields between the pilot and his door.

Civvies: Civilian clothes.

Clear: Yelled prior to starting an aircraft after looking to be sure everyone is clear of the area.

Click: One thousand meters.

Collective: Operated by pilot's left hand for control of blade pitch for climbs and descents. The throttle control was also operated here.

Cong: South Vietnamese communist troops.

C.O.: Company Commander.

CP: Command post.

CQ: Company Quarterly. Man on duty twenty four hours per day to do necessary company duties, including waking and messages to crews.

Crank: The initial starting of aircraft engines.

Cyclic: "Joy stick" control used for directional control of helicopter.

Delta Mission: A mission behind enemy lines.

DEROS: Date of expected rotation out of service.

Deuce and a half: 2 ½ ton, 6 wheel drive military utility truck.

DFC: Distinguished Flying Cross.

EGT: Exhaust gas temperature.

FAC: Forward Air Controller.

FRAGS: Fragmentation grenades.

Freq: Radio frequencies.

Gaggle: A flight of aircraft.

Gooks: Nickname for Vietnamese.

Grease Gun: Short .45 caliber sub machine gun.

Green Beanies: Green Berets.

Grunts: American soldiers in the field. Spoken with a great deal of respect.

Gunship: Huey helicopter armed with a 20mm cannon, two 7.62mm Gatling guns, 76 aerial rockets, and one or two gunners armed with M60 machine guns.

Hootch: Vietnamese hut constructed of bamboo and local grasses.

Hot Massage: Prepping an LZ by bombers, fighters, and artillery prior to helicopter aerial attack.

Huey: Bell UH-1 helicopter.

Incoming: Enemy fire.

Input quill: The connecting shaft between the engine and transmission.

In-trail: Aircraft flown in formation one behind the other.

KIA: Killed in action.

Lightning Bug: Flare ship for nite hunter Missions.

Listre Bag: Thirty gallon canvas water bag suspended from tripod.

LRRP: Long-range reconnaissance patrol.

Loach: Nickname for light observation helicopters (LOH), whose job was to fly low and slow searching out the enemy.

Log Runs: Logistical supply missions flying food, water, ammo and whatever else was needed by the troops in the field.

LZ: Landing zone.

M16: 5.56mm automatic rifle.

M60: Machine gun firing 7.62mm rounds.

M79: Hand held 40mm grenade launcher.

medivac:: Medical evacuations.

Military Time: The 24-hour clock is used by the military. Starting with midnight as 2400, 1:00 a.m. is 0100, etc. and counting up to 2400 again.

Mini Gun: Six 7.62mm barrels mounted on each side of a gunship. The barrels turn in a rotary fashion, sending out wicked streams of destructive fire.

Montagnards: South Vietnamese hill tribesmen related ethnically to Polynesians. Heavily recruited as mercenaries for SOG and other Special Forces units, called "Yards" by Americans.

MOS: Military Occupation Specialty.

Newbie: New replacement in the unit.

nite hunter Mission: Two slicks plus 1-2 gunships. High slick drops flares over a suspected enemy area with rivers. Low level bird has sniper laying on floor with sniper rifle equipped with Starlite scope to spot the enemy sampans. Sniper shoots tracers to mark sampan, gunners open up and drop white phosphorous grenades on the sampan, while gunships roll in and finish the job with rockets and minigun and canon fire.

NVA: North Vietnamese Army.

Old Man: Slang used for the Commander of a unit.

POL (Petroleum Oil Lubricants).Dump: Designated refueling area.

PSP: Perforated Steel Planking.

PSYOPS: Psychological Operations.

PZ: Pickup zone.

R & R: Rest and recuperation.

Rabbit: Low ship with sniper on board with Starlight scoped rifle.

Racetrack Pattern: Usually an oval pattern flown by aircraft that are in an area for holding position while awaiting orders.

Revetment: Parking place for helicopters. Sandbags were piled about four feet high along the pad on the front and two sides to help protect it from flying bullets and shrapnel.

RF or RRF: Ready reaction force. Team on standby alert.

RPG: Rocket propelled grenade.

RTF: Return to service flight after maintenance.

Sampan: Local boats of various sizes built by the Vietnamese from local materials.

Scout: Small helicopter used for low level observation.

Section Eight: Medical discharge for being mentally incompetent.

Short: Nickname for a short time left in country.

Short Shaft: Drive shaft connecting the transmission to the engine.

SITREP: Situation report of enemy movement.

Six: Designation for the man in charge of mission.

Sky Troopers: Infantry supported by helicopter.

Slick: Huey used mainly for the transportation of troops and material to and from the field. Crewed by two pilots, one crew chief/gunner, and an additional gunner.

Sneaky Pete: Operations into Laos and Cambodia by SOG teams.

SOG: Studies and Observations Group consisting of Special Forces Teams.

Sorties: Each flight within a mission.

SOS: Military meal of chipped beef on toast. (S--t) on a shingle.

Spider Holes: Well camouflaged holes in the ground used by the enemy for quick escape and evasion, often leading into a tunnel complex. They often popped out of a camouflaged hole to take a couple shots and then ducked back in to hide.

TAC AIR: Tactical air strike.

TOC: Tactical Operations Command.

Top: Company First Sergeant.

V Device: When the letter "V" is seen on a medal or ribbon, it represents a Valorous act by recipient.

Victor Charles: Viet Cong. Military men made up of indigenous South Vietnamese Communists.

WIA: Wounded in action.

Willy Peter: White phosphorous.

White Robe Six (WR6): Reverent call sign that flight crews have created for God.

Xin Loi: Vietnamese for "Sorry about that."

XO: Company Executive Officer.

Yellow One: Lead ship in an aerial assault flown by the flight leader.

CHAPTER 1

LACK OF ADVENTURE

Fall 1966
Michigan State University
East Lansing, Michigan

Though my heart wasn't in it, following a summer road
construction job right out of high school, I headed for Michigan
State University. I wasn't exactly the Valedictorian of my high
school class, but most of my friends left for school, so for lack of
anything better to do I decided to join them. I made friends quickly,
despite not being much of a party animal.

I'm having a great time. My grades prove it. First semester
and I'm bored beyond belief. Textbooks make me crazy! I don't
know what I want to do with my life. I just feel a need for some
excitement.

Every time I watch the nightly news and see the helicopters
in action and hear the harrowing stories, I know I want to go to
Vietnam and somehow get involved with choppers. I don't know
much about it, but that isn't going to stop me. I want action and feel
the war can provide that. One small problem…how can I break this
to my folks?

My Dad, an old B-17 pilot, has always told fascinating flying
stories. Surely he'll understand my desire for a little adrenaline rush.
My Mom, on the other hand, may not feel quite the same way. I'll
call them tonight. I won't mention my grades. I've likely set an all
time record here at MSU and I certainly don't plan to mention that
I'm on the top of the Dean's list…the wrong one.

When I make the call, collect of course, both Mom and Dad are home. After the small talk, I hurry into my pitch before they have a chance to ask about my grades. After explaining my unhappiness with the rigors of school, the "left-wing" profs, my boredom and my desire to have a little excitement in my life, Dad responds.

"Have you thought about the military?"

Is this easy, or what? With Dad explaining that two or three years of military discipline might help me decide what I'd like to do with my life, I'm sold.

Mom is as silent as a stone…but I know what she's thinking. When asked what she thinks, she has only one comment.

"If you enlist, you'll probably have to go to Vietnam, ya know. I'm not sure I like that idea."

I assure her that if I am sent to Vietnam, God will look after me. After all, consider the number of guys who have come home from there unscathed. We don't discuss those returning daily from Vietnam in body bags. It's a done deal. We agree that if that's what I want to do, it's my life. I'm a big boy.

I stay for the balance of the semester, but am unable to concentrate on my studies. All I can think of is flying low level over the jungle in a helicopter. How much fun could that be?

During Christmas vacation, I visit the recruiter. He makes the usual promises, and I believe all of them. I'd love to be a helicopter pilot, but right now the army is recommending two years of college. This isn't a requirement, the recruiter assures me, just a suggestion. Deciding that I really don't want to compete with the warrant officer candidates who have more college than I, my decision is to be a helicopter crew chief.

That will get me on flight status and to Vietnam more quickly. The adventure of my life would soon begin!

CHAPTER 2

CHARMED LIFE

Up to this point in my nineteen years, I've lived a pretty charmed life. Growing up in the north woods of the Upper Peninsula, I've spent most of my spare time hunting, fishing, and trapping. What more could a young man ask than to top it off by going to war?

Boy, did I have my head in the sand!

I have the idea that being a crew chief aboard a helicopter will give me all the thrills that I'm seeking. Any thought that I might be wounded, captured or killed is nonexistent for me. And that's what made it even more tantalizing... anticipating the unknown. Little did I know what this adventure might entail, or how drastically it would change my life!

I grew up in a great family with one younger brother, Bruce and four sisters; Fran, Mary Jane (MJ), Lin and Barb. I was third in line. I got along well with my siblings. I had to. We grew up in Carney, Michigan, a small town of about 300. Though there were plenty of kids around, we all had to make our own fun. We had a terrific time together...spring, summer, fall or winter...it didn't matter. It was a great place to grow up.

In the spring, my buddies and I would get together and, donning long johns, jeans, a couple of sweatshirts, and tennies, we would head for Guard's Creek just after the ice went out. The water was fast and furious. Did I mention ...cold? Braving the frigid water for the great adrenaline rush, we plunged in one by one and body surfed downstream in the swift current. We would "surf" until numb and then swim to the bank. We each carried a waterproof Boy Scout

3

matchbox and with our frozen, shaky hands managed to get a fire started. After an hour or so, we thawed out.

In the summer we fished endlessly. When the apples were ripe, we had apple fights. We also amused ourselves by going down to the railroad tracks and throwing apples at the occasional guy we saw hitching a ride on a flat car.

After the apples fell, we hunted and trapped every chance we could get before the harsh winter set in. Even after the streams and ponds were frozen over, we continued to hunt and trap. Snowshoes were often needed to participate in the outdoor sports we enjoyed, but winter didn't slow us down. We built duck blinds on the frozen pond by chopping holes in the ice in order to drive poles in the mud while standing on the solid ice. This was much easier than trying to do it from a rocking boat or canoe.

Playing hockey on the local duck pond and ice-skating up the river on a clear moonlit night was one of our favorite pastimes, particularly with a date in tow.

When ice storms followed a severe snowstorm and covered the deep snow with a layer of crust, we would wrap binder twine on the tires of our bicycles. With the added traction, we'd race over the hardened snow down a farmer's steep hill. Whoever broke through first, lost the race.

We spent hours building ski jumps and "going for the record." I spent a fair amount of time on crutches. What a great life!

Later on in high school, I worked for my father in the rustic wood fence manufacturing plant that he owned with my Uncle Vince. That cut into my program, but the money was nice for an occasional date or box of shotgun shells, depending on the current need.

Terrific Christian parents raised our family. When the doors of our small country church were open, I was expected to be there with the rest of my family. With the church right across the street, it was difficult to come up with an excuse to skip out. I recall one blustery Sunday when we were one of two families in church. The snow was deep and the drifts deeper, but we were there with the Guard's, another die-hard family. After a little small talk, we all trudged home through the snow. That was great…a Sunday off. I went rabbit hunting. What a break! Even though I was spiritually committed and my faith was strong during my teenage years, I

4

always felt close to God while out enjoying His creation. I did that whenever the opportunity presented itself. I loved the outdoors.

I had a good sense of humor and loved playing jokes on anyone I could snag. I especially enjoyed this with girls…they're so gullible! Little did I know that later in life, my sense of humor would change, making it difficult to laugh about many things others thought to be so funny. If there is anything that changed in my life after having gone to war, that is the one thing my family and close friends seem to notice the most.

Several of my buddies either enlisted or were drafted. Their lives have changed as well. Some were maimed for life…either physically or emotionally. Others are buried in the local cemetery on the hill, on the north end of town.

Why can't the governments of the world find a better way to settle their arguments?

CHAPTER 3

FORT BLISS TORTURE

20 February, 1967
Fort Bliss, Texas

"I'll be your mother for the next six weeks. Don't even think about coming to me and whining about your personal problems! If you don't like the way I treat you, suck it up…that's just the way it is. You might like it here, and you might not. Personally, I don't care. I'm here to do my job and that is to transform you from the sorriest looking, out-of-shape boys I've ever seen, into a lean, mean, fighting machine."

"Now, get your sorry butts off the bus!"

After that welcome to basic training by our drill sergeant, all of us new recruits are ready to go AWOL before we begin our training. It'd be a piece of cake. Mexico is just down the road. The worst of that would be getting caught by this 6'4" black bulldozer. He looks like he eats boulders for breakfast after a ten-mile run. His body has large bumps all over it, and none of them look very soft.

Standing at attention during our first formation in the blazing sun, we're again reminded how absolutely worthless we are…in a language only a drill sergeant knows, containing more expletives than I knew existed. Admiring all our various hairdos in a way only a "mother" could, he told us to enjoy them for the next few minutes. We would soon be going to the hairdresser.

Once the formalities are complete, our leader asks if any of us has had prior military experience. All our hands stay at our sides.

6

When asked how many of us had been in the Boy Scouts, some of us half-heartedly raised our hands.

"Now we're getting somewhere. All right, how many of you have attended college?"

Several of us again sheepishly raised our hands.

"Anyone ever participated in R.O.T.C.?"

My hand went up along with one other.

"O.K. You, you, you and you will be our Company Squad Leaders."

For what it's worth, he pointed at me first, followed by the other R.O.T.C participant, and then he pointed out two of the other Boy Scouts. To him, that's good enough. We might know something about formations and how to march. Perhaps he thinks we can help whip the others into shape. At first I thought this would be a privileged position, and it was…we didn't have to pull K.P. or guard duty. However, we were to be a "junior mother" to all the men under us. Interesting.

After spending several days getting used to "Mom," we kind of thought we knew what to expect. However, "she" never ceased to amaze us with "her" little surprises. We soon learned that ALL of us had to adhere strictly to this guy's wishes or the hammer would come down in one way or the other…sometimes in both ways! We soon learn the joys of being rudely awakened by this nut in the early hours of the day…like between midnight and 0330 hours. We're out in the parking lot in no time, forming up for a nice little walk. This usually starts out as a march, quickly followed by an order to…"Double-tiiiime, harch." (His special word for march.) After six to ten miles, depending on Sarge's mood, we have a lot of stragglers who are harassed unbearably as they hunch over, vomiting. Eventually, we get in shape and can take it without loosing what we had for chow the previous night.

We learn all the idiosyncrasies of the chain of command, various and sundry rules, and codes we have to memorize. Of course we learn how to keep our weapons clean and use them not only to fire at the enemy, but for P.T. and bayonet training. There is also training with "pugil sticks." These are stout sticks about five feet long with large padded ends. We take turns in a circle beating each other to a pulp. Fortunately, we wear helmets and are told not to hit each other in the head or groin. Right! This is meant to teach us to

7

use our weapons in close quarters to beat the enemy to death before they do the same to us. Bayonet training seems like a big joke in the days of our high tech military and long-range weapons. However, several of the men would soon thank the good Lord they had the training. In many cases, it saved their lives.

The rifle range is fun for a lot of us who have spent half our lives growing up with guns. For others, mostly city boys, it is humbling. The down-range targets have pits below where we take turns keeping our heads down until the shooting stops. We pull the targets down to be scored. Several of us come up with the idea to hold up a perfect score if there are no holes in the target at all. Those targets with the bull's eye shot out didn't score too well. It makes for a lot of cocky guys loosing their cool and continually readjusting their sights. In actuality, it isn't at all beneficial to the non-shooter who needs to learn to be an expert marksman if he is to live through the coming months. The drill sergeants soon catch on and ride herd over the perpetrators. Fun while it lasted. Actually, I think our "mothers" got a charge out of it. They all have a sick sense of humor.

When it's time to go on bivouac, explained as a little "camping trip" for three or four days, a lot of us are excited. Boy Scouts in the company all have fond memories of camping.

Loading the whole gang into the back of a cattle truck is a tight squeeze…standing room only and tightly sandwiched at that. No danger of falling down while going around the corners. After what seems like an interminable ride on the dustiest road known to man, we arrive at our destination feeling pretty ill. The White Sands Missile Range extends for miles along the New Mexico desert. Nothing but sand, scorpions, rattlesnakes, cactus, scrub brush, and… did I mention…scorching sun?

After setting up camp, we spend the rest of our time learning the basics of just how and why the Army does things the way they do; from setting up tents to how to crap in the desert... we learn it all. We're divided up into teams to play a series of war games with blanks in our M14s. Doing this in the daytime is all right, but the dark hours are really spooky. We're taught the "night walk." I'm used to hunting, so stalking isn't new to me. But this night walk is rather unusual, though effective, I guess. In a war zone, you always have to expect the unexpected and this particular technique is used in hopes of detecting mines and booby traps before they find you. Walking more slowly than a melting glacier, we're trained to take high steps while pointing one foot downward setting it down softly, then listening and feeling for what could ruin your day. Then you slowly move your arms up and ever so slowly down in front, feeling for wires. The next foot follows and you repeat the sequence. If done correctly, one doesn't cover a lot of ground, but hopefully you remain alive.

Having spent a great deal of my youth outdoors, I am able to help members of my squad who have been raised in the city and have few, if any, outdoor skills. Some of them have trouble coping with the desert situation. So do I. I've never "camped" in a desert. But we get through it and learn a lot as a result. In addition to mastering specific techniques, we gain a lot of knowledge about ourselves and how we might react under fire.

Cruising into the last week of Basic, our leaders begin to ease up a bit, at least with respect to some of their comments. Some semblance of hope comes from the drill sergeants. They have us pretty well whipped into shape. We no longer trip over each other when we march, and don't heave our guts out on a forced march or run. We've lost our "baby fat" and actually looked pretty trim in our uniforms. Most of us know how to please the drill sergeants without having to do extra push ups and can really put a shine on our shoes. Every day we had watched with envy as the planes flew over. We soon would graduate and board a bird to freedom.

At graduation we surprised not only ourselves, but also our drill sergeants. We looked sharp!

CHAPTER 4

SAMPAN ON THE CHESAPEAKE

21 March 1967
Ft. Eustis, Virginia

A few months ago while in the Recruiter's office, having enlisted for "Helicopter Repair and Maintenance School," the Recruiter told me that there would be no problem getting into the training that I so desperately wanted. What he hadn't mentioned was that the attrition rate of helicopter crew chiefs was very high. Consequently, I had to figure this out for myself months later. Those of us headed for this training in either Ft. Eustis, Virginia, or Ft. Rucker, Alabama, are not offered the privilege of even a short leave following Basic. The skills we're about to learn are desperately needed across the pond. In my particular case, I'm ushered to the airport late in the afternoon after graduation, flown to Virginia Beach, VA, and then bussed to Ft. Eustis.

Climbing aboard the plane is an experience surpassed only by boarding the Freedom Bird in Cam Rahn Bay, Vietnam, after finishing my tour there. It is such a pleasure to get on board with other G.I.s and civilians. There's no Drill Sergeant to greet us. The smiling faces of the flight attendants are a welcome sight. Even the evening meal on the plane is like a gourmet meal after having eaten nothing but Army chow for the past six weeks.

Settling down for a much needed nap after eating my supper, I'm very restless in anticipation of my next assignment. I finally fall asleep and don't wake up until the aircraft wheels squeak on the pavement at Virginia Beach at 2105 hours.

Off loading at the terminal, those of us headed for Ft. Eustis are greeted by an N.C.O. (non-commissioned officer) who leads us out to a Greyhound bus bound for our new duty station. This is a luxurious way to travel after having had the experience of the cattle trucks back at Ft. Bliss!

It's so nice to see green vegetation playing in the headlights along the route after having been subjected to desert conditions for so long. It almost looks like home.

Arriving at the base, we grab our duffel bags and are ushered off to the barracks where we each choose a bunk and crawl in, knowing reveille and in-processing will come in just a matter of hours.

While in basic training at Fort Bliss, Texas, I met Dale Erickson a tall, blond-headed, dark eye-browed Swede from Lead, South Dakota. "Swede" is soft-spoken. We shared a lot of the same interests, including girlfriends back home with whom we were hopelessly in love. We shipped off to AIT where we would both achieve the same MOS, 67N20, Helicopter Repair and Maintenance.

With Dale at my side during breakfast, we're sitting next to what we believe to be the thinnest man to ever wear a set of fatigues. Standing about five foot ten, Delton Tollett is a genuine Okie. He not only has the accent, but his sense of humor is outstanding. His face looks like it was carved out of an apple a while back and is already beginning to wither, even at such a young age. He's had a hard life. We hit it off immediately. This guy has the shiniest boots I've ever seen. His fatigues are starched like pieces of crisp bacon. Del is obviously 100% military material.

Standing in line for what seems like hours following breakfast, we're each being processed into our new home. While in line, Dale, Del and I meet a blond haired fella from Idaho. Built like he was raised on a farm and knows what hard work is all about, Tom Henderson is a soft-spoken, rather shy individual. Like us, he enlisted for this training, and of course, expects to go to Vietnam with the rest of our class. After a brief conversation, we find out that Tom is a hunting fanatic. We'll get along just great. Though the rest of our little group hasn't discussed the possibilities of becoming a statistic in the war, Tom brings up the fact that though he really wants the experience, he is extremely apprehensive. In talking with him further, we find that he is engaged and plans to be married when

11

he gets back from his tour in Vietnam, if that's where he goes. I think he's more concerned for his fiancé than for himself.

Admittedly, I didn't apply myself in my one semester of college. My heart certainly wasn't in it. However, I can see a definite difference in the military instructors here at Eustis over those I had in college. After several days, I find that these guys do a great job of teaching. I realize my motives for learning are better here. I want to learn how to repair and maintain helicopters. My life, and the lives of others will depend on it. I didn't want to learn whatever the profs were trying to cram down my throat at Michigan State University. Due to the limited amount of time allowed to learn a particular MOS, military instructors only teach you what you have to know to accomplish your mission. There are no prerequisites, other than the fact that you have to be Government Issue. Consequently, the amount of time to learn a particular task is shortened considerably by only having to learn the nuts and bolts of the subject.

We not only learn how to repair the Huey, but also learn that as helicopter crew chiefs we will be responsible for weight and balance of the aircraft for each mission. As soon as we arrive in Vietnam, however, we find out differently. If the aircraft won't hover due to being overweight, you do a running takeoff. If that doesn't work, or you don't have the necessary takeoff area, you throw some equipment or people off until you can get airborne. So, even though we can accurately figure the weight and balance, for our purposes, it's a joke. In Vietnam, common sense plays a big part in safety.

The importance of a thorough preflight and daily inspection are hammered in. Spotting your problems on the ground sure beats finding them while in the air! We will soon discover that we'll have enough problems to face while airborne.

Several days are spent in the sheet metal shop learning how to fabricate metal patches and rivet them in place. Patching plexi-glass is also taught. In actuality, both of these skills were put to good use on a regular basis later on in my career.

After the majority of the maintenance and repair is behind us, it's time to go to the rifle range and learn to fire and clean the M60 machine gun. This sucker fires a 7.62mm round and spits them out at six hundred rounds per minute! We spend the better part of a day learning the idiosyncrasies of this weapon and how to fire it accurately. We only have stationary targets, but it's a thrill to see how rapidly we can make things disintegrate. I am looking forward to firing this thing from a helicopter flying at 120 mph! We're instructed to fire the 60 in short bursts. Holding the triggers down for more than a couple of seconds causes the barrel to warp from the heat! That was soon proven by a couple of my buddies in the heat of the battle.

At the end of the day, we're told that we will each get a helicopter ride and experience firing the machine gun from a moving ship…with blanks, since they don't have a live aerial shooting range.

Early the next morning we're bussed out to the airfield where a couple of Hueys are waiting on the tarmac. The M60's are already mounted. We're introduced to the four pilots. The well-tanned warrant officers are decked out in their gray Nomex flight suits. The N.C.O. in charge tells us that these guys have recently returned from leave, following their tour of duty in Vietnam where they flew combat missions on a daily basis.

One of the pilots briefs us on safety etiquette in and around a helicopter, such as: always duck your head when walking under the rotor blades, never walk behind a helicopter while it's running or the tail rotor will ruin your week, never approach a running chopper from the uphill side (where the rotor blades are closer to the ground), seat belts, fire extinguishers, and exit strategies in the event of a crash.

With only two helicopters available, we had to take turns so we would each get a lesson on the machine guns, one gunner on each side. Technically, the crew chief usually rode in the left seat, with the gunner on the right. For this exercise, it didn't matter.

As each flight comes back, most of the trainees are beaming! They love it! A couple exit the aircraft and immediately show us what they had for breakfast. This must be quite a ride. By the time my turn comes up, along with my partner, it's about lunchtime and the pilots of our ship almost seem like they're bored.

Bob Parent is riding right seat and serving as gunner. He's a stout eighteen-year-old Bostonian who sports a great mustache that he keeps trying to curl in between his tobacco spitting scenes. He's

13

a jovial guy who, though unknown to me at the time, I will find myself grieving over in the months to come.

Departing the area, we first climb to 3500 feet and then, after a short time, the pilots confirm that our belts are tight. Diving a Huey from that altitude to tree top level is better than the best roller coaster ride I've ever been on! The pilot smoothly pulled out of the dive just over the tree tops along the coastline and then commenced sharp turns not just over the trees, but out over the bay as well. What an exuberant feeling! From all reports, this is how most of the flying is done in Vietnam, (should I be lucky enough to go there). The purpose of fast low-level flight is to attempt to stay out of the "bulk" of enemy small arms and machine gun fire. I wonder what the instructors mean by the term, "bulk."

Though I'm thoroughly enjoying my first helicopter flight, I begin to wonder when we would fire our machine guns.

Suddenly, the pilot pulls pitch, shooting us skyward. Reaching 3500 feet again, we're flying along peacefully watching the boaters below who are enjoying a pleasant, quiet morning, fishing and just cruising along. Suddenly, the Aircraft Commander comes on the radio.

"Sampan twelve o'clock."

My stomach moves quickly to my short haircut as the pilot immediately dives toward the unsuspecting fourteen foot fishing boat.

"OK Chief, (that's me in the left seat) when we get over the sampan, I'll circle to the left. I want you to sink that enemy boat. Shoot to kill!"

He's joking right?

We drew nearer to the unsuspecting elderly couple about to eat their picnic lunch while minding their own business fishing just a short way off the coast. They obviously see the Huey rapidly approaching and offer a friendly wave…proud Americans supporting our military effort. Assuming we're just going to give them a buzz job, the couple is enjoying the thrill while the pilot cranks the aircraft over into a tight left turn.

"Let 'er rip, Chief."

This guy's serious!

With a powerful amount of adrenaline pumping through my veins, I cut loose with several short bursts. The muzzle flash shooting out the end of the barrel looks vengeful, even though I'm only firing blanks. I feel like I'm in another world…I've never fired a weapon at humans before! Both straw hats fly into the water. In their terrified struggle to try to hide from the ensuing "battle", the picnic basket spills onto the floor of the boat while the passengers scramble about not knowing what to do. Seeing how frantic these folks are after several machine gun bursts, I hold my fire.

The pilots are laughing hysterically. I'm wondering if a tour in a war zone gives everyone a sick sense of humor.

Realizing I'd had enough and didn't know what to do next, the pilot entered a steep turn in the opposite direction.

"OK gunner, your turn."

Knowing the pilots aren't just kidding around, the gunner laid his blanks on the poor couple. The elderly gentleman is now standing up in the boat, saluting us…and I don't mean a military salute! Without a doubt, he and his lady friend would shoot us down if they had a weapon! I wouldn't blame them. Even though this is a thrill at first, it turns out to be a cruel joke. I wonder if word will get back to base and these pilots will be reprimanded.

After graduation the next morning, we're told to pack our gear and be ready for departure in the next day or two to our next duty station. Orders would be posted on the bulletin board outside the Orderly Room after breakfast the following morning.

Many of my classmates anxiously skip eating and go to the bulletin board in anticipation of receiving their orders. As promised, the orders come out right after breakfast. All of us expect to have a leave that we have each requested. We also expect that our next duty station would be Ft. Lewis in Tacoma, Washington. This is the last stop before…Vietnam…the place that many of us had NOT requested! Crowding around the list of orders, some of us are elated, myself included. A two-week leave, fly to Tacoma for out-processing, and then board the big bird to Vietnam. Others have fear in their eyes, others terror, and some even have tears streaming down their cheeks. Reality has set in. Ultimately, within a month we'll all be going to Vietnam for a year to do what we have just been trained to do. Some of us will come home early, some with horrendous physical and/or mental wounds…the remains of others will be returned to their families…wasted by the enemy.

As promised, I'm granted a short leave, where I spend an intense two weeks visiting my family and friends, and of course Cindi, my girlfriend. Though we all have a great time together, it passes too quickly.

On the day of departure for Ft. Lewis, the holding pen for those of us continuing on for assignment to the Republic of Vietnam, there are hugs all around. Final farewells are wet with tears. None of us knows for sure if this will be our last words ever spoken to each other; but that thought certainly passes through our minds. The attrition rate for helicopter crews in the war is nothing to be proud of.

The 30-minute drive to the airport with my folks was fairly quiet. Each of us was alone with our thoughts. After checking my bags, the three of us hugged, and Dad prayed for my safety and God's protection over me in the coming months. He quoted from Psalm 91, verses 1-7:

1. He who dwells in the shelter of the Most High will rest in the shadow of the Almighty. 2. I will say of the Lord, "He is my refuge and my fortress, my God, in whom I trust." 3. Surely He will save you from the fowler's snare and from the deadly pestilence. He will cover you with his feathers, and under His wings you will find refuge; His faithfulness will be your shield and rampart. 5. You will not fear the terror of night, nor the arrow that flies by day, nor the pestilence that stalks in the darkness, nor the plague that destroys at midday. 7. A thousand may fall at your side, ten thousand at your right hand, but it will not come near you.

It was the final seal on my departure, and very fitting, I thought.

Tears filled my eyes as the aircraft engines barked and the smoke cleared.

Will the next year ever come to an end?

11 August, 1967
Carney, Michigan

Dear Bill,

Mom and I stood by the airport fence in Menominee watching your plane until it was a tiny speck in the sky and finally disappeared from sight. You were off to Vietnam and the wildest adventure of your 19 years. It was a sad and melancholy day. We didn't feel like going home so we just got in the car and drove, with no idea of where we wanted to go. We finally wound up at the old iron smelting and shipping port at Fayette. The history of that harbor helped a little to take our mind off the fact that our eldest son had gone off to fight an ugly, nonsensical war.

Will we worry about you? Sure we will, although we know you will keep telling us, "Don't worry about me, I'll be alright." You know we committed you into the Lord's care when you left (and all your life) and we claimed the security of the 91st Psalm verses 1-7. That was the scripture I chose when I went off to WWII. Read it often and claim it as your own. You can be assured we will be praying for you faithfully many times through the day, and whenever we wake at night. We know you are a competent soldier and have placed your faith in the Lord. God bless you and keep you.

We love you Bill,

Dad

CHAPTER 5

THE LONG-ANTICIPATED ARRIVAL

13 August, 1967
Cam Rahn Bay

While in processing for Army Basic Training at Ft. Bliss, Texas, the clerk was kind enough to ask my first choice of assignment. We all thought it was mighty accommodating of Uncle Sam to ask such a question. Hawaii seemed to be the first, second, and third choice for most of the guys. Big dreams cost the same as small ones, so why not. However, there are a few oddballs…like myself.

"What would you prefer for your first choice of assignments, Private?"

"Vietnam, Sergeant."

"No Private, you misunderstood. I asked for your first choice, not your last."

Feeling a little cocky and perhaps with a touch of youthful pride, I reply, "Sarge, that's not only my first choice, but my second and third as well."

With a wide grin, this clerk probably thinks I'm nuts and should be recommended for a section eight. He says, "Well son, you're one of few in this line of young men who will get exactly what you asked for."

Reality begins as the rear door of the Boeing 707 opens to the flight of stairs leading to the tarmac at Cam Rahn Bay. The humidity hits us like a stream from a fire hose. It's 1920 hours, with the mercury reaching 100 plus. Given the uncertainties about what lies ahead, none of us has slept much since leaving Seattle twenty four hours earlier. Judging by the feel of the oppressive heat, there won't be much sleep for the next twelve months. Upon leaving the false security of the aircraft, our conversation is minimal. Though a few of us have actually volunteered for this assignment, most have not. We file out onto the tarmac with an overwhelming sense of trepidation.

Single file and quiet, we march to a waiting bus that transports us across the airfield to a wooden barracks. It's a spartan building with wood siding four feet up, the studded walls and two by six rafters exposed on the inside. Screen covers the upper half and it's topped with a metal roof. The floor is concrete and sixty or so school desks are lined up in neat rows as only the military can do. "In-Country Processing" is where I begin to sense the absurdity of this war. Didn't we just spend days filling out mountains of paperwork before leaving the States? All for naught it seems as we tackle more of the same. I'm so tired of filling out my permanent address…I should have brought a rubber stamp. I guess the military wants to be doubly sure where to send all the excess money they're overpaying us. They also want to know whom to notify in the event of an "accident." And somewhere in the fine print I think they're asking where to send my body, or what may be left of it, should I happen to return to Cam Rahn Bay "prematurely." But somehow, that seems like a remote possibility.

Following the seemingly endless drudgery of paperwork, we head to the mess hall for popcorn and cokes. Is this any sign of how we'll be treated for the rest of our tour? Somehow, that's very doubtful.

Hitting the rack after our midnight snack, I finally have time to think. For the first time I realize how anxious I'm feeling. My thoughts immediately take me back home to my loved ones. My family is a very close-knit one, and already I desperately miss them. And somewhere, far away, is Cindi, my girlfriend of three and a half years. I used to think two hundred and forty miles was a long way to travel to go see her and now I'm half way around the world from her. Twelve months is beginning to look like a very long time!

In the middle of the night the bad guys add to my sleeplessness by cutting loose with two mortar attacks. I haven't been here long enough to know just how close these attacks are.

Later I learn they're launched just outside the perimeter, about a half mile from my hootch. And the next morning we're told Charlie does this almost every night just to keep the local G.I.s on alert. Works for me!

Room service hasn't yet made the expected wake-up call, but as dawn approaches, the almost continuous roar of bombers, fighters, and helicopters cranking and departing makes sleep impossible. The sounds are tantalizing enough to get me out of the rack to make the short walk out to the flight line to take it all in. The smell of jet fuel fills the air.

This is what I came for...not the smell of jet fuel...the excitement!

My mind races through mental images of the possibility that some of the departing Crew Members might be wounded, shot down, never seen again, or...come back in body bags. I try to push these horrid thoughts out of my mind. I'm beginning to recall the news clips of so many men arriving home in boxes. Until now, I think I had ignored that I had ever seen those pictures, and then I see a deuce and a half pull up to a cargo plane on my left and humbly watch while many long narrow boxes are loaded on the aircraft for the "Final Flight" home.

This "Police Action" is beginning to look grim.

CHAPTER 6

FIRST IMPRESSION

15 August, 1967
An Khe

Within a few days of arriving in the war zone, my buddy Dale Erickson and I were assigned to the same outfit, C/227th Aviation Assault Helicopter Battalion, First Cavalry Division…the BEST! Here our personalities, not to mention our very lives, would be transformed forever. There was no turning back! Though kept extremely busy, we shared a lot of our precious spare time talking about home and our girlfriends. Dale plans to be married as soon as he gets home in August, and he asked me to be his Best Man. We are serious buddies for sure.

It's 0500 hours and those of us who are being assigned to points further north board a C130. I'm headed for An Khe located in the Central Highlands about one hundred and twenty miles north of Cam Rahn Bay.

My orders read that I'm being assigned to the First Air Cav. From all that I hear, the Cav is the place for action. They have been in numerous historic battles. My adrenaline pumps wildly as I look out the window of the aircraft and see my dreams coming together right before me!

Our Air Force crew lands at several bases along the way, unloading replacement troops and picking up others who are either being reassigned or sent home following their year's tour. In this war, we are not only dispensable but also very transient and are assigned and reassigned wherever we are needed for either our particular specialized training, or to replace those who have been unfortunate enough to be WIA or KIA. I'm learning that aircraft here are used like taxis.

Even we "new guys" recognize the replacements by their fresh, unstained jungle fatigues and clean boots. Picking up other troops at our various stops it becomes equally clear who the old timers are. Those who have been in-country for awhile are given away by their sweat-stained fatigues and deep "farmer tans". What a contrast!

One thing that seems a bit strange to me is that many of these guys take off their flak jackets, or their helmets and sit on them.

Though I'm very curious, I'm too embarrassed to question any of these seasoned war heroes. I'm sure I'll figure it out for myself before long.

After having flown the entire trip at about twenty five hundred feet, we're approaching An Khe. I stare out the window. I'm mesmerized by the hustle of this LZ that is to be my home for the next couple days. Though not nearly as large as Cam Rahn Bay, it's perched on a fairly large plateau. There are a slew of helicopters as well as fixed wing aircraft parked inside three-walled enclosures of sandbags stacked four feet high. These revetments are a feeble attempt at protecting the ships from shrapnel during attacks.

In addition to the aircraft, probably numbering between eighty and one hundred, there are all types of heavy equipment including trucks, bulldozers, graders, cranes, backhoes and sundry smaller vehicles. Tents are everywhere. Along the perimeter are pup tents, occupied by the grunts who are on guard duty. Larger tents all over the camp not only house the balance of the troops, but are used as mess halls, maintenance facilities, and of course, field hospitals. There is constant air traffic in and out of this dirt-ridden place. Bird Dogs are small single engine fixed wing aircraft used for observation. There are several types of helicopters. Huey slicks used as troop transport, re-supply and medivac. These are the air taxis of the Cav. Gunships are loaded with thirty four rockets, a 20mm cannon, twin .30 caliber miniguns, and topped off with a pair of M60 machine guns on either side. They're manned by a door gunner and crew chief. The Loaches are used for observation, marking targets and raising havoc with Charlie whenever they're fired upon. I see CH 47 Chinook tandem rotor helicopters parked out on the red clay landing zone. These are used for troop and material transport into more secure areas. There are also a couple of Sky Crane helicopters used for picking up huge external loads. They can also carry a large pod externally that is used as a portable clinic, converting it into a flying field hospital if so needed. All of these aircraft combined are coming and going like bees to a honey tree.

Huge clouds of red dust are everywhere while aircraft take turns arriving and departing. This LZ expands over several acres of dirt. Since this is a fairly large base, there is even a tower with air traffic controllers dealing with this seemingly unorganized mayhem like well-seasoned conductors at a concert.

This is fascinating. I can't wait to get my assignment to a Huey as crew chief and door gunner! As exciting as this is, I can only imagine what it will be like to actually be based in a more remote area and be a part of these missions. So far, this seems even more adventurous than I had anticipated. This forsaken countryside, the sights, sounds and smells seem to be overtaking my feelings and emotions. There is so much hitting me at once. I feel like I'm going to burst! This is going to be great!

A couple of hours after arriving, I meet a grunt who tells me his story of having been lucky enough to return from a mission a few days ago. He tells of his unit being flown into an LZ about fifteen miles to the west of An Khe. There are six Hueys assigned to the lift. All are shot down on the initial insertion. Tally for Charlie: six helicopters, six men dead, and twenty four injured. Hearing this, my gut churns. I wonder if I have made the mistake of my life by volunteering for such hazardous duty.

Surely this grunt, that I didn't even know, is exaggerating on the losses. It's obvious I'm a Newbie and he just wants to fill me with fear.

It's working!

20 August, 1967
An Khe

Dear Mom and Dad,

My impression of the Army up to this point is all spit and polish, but I'm quickly realizing that a war zone is a different world.

There is so much going on here that there isn't time to keep everything as clean as we did back in the States. When it's time for meals we have to not only cross a small bridge over the open sewer that runs past the mess tent, but in addition we must pass by the grease pit for the mess hall.

Believe it or not, someone decided that in order to get rid of the deficant from the outhouses, it is to be burned. We have a daily detail that pull the split fifty five gallon drums out the back of the outhouses, douse them with diesel fuel and light it off. Only in the military! If you add every imaginable insect to this horrid mess, you may get the idea that disease would be hard to avoid while over here fighting for freedom. If I can survive this, dealing with the V.C. should not be more than a minor inconvenience.

Officially I am now assigned to the "Ghostriders" of Charlie Company, 227th Assault Helicopter Battalion, First Air Cavalry. Now that I have my assignment, I'm told that "Charm School" begins tomorrow. That's where we're to unlearn everything we've been taught in Basic Training regarding survival in a war zone. Now that we're here, they want to take us out in the jungle and teach us what we really need to know to survive.

Charm School was interesting. The monsoons have begun, so I'm finished complaining about the heat, having spent a few days and nights in the mountainous jungle where it rained the entire time and was relatively cool. Even though I wouldn't want to be a grunt, as my instructor so aptly explained, "What do you think you flyboys will be when Charlie blasts you out of the sky?" He had a point. While on patrol, we were taught some of the finer points of booby traps, including how they're set up and how to spot them. Charlie is a master of camouflage! It's not hard to see that we're fighting a hard-core enemy who'll stop at nothing to score.

Late in the afternoon we set up our ridge line perimeter consisting of a double row of concertina wire, claymore mines, flares and of course foxholes. Digging foxholes large enough for four men is a real experience during the monsoons. Not only was the ground very rocky, whatever wasn't full of rocks was red, slimy clay. We set up a couple of ponchos overhead in an attempt to keep the majority of the water out. A wasted effort.

We were told to keep two men awake per foxhole and on guard at all times, using a two-hour off/on duty schedule from sunset to sunrise.

Sundown. Gotta go.

Love,

Bill

The visibility during the horrendous rain, coupled with the impending fog rolling in is making me very uneasy. I have no idea who or what is out there beyond the perimeter. With darkness quickly approaching, the knot in my stomach is growing rapidly. Even though I have always considered myself quite adventurous, the fear of the unknown is beginning to wear on me. Will we be mortared tonight? Will the mortar attack be followed by a ground attack? Can the Gooks really get through all of that concertina wire which we put up a few hours before? Are they really capable of disarming the mines that have been placed outside of the perimeter? How can they be this dedicated? After the first night of this nonsense, it was apparent we're not here to catch up on our sleep.

CHAPTER 7

LZ UPLIFT

24 August, 1967
LZ Uplift

Dear Mom and Dad,
     Today I hopped on a north bound Huey and was flown 70 miles north to LZ Uplift. This will be my official home for a while. One thing I am finding out about the Cav…we're nomads.
     Though Uplift resembles An Khe in many ways, Uplift is much smaller and more remote. It's nestled in the mountains and surrounded by jungle. If you look beyond the perimeter, the surrounding countryside is beautiful. Inside the perimeter wire, there is nothing but tents, mud, and a slew of helicopters…mostly Huey slicks and gunships.
     I'm basically settled in and have met several of the flight crews. It's good to finally get an actual assignment and meet my new "family".
     Our unit flies slicks that are used on varied missions. We transport grunts to and from the field primarily, and re-supply them. We are also called upon to transport the wounded and dead, and fill in wherever else the helicopter can be utilized.
     Psyops, nite hunter Missions, Command and Control and Search and Rescue are all pretty much daily missions. After all those are completed, in our spare time, we do whatever else it takes to support this monstrous war machine.
     Until a shipment of new Hueys arrive, I'm flying with another crew chief as his gunner. Our first mission began this

morning at 0500 hours...We flew a unit into an area about five miles from here. It wasn't considered a hot LZ, and we didn't receive any fire while delivering three helicopter loads of grunts.

Following the mission we landed in a rice paddy on the outskirts of a nearby village. We shut down while waiting for the inserted unit to call requesting reinforcements, supplies, extraction of the entire team or extraction of dead or wounded.

Our men happened on an NVA unit that was holed up in a cave. Six of the enemy were captured. Our ship was called in to extract these hardcore NVA. Arriving at the LZ, we discovered that the grunts had tied the enemy's hands behind their backs and blindfolded them. After they were loaded on board, we flew them back to Uplift for interrogation.

While escaping from their hideout to surrender to the Americans, these soldiers had all been shot by their own men. One was wounded severely. They all appeared between thirteen and twenty years old and had not bathed since last year's monsoons. These guys get first prize for the worst thing to ever reach my nostrils! According to the interpreters, the Gooks had been told that if the Americans captured them, they'd be eaten alive. Apparently, they preferred that over the treatment they were getting in that cave. After all, they surrendered only to be fired upon by their own comrades.

One of the items we picked up while flying our resupply today was a parachute that had been found by the grunts. It belonged to an Air Force jock that had bailed out and hasn't been found. One of our pilots is going to try to send it home to his wife who he says makes panties from the material.

The food here is even worse than army food in the States. Whenever we can get C rations, we chow down on those. If any of it needs to be heated, cans of peanut butter that come in small tins included in the boxes of C rations are lit. Being military issue food, it is not exactly of the highest quality (as you may remember from your WWII days), all the oil separates, comes to the top, and burns quite well. We also use insect repellent, a better heat source than a bug repellent.

I know it's easy for me to say, but there is no need for you to worry. All is well.

I love you,
Bill

CHAPTER 8

MAD MINUTE

25 August, 1967
LZ Uplift

Dear Mom and Dad,

    While I was on guard duty last night, we had two "Mad Minutes." At prearranged times, based on intelligence, we opened up with everything we had including artillery aimed point blank toward the outside of the perimeter and loaded with beehive rounds. These consist of hundreds of tiny steel darts, which ricochet off of anything hard. Getting hit by one of these rounds would turn anyone to mince meat at the blink of an eye. After a full minute of firing the smell of gunpowder was overpowering! Following guard duty and a few hours of sleep, the First Sergeant woke me up with good news. Since I had been on duty for thirty hours straight, I could join Miss America and her entourage for lunch. They were on a USO tour and stopping by Uplift. I decided that I was homesick enough without seeing all those round-eyed women, and really needed more sleep, so declined.

    At 1215 hours I joined the crew chief to help prepare for the next flight. At 1300 hours the Battalion Commander decided to have a "Mad Minute" to impress the girls. As usual, we cut loose with howitzers, mortars, machine guns, and automatic weapons. In the middle of it, four gunships flew over and unloaded forty-eight rockets apiece, and fired miniguns and 40mm cannon fire at the mountain. The continuous roar and pungent smell of gunpowder can't even be imagined! As the rounds hit the mountainside, beautiful triple canopy jungle was turned into a twisted pile of smoking debris. I doubt that the gals were impressed by our macho display of power.

Tonight after cleaning my M16 and both M60s, I attended a briefing on the daily missions in our unit. The tally is: twelve NVA killed, twenty four captured, four .50 caliber machine guns and twelve AK47s were rounded up, along with seven grenade launchers, two M60s, a couple of Ml6s and three .30 caliber rifles, in addition to a pile of ammo, gas masks, and numerous other field gear. It's apparent, the enemy is, or at least was, well equipped. Even though the majority of supplies captured were of Chinese Communist manufacture, several items had once belonged to the Americans.

Included in the report this evening was the fact that the NVA remaining in the cave refused to surrender and that, according to intelligence, they had a well-fortified command center inside. The decision was made to bury the entrance. What a gruesome war! Knowing the enemy, they probably had several other hidden escape holes and are long gone. At any rate, we are to haul several gallons of yellow and black paint out to that location tomorrow so the grunts can paint a big Cav patch on the mountainside as a reminder to the enemy that we are here.

Will write again as soon as I can.

Love ya,

Bill

CHAPTER 9

ROYAL SCREW-UP

31 August, 1967
LZ Uplift

Dear Dad,

I'm beginning to feel like a zombie! In addition to four hectic days of flying and being shot at on almost every lift, we have had mortar attacks every night! It's put us on edge and we often get on each others nerves. There are a lot of arguments over petty things between some of the men. We all miss home of course. Top that off with insufficient sleep, frequent attacks, seeing buddies getting blown away and the fear of the unknown is working on all of us. I guess the stress is getting to me.

Lack of mail was also getting me down. I know you are all sending letters, because you promised you would write often. No one had received mail for ten days. We are told that every time we move to a different LZ, that it will take up to two weeks for our mail to catch up with us.

Most of us got letters today! Thanks so much for being faithful in writing. You have no idea how much that means to me! It is often sad during mail call to watch the disappointment on the faces of those who don't get anticipated mail. Some guys don't get any mail. That's really sad. I can't imagine that!

You won't believe what happened this morning! Mike, my crew chief, and I had just begun the process of checking our machine guns out from the armorer at 0630 hours for a scheduled flight at 0800 hours. We planned to get the ship ready, mounting the guns, loading up with ammo, frag grenades and smoke grenades, along with all our personal gear and then having a leisurely breakfast before the mission. As that great plan was culminating, we were ordered to get to the flight line immediately for an emergency medivac. No, we are really not a medivac ship, but if those ships are tied up or we are closer, we do what is needed in an attempt to get the wounded back to a hospital ASAP.

Mike and I grabbed our gear and headed for the ship as fast as we could in the slimy mud. This was a good two hundred yard jaunt while loaded down with not only a machine gun and M16 each, but all our other gear as well. When we arrived at the ship, the pilots were already there…they got to ride in a jeep…and had already cranked. They were in a big rush because the grunts we were to pick up were reportedly in bad shape. As we clamored aboard with our gear, there was only enough time to place our M60s in the mounts before we came to a hover and blasted off.

Normally, I have a secure place for everything on the aircraft so I know exactly where it is when I need it. I was sweating profusely from the run, exhausted enough from the last several days and nights of action, and…I screwed up royally! I usually fasten my M16 against the wall with a cargo ring, but only had time to stand it against the wall. As we cleared the perimeter and I was loading my 60, the aircraft broke to the east in a hard turn and I saw my weapon leave the aircraft. I made a lunge for it and had it not been for my monkey harness, I would have gone with it! I leaned out to look, but was unable to see where it fell. I notified the pilots and they called the crew of the gunship that was behind us.

"Bandit One did you happen to see a weapon fall from our ship?"

"Roger, Yellow One. It looked like it landed just inside the perimeter."

At least that was some relief. There is a village right outside our perimeter and I could just see it falling into the hands of a Gook!

After flying a total of three medivac missions, I borrowed a buddy's M16 and spent three hours in a steady rain searching for my rifle…with no luck. I searched inside and outside the perimeter, and in the village, in the off chance that someone had not picked it up and claimed it. I can just picture one of our men getting zapped tonight with my weapon! If that happens, I hope it's me!

I have vivid memories of you teaching me gun safety when you let me hunt with you, Dad. I know how important that is. I never dreamed that I would drop a gun out of a helicopter! How stupid of me!

Finally, I had to swallow hard and tell my platoon sergeant my story. He was almost as sick as I was. He didn't waste any time taking me to "Top" who of course chewed me royally. From there we went to talk to Captain Woods, the X.O., who was next up the ladder since the C.O. was out flying. Personally, I would have rather been lectured by the C.O., as Captain Woods has a bad reputation. I felt as though I deserved whatever punishment he wanted to administer…until he excused himself after hearing my story and came back a minute later with a nine foot steel fence post.

"Peterson, this will be your weapon until you find your M16 or until you pay for a new one."

I had to argue with this insane man that I had looked diligently for my rifle, admitted that I had really dropped the ball, and I had no money with which to buy a new weapon, but would gladly pay for a new one at the next payday. I told him that I felt his punishment was unreasonable and asked him to reconsider. He smirked as he said his mind was made up and his orders were that I would carry that post wherever I went. I swallowed hard, took the "weapon" and saluted as I said... "Yes Sir." I did an about face and walked out the door with my new weapon in hand, tail between my legs, and secret hopes that if the Gooks had found my weapon that they would use it on this guy!

Naturally, I was down in the dumps over this entire episode, but reluctantly decided I would play his silly game.

I went out to my ship to clean the 60s, while I thought how absurd this place is.

I wish I had stood up to Captain Woods and asked permission to see the C.O. when he returns.

After fuming for a couple hours, I went to Sgt. Decker and told him I was all finished playing Woods' childish game.

"Congratulations, 'Pete'. I didn't think you would hold out this long. Captain Woods told me to have you write up a statement explaining what happened; it'll be investigated, and will probably be considered a combat loss. Don't sweat it. By the way, you can drop off the fence post by the bunker on your way to the armorer. I've already told him that you'd be comin' by for a new weapon."

What a relief! Now I just hope the weapon I dropped is either found by one of our troops or smashed sufficiently by the impact to not be serviceable.

It's already 1930 hours and I have guard duty from 0200 hours until 0300 hours, followed by KP all day tomorrow. I am told that as soon as I get my own ship, I won't have to pull KP anymore. That's certainly worth looking forward to! I'd best hit the rack before I hear the all too familiar..."Incoming!" Hope I don't have to spend another night in the rat-infested bunkers!

Last night, a snake crawling over his neck suddenly awakened one of the warrant officers. He was in the tent next to mine and of course woke us all up with his screaming as he left not only his bunk, but the tent as well. No sense of humor! The snake left as quickly as the pilot, so I suppose it's still crawlin' around here somewhere. Wonder who'll be next!

Love,
Bill

CHAPTER 10

CANCELED MISSION

3 September, 1967
LZ Uplift

Dear Mom and Dad,

First I gotta tell you the greatest news of all! After a full day of flying, I came "home" to nine letters! Almost everyone received several letters today. It's a happy camp!

After coming in from guard duty this morning, twenty of us were flown to LZ Dog for a parade. Can you believe it? I came half way around the world to fight a war, and they put me in a parade! General John J. Tolson flew in for the "awards ceremony." The temperature was somewhere around 110 degrees while the General presented a major and a colonel with the Distinguished Flying Cross for "extracting troops while under heavy enemy fire." So, what's new…we do that almost every other day! The crew chief and gunner were awarded the Air Medal with Valor. This seems to be the norm. Even though as a crew we all work as a team, more often than not, the officers are awarded the more prestigious medals.

The First Platoon Sergeant is scared to death. He's been here about five months. After sunset, he can only be found in one of the bunkers…usually, he chooses the one built by the crew chiefs in our tent, because it's one of the best constructed in the whole company. We doubled the sandbagged walls, used coconut trees for rafters, laid PSP, and triple-sandbagged the roof.

Anytime after dark, if this clown has an errand to run he asks one of us to do it because he's terrified to venture out…says he is

35

too "short." Personally, I'd like to make him "shorter"! He is the only man, if you can call him that, who sleeps in a bunker all night rather than a tent!

7 September, 1967

We flew two hours beginning just before dawn this foggy morning. While refueling, we noticed that we had a pretty bad leak in the transmission quill, where the engine and transmission are linked together. We grounded the ship, which of course made the pilots happy. All the other ships are flying, leaving no additional birds for the mission. While the pilots were out lounging, Mike and I spent the morning replacing the quill.

This afternoon I was asked by another crew chief if I would replace his gunner who was wounded this morning. I must admit, that kinda made my skin crawl. But, I agreed and we flew seven more hours. The pilots of this ship were lousy! While leaving an LZ under a fair amount of small arms fire, they got excited and hit some tree branches during our hasty departure. Although we felt a real bad vibration on the return flight, we made it back to our base at Uplift and inspected the damage. One rotor blade was totaled, so we replaced it and went out to finish the day. It's never boring!

We would have had a lot longer day if a severe weather system hadn't blown in about an hour after dark. We had three more assigned resupply missions, but fortunately for the crew, the pilots used their best judgment, and decided to scrap the missions. What began as heavy rain rapidly turned into a violent thunderstorm and visibility was the pits!

Canceling a mission for any reason is always a tough call when we know how desperately the grunts need to be re-supplied. But when all the odds are stacked against the aircraft crew, it's senseless to risk additional lives and equipment.

After cleaning the 60s in the ship by flashlight, the crew chief and I sloshed through the mud back to the mess tent for a cup of coffee. As you know, that was never my favorite drink, but it sure tasted good this evening. After relaxing for a few minutes, I realized how well the drain holes in my jungle boots work...for letting the water in. Later, when I removed them, it was no wonder the water

36

wouldn't drain out with all the mud caked inside! I don't think mom would care to do my laundry over here.

I'll try to finish this in the morning. Goodnight.

8 September, 1967

The torrential rain continued all night. None of us slept well with the water drumming its steady cadence on our tent, while it ran down the aisle between our cots. We figured it would have been an ideal night for Charlie to pay us a visit, so we were "pumped" anyway. Guess Charles didn't want to venture out either. Other than the sound of the thunder and the downpour, it was a welcomed silent night. No incoming.

We flew a colonel to Qui Nhon this morning. While we waited for him, the pilots, crew chief and I found a genuine American restaurant nearby. It was a brick building built by the Navy. Guess they have nothing else to do. This place even had fans! We were thrilled to get burgers and fries again! Most everyone in the restaurant was dressed in civvies. We sure turned heads when we walked in. Our muddy fatigues were torn and fairly ratty compared to those worn by our Navy comrades whom we saw walking about the base. Our Cav patches got their attention. They asked if the rumor that the Cav was seeing a lot of action was true, and we assured them it was. This place is an R&R Center and never sees any action. Lucky for us, they asked a lot of questions and were sufficiently awed to pitch in and buy our lunch!

Love,
Bill

CHAPTER 11

PEAKED EMOTIONS

12 September, 1967
LZ Uplift

Dear Dad,

    After flying from 0500 hours until 1900 hours, I think it's time to ask for a raise!

    Our ship flew combat assaults all morning and then spent all afternoon and early evening flying supplies out to the same guys we inserted. After dropping off supplies, several of the return flights were medivac missions. Body bags are a necessary part of the cargo we drop off almost daily to the men in the field. However, this particular unit had been hit pretty hard and had run out of the olive drab, zippered, rubberized body bags. Among those we transported back who had been killed in action, were a number we recognized as the same men we had dropped off this morning. On the first lift, there were eight mortally wounded soldiers loaded on our ship. Several of the wounds had been inflicted by small arms and machine gun fire. One grunt had stepped on a mine, grenades had killed two, and one died after being hit by a mortar round.

    It tears my heart out every time we have to do medivac flights. I'm beginning to feel guilty every time we do a combat assault, knowing before hand that several of the men we take into the depths of enemy territory will not return unscathed. Not only that, they may not return at all. During their ride in our helicopter, or another, their eyes may not reflect the fear that is evident among so many during an air assault. Instead, on their next ride out of the jungle, their eyes may be closed inside a body bag, or hidden by a poncho liner covering their body. Eerily, their eyes may be all too visible while they lie on the deck of the ship, that final distant look staring blankly into what lies beyond.

On the flip side, others are laughing as they crawl on board, and some seem to show no emotion at all. Those who laugh and carry on while we transport them on missions of death are usually those who have been in country for several months, or possibly they are here on their second or third tours of duty. Often these men either think they're invincible or believe they're not going to make it back to their loved ones anyway, so why not enjoy life for a few more hours, minutes or perhaps seconds. This is a deadly game. Personally, I think those grunts are in denial. If they've been on many assaults, they know what's coming. And it's never pretty.

Regardless, every man who joins us on a helicopter assault will never be the same. Combat changes one…forever.

Watching my comrades load the unfortunate soldiers onto our chopper, my emotions peak. Holding back the tears doesn't seem to be an option. We depart the PZ to a more secure LZ. There the dead will be processed for their silent trip back to America. Glancing down from my gunner's seat, I have trouble taking my eyes off these heroes. Wondering what may be going through the minds of these brave men in the final moments, I'm horrified to see their bloody, tattered, muddy fatigues flapping in the breeze while we cruise along at 100 knots over the tree tops in an attempt to avoid drawing ground fire. Steam rises from the belly wound of one of the troopers hit by a mortar just a few short minutes ago. Blood is blowing across the deck of the aircraft and running past my feet. The horror of it all!

It's been a long and emotionally draining day. But seeing all these guys who've been badly wounded, many maimed for life and others killed in action, I have nothing to complain about. I'm happy to be alive.

Dad, I'm sorry but it's just too depressing to finish this. You wanted to know everything that I experience while here, but I just can't go on. I may not even send this…

I love you…please don't worry.
Bill

CHAPTER 12

DENIAL

18 September, 1967
LZ Uplift

Delivery of several new Hueys has begun. More powerful than the D Models that we're currently flying, they'll be better suited to the daily flying we do. With the demands of our missions, air assaults, transporting WIAs and KIAs, emergency ammo resupply, and numerous other flights, we're forced to overload and over-stress these choppers. There are times when, because of enemy fire, only one ship is able to make it into a hot LZ to pick up troops though three or four may be sent into the fray initially. We attempt to take not more than eight Americans out at a time. But when conditions dictate, in an attempt to get the last man out, we will stretch that limit and take a chance in our efforts to save a life if at all possible. When the extreme heat, humidity, and at times, higher altitudes are added to the equation, the D Models are underpowered. Any machine has its limits.

As a result, our company lost one ship yesterday in a crash that the "Brass" is blaming on overstressed short shafts due to overloads. Both pilots and the gunner were killed in the crash and the crew chief is in critical condition.

We lost another aircraft this evening. No details, other than that the Aircraft Commander is dead. It's stressful enough to worry about being shot out of the sky on a daily basis, but of course with the complexity of helicopters, we're always faced with the reality of

40

mechanical malfunctions. Our mechanical problems are fewer than expected even though we don't always have the desired time for preventive maintenance.

19 September, 1967
LZ Uplift

In the past eight days we've lost seven choppers. Three crew members were killed and five injured.

Happy Valley is the target for our CAs today, lying just north of An Khe. The US hasn't been in this area for at least two months, so the real estate pretty much belongs to Charlie. Once the Americans move out of an area, it doesn't take long for the enemy to get re-established.

After takeoff, our flight of twenty slicks, each loaded with eight grunts and accompanied by four gunships loaded to the gills for a fierce firefight, attempts to maneuver into some semblance of a formation. The single-ship LZ is nestled in a small saddle on a ridge line at an altitude of thirty one hundred feet, so our gaggle (flight of aircraft) is spread out sufficiently to allow the aircraft ahead to make its approach, land, and deposit its load of freedom fighters. The spacing needs to be as precise as possible to enable each aircraft to depart just prior to the next one in line touching down. If this all takes place according to plan, there is constant suppressive fire from the slicks and gunships in an attempt to keep the enemy at bay, until all the men have landed in the LZ. If there's a gap between aircraft it opens the door for Charlie to set up and draw a better bead on the arriving…or departing aircraft. If an aircraft is shot down at a single-ship LZ plan B is set in motion. If there's another suitable LZ nearby it has been discussed in the pre-mission briefing and the coordinates are marked in grease pencil on the Plexiglas covering the pilot's flight chart. Plan B calls for inserting the remaining troops into the secondary LZ, from where they are to make their way to the original LZ. Without a suitable nearby LZ where the choppers are able to land, troops are occasionally rappelled into the LZ from the hovering aircraft. This is not only dicey for the big bird with the rotating disc, but also very dangerous for the men on the ropes who can easily be picked off by enemy snipers.

41

The target area can be seen from a distance shortly after takeoff from our base while eight-inch guns from a nearby fire base prep the site. Combat assaults are very well organized and this is no exception. Arrival at the LZ is set for an exact time so that the artillery batteries know precisely when to stop firing.

Following the last artillery explosive round, a Willy Peter round is fired. Rather than the dark gray smoke left by the first rounds fired, WP leaves a pure white plume of smoke…a guarantee that Arty is finished with its fire mission.

Following this, our Huey gunships take turns pounding the LZ with round-robin gun runs rolling in hot with ARA 20mm cannon, and minigun fire. While the slicks approach with their troops on board, the gunships continue their attack right outside our doors as we approach the LZ.

There is nothing more exciting than a helicopter combat assault on an entrenched enemy. The constant wop…wop…wop of the rotors, turbine engines whining behind you, coupled by not only friendly fire, but tracers streaking toward you, knowing there are four more bullets between each tracer…the adrenaline rush pulses wildly through your body. Once I am into the thick of the battle, my concerns over possible death are gone…I become one of the gears of the war machine and work in sync with all the other gears while we desperately work to achieve our goal of getting our men on the ground safely. Once the grunts have abandoned the aircraft, some of the pressure is off…we are no longer responsible for these soldiers…until…we have to resupply them, pick them up for another assault on the next hot spot, or so often, return to evacuate the wounded and sadly pick up the full body bags.

When close enough to the LZ to be effective, we cut loose with our machine guns to further suppress the LZ and surrounding area. This not only gets the adrenaline flowing freely, but other body fluids have been known to be released unwittingly. With green tracers streaming up at our aircraft from this hot LZ, there isn't time to check my pants.

There's enough underbrush in the LZ to make landing hazardous. The rapidly spinning tail rotor is very susceptible to damage should it strike so much as a small branch. If that happens, or debris is sucked into the spinning rotor blades, the chopper could easily crash. If a tail rotor blade is even slightly nicked, the resulting high frequency vibration could damage the tail rotor gearbox, not a pretty picture.

Each ship has to hover as the infantrymen jump the five or six feet to the ground. On the first lift, the lead chopper comes to a hover enabling the eight men to bail out…directly onto a camouflaged mine. A loud explosion flings all eight unsuspecting warriors into the air like rag dolls.

Fortunately, the aircraft is hovering just high enough to avoid anything other than the extreme concussion from the explosion. Like a dog shaking a snake, the aircraft shudders violently, but very competent pilots keep the vulnerable chopper in the air. Despite drawing heavy machine gun fire, the Huey escapes over the tree line without further incident.

The location of the enemy gunners is spotted by the gunships and with their miniguns blazing, pairs of rockets leave their tubes, silencing only some of the North Vietnamese gunners. While the fierce B Model gunships hose the area, a call is heard over the radio. It's the "Old Man". He's flying high above the battle, giving directions for the next tactic. It's a deadly chess game with the men below used as pawns and often placed in severe jeopardy.

The gunships go on with their battle while the mission continues as planned. Most of the twenty ships have reported ground fire. Several are hit, but still flyable.

The pre-mission briefing called for each of our aircraft to return four times to the same LZ with additional troops and supplies. Generally, the initial assaults are the worst.

Without friendly troops on the ground supplying cover fire, the enemy is kept at bay by the gunships and suppressive fire from our slicks, but often, that's not enough. These little rascals are determined fighters. On the other hand, once troops are on the ground, the gunners have to be much more cautious about where supportive fire is aimed.

On our third trip into the LZ and with a full load of troops, we take several rounds and lose hydraulics. The master caution light comes on instantly! The ship shudders while the AC, Lt. Lawton, makes a sharp nose-dive to the right, with the main rotor blades almost striking the ground. As the Cong open fire with automatic weapons, the pilot regains control, gingerly eases the ship over the triple canopy jungle, and dives down the side of the ridge in an attempt to gain more airspeed for better control. There isn't time for the grunts to bail out, much to their dismay. Judging by the color rapidly dissipating from their faces, you can tell they would rather be on the ground taking fire than be airborne in a squirrelly helicopter!

Staying airborne after experiencing loss of hydraulics is taught in flight school. Though manageable, the controls become very stiff without hydraulic assist. The normal soft touch in control movements required for smooth flight is now replaced by brute force. Lt. Lawton is joined by the co-pilot, Mr. Gordon, to assist on the controls.

Our skilled pilots keep cool heads and though we have a harrowing flight, we make it back to the PZ. Without hydraulics to make for a smooth transition from flight into a hover and landing, a running landing is called for. Maintaining 45 knots of airspeed, we make a shallow approach to a fairly large LZ. With tense nerves, our pilot slides the helicopter skids on the ground and makes a rough, but safe landing.

After a quick inspection, I find a bullet hole through one of the main hydraulic lines. After using the radio to call back to maintenance for a part, we wait for an hour while a new line and more hydraulic fluid are flown out to us in another Huey. Within fifteen minutes, we have the ship repaired and back in the air enroute to the LZ again. Though fired upon again on the initial approach, we don't take any additional hits and deposit our passengers safely in the LZ, their new home for the next couple of days.

CHAPTER 13

BREAKFAST WITH THE GRUNTS

20 September, 1967
LZ Uplift

Dear Family,

    The last week has been tough on aircraft for us. Today during one of our air assaults, the right cargo door of one of our gunships left the aircraft and flew into the tail rotor. The tail rotor was wiped out! Fortunately, the pilots remained calm and flew 30 minutes to the ocean where they jettisoned all doors, guns, and ammo to reduce not only the weight of the aircraft, but also some of the hazards in the likely event of a crash landing. They decided it would be wise to dump everything in the South China Sea to keep Charlie from getting his grimy little hands on it. After jettisoning their load, the crew headed for LZ Two Bits where they made a running landing. Without a tail rotor, a helicopter will spin like a top. If the airspeed can be kept up, the streamlining effect of the tail boom keeps the chopper straight, and given enough room, the bird can be landed much like a fixed wing aircraft.

    A lot of the pilots here don't have much experience, but most are very talented and do a great job. However, as luck…or no luck... would have it, this ship hit the dirt strip at about a twenty degree angle, bounced, and landed on its left side. As you might expect, that didn't do the paint job any favors. When these machines hit the ground, rather than make a graceful landing, they come unglued rather quickly. There were helicopter parts scattered everywhere!

Miraculously, the four-man crew walked away with only minor injuries.

The manufacturer of the Bell Hueys sent a Tech Rep here yesterday to try to figure out why we're having so many problems with our short shafts linking the engine to the transmission. He didn't know much more than we already knew through experience. Personally, I think it was the manufacturer's way of trying to smooth things over with a little political maneuvering. As quickly as we lose helicopters and crews in the field lately, politics doesn't mean much to us!

When I signed up to come fight in this God-forsaken war, I expected to find tropical heat for my full tour. We landed on a 4300-foot ridge this morning and shut down to share breakfast with the grunts whom we've been re-supplying for the past several days. It was quite cool, in fact down right cold! Wouldn't you think that the good 'ole Army would have provided all flight crew members with flight jackets, rather than just the pilots? As soon as we haul another load of captured field gear and weapons, we plan to locate some Navy personnel and do some horse-trading. The guys on the Navy base don't get to see a lot of action, but always have great equipment. They're always eager to trade anything they have for captured enemy weapons and field gear.

The cook offered me $40.00 for my Randall knife today. When I told him it wasn't for sale, he said he hopes I get zapped so he can claim my knife. He'll have to stand in line. There are so many guys who would like to have my knife that I sleep with it under my pillow. If you could write to the manufacturer and have him send some catalogs, I'm sure I could get plenty of orders.

Well, I have one sortie to go today before my day is supposedly over, so I had better get this in the mail and get out to the flight line.

I haven't had any mail for a couple days. Can't decide if I'm more homesick with or without mail, but it sure is nice to get some.

If Barb would like to send some of her special cookies this way, I'm confident they won't go to waste.

My love to all,

Bill

CHAPTER 14

DAILY LIFE

22 September, 1967
LZ Uplift

Dear Dad,

We just finished our first CA mission of the day…a "cold" LZ for once, so a rather boring morning so far. We have shut our aircraft down while waiting to see if the guys we inserted make contact. If they do, we'll have to fly out some reinforcements and/or pick up the wounded. While I wait, I'll see if I can at least get a short letter out. But, as soon as I get into this, I expect the pilots to get a call, yell "CLEAR!", crank, and take off on our next adventure. We rarely get to sit around for very long.

This morning one of our ships was called out to a remote LZ where an NVA had been captured during an early morning firefight. He had been wounded, so we were asked to medivac him back to our base. The C.O. wanted to not only get medical attention for this guy as soon as possible, but following that, he wanted to have him interrogated. Well, not only did the enemy not make it to Uplift for medical attention, but the crew didn't make it either. While the ship was on "short final" for our LZ, the prisoner apparently had a grenade hidden and pulled the pin. The aircraft blew up in midair, killing the NVA, crew of four and one other passenger. It is beyond me how anyone can commit suicide to support his cause. Some of these NVA are as dedicated and hard-core as they can be!

Gotta crank...

The Company we inserted at daylight made heavy contact, so we had to fly some help out to them. This trip drew a little attention…a bit of automatic weapons fire on short final. Lousy shots…today.

Did I tell you that a grunt found my M16? After falling two hundred feet at eighty knots, it had a broken stock, loose pins, and damage to the receiver. I will be getting it back from 27th Maintenance tomorrow.

We flew several sorties to a village on the coast just northeast of Uplift today. This village is beautiful with all its little grass huts nestled between the multiple sand dunes. Numerous round fishing boats made of reeds are overturned along the beach to dry. Cooking fires emit curls of smoke through the palm trees barely waving in the slight breeze. Whatever the South Vietnamese are cooking for breakfast smells great.

We hauled ammo and hot breakfast in and returned to Uplift with several loads of P.O.W.s. We also flew several loads of ARVN troops out to the village. At the end of the day, one of the ARVN soldiers handed me a sack to deliver to their Commander who was back at their base camp. Whatever was in the bag smelled like it had been dead for awhile. When I opened it to check to see what our precious cargo was, I discovered a twelve inch fish. A note on the outside in Vietnamese said, "Number One fish for Boss." The Commander seemed thrilled with the gift. Some people are very easy to please, I guess.

Time for a nap!

Love,

Bill

23 September, 1967
LZ Uplift

Dear Mom and Dad,

 If there's time between swatting mosquitoes, I'll attempt to get a letter off. The bugs in Michigan are horrible, but the bugs here are bad enough to make one consider suicide.

 I'm at LZ Dog again. I'll be here three days and hope to finish repairs on an H model Huey during that time.

 I went into town this afternoon for a haircut. The barber spoke broken English and was very chatty. He wanted to know how many days I had left on my tour, and when I told him three hundred twenty two he said, "Oh, xin loi!" (sorry about that). He wanted to know my life history! Asked about my family even! We showed each other pictures from our wallets. His wife had been killed a couple months prior and he has five children whom he gloated over. He said they live in another smaller village and that he's in Bong Son trying to earn a living for them. We continued to chat while he cut my hair and we became fairly good friends in just a few minutes. I guess I was feeling sorry for him. I gave him $5.00 for a $1.50 cut and a handful of Tootsie rolls for his youngest children. He was so elated, he cried, which of course made me cry. While we shook hands, he patted me on the back and asked me to be sure to stop in next time I was in the area for a free haircut and shave. Guess I'm getting a soft spot in my heart for these unfortunate people.

 After I left the barber, kids who had been watching this whole process through the doorway, mobbed me. They all wanted candy, so I emptied my pockets. These kids are so cute and underprivileged. When I look around, I wonder how they can smile at all. They live in an environment where they never know when their village will meet with more strife. Many of them have lost parents, brothers, and sisters in this senseless war. Many of those left have been wounded either by the enemy or by "friendly fire."

 I feel like maybe I've reached my peak as far as being lonely… How can it get any worse? As you mentioned in your last letter, Dad, "You kind of get used to it after awhile." I'm not sure that I ever will.

 I found my slingshot in the bottom of my duffel bag today. I should be able to have some fun with that!

A care package came from Cindi today. She seems to be a pretty good little cook…She sent a couple dozen cookies. Packages like that never last long, but I really don't mind sharing. We all cherish boxes from home and generally share equally.

Must get some sleep while I can.

Love,

Bill

25 September, 1967

LZ Uplift

Dear Dad,

Along with the letter I received from you today were the prints from the negatives that I sent you of the bullet holes in our aircraft. Thanks for having those printed for me. Several of the guys would like copies. When I return the photos with captions, I'll also enclose an order for you to fill if you don't mind. I really appreciate your willingness to do this for me.

You asked several questions regarding living conditions and missions. There are twelve men in my tent-all gunners. The crew chiefs occupy a tent next to ours. We actually have three gunner tents and three crew chief tents in our company area. We have 35 slicks to crew. We sleep on cots with mosquito nets and keep the majority of our belongings in a footlocker. Not a lot of extra room, but more comfy than the poor grunts out in the field. I really feel for them. They've got it tough!

Each crew chief is assigned his own ship, while the gunners and pilots rotate between various ships…why, I'm not sure. It doesn't help much to question the Army. I guess that hasn't changed much since WWII, has it? However, there is some talk about assigning a full crew to each ship.

Generally, all ships fly every day, but we try to keep one spare bird available whenever possible to cover a ship which may go down due to maintenance or a well-placed shot.

So far I've not seen the enemy while in flight, even though we have received plenty of ground fire. When we return fire, we are basically suppressing the area in an attempt to keep Charlie's head down until we can "get out of Dodge." After the grunts are dropped off and do a sweep of the area, they call in a body count report to let us know how much damage we've done. So we're diminishing the enemy's numbers, for whatever that's worth.

Each crew chief/gunner carries twenty five hundred rounds of machine gun ammo for his M60, a dozen twenty round magazines of .223 caliber for his M16, eight to ten smoke grenades for marking LZ's and enemy positions, a couple of frags to drop on huts, sampans, or troop concentrations that we might encounter, and two or three Willy Peter grenades that are great for suspected munitions caches. It's amazing how many secondary explosions we get when these are used.

The word is that we'll be moving to another LZ before long. No word as to where yet…typical Uncle Sam….keep ya guessing.

In addition to our slicks and several gunships based here, there are about ten OH13 helicopters used for observation. These look a little like they're made by Mattel and appear extremely fragile. These aircraft, in reality, are very maneuverable and a real asset to us. The OH13 pilots fly low and slow to try to locate the enemy by drawing ground fire. How would you like to have that job? Often, Charlie is smart enough to not fire at these choppers. He's waiting for the main course…the slicks that carry the troops and supplies.

There isn't room at Uplift for a fixed-wing strip…choppers only. There are a couple LZ's not far away with landing strips that support us as needed.

We have a Battalion Chaplain who comes out occasionally either to chat with the men or to conduct church services. But so far, I've been out on missions whenever he's been here. I haven't been to any services, but have heard they're very good.

Time to crawl under my mosquito net…Will try to finish this tomorrow.

Good morning,

Up at 0430 hours. A G.I. bath, quick shave, dehydrated eggs, Tang, and a couple pieces of toast for breakfast, and out to the flight line to prepare for takeoff.

After being out of bed for two hours, it's time to crank, but we're waiting for a thick, milky fog to lift. Our first mission will be to fly hot breakfast out to a company in the field.

When I finish my tour here, I'll have eighteen months left on my enlistment. Because crew chiefs are so badly needed here, it's very possible that I will have to come back for a second tour. At this point, I hope that won't happen, but I wanted to prepare you for that possibility. I have also written to Cindi to let her know that we may have to change our tentative plans for marriage. We'd really like to get married within a year after I return, but I wouldn't want to do that if I have to return to Vietnam. That wouldn't be fair to her.

Dad, I've given serious thought to what I might like to do when I'm finally out of the service. I want to thank you for inviting me to join you in your fence business. I am honored and will take that under serious consideration. At this point, I would like to finish college and then consider coming back home to work with you…but no promises yet. Things can change quickly, as you know.

We've been on two missions and back since I started this letter and have had a couple breaks in between. It's chow time, so I'll wrap this up.

I want to thank both you and Mom for being the most wonderful parents anyone could ask for. Now that I am on an extended stay away from home, I can look back and be very thankful for the way you raised me. Thanks for all the support, encouragement, and love you have always shown me.

With much love and admiration,
Bill

CHAPTER 15

MYSTERY MOVE

29 September, 1967
LZ Uplift

Dear Mom and Dad,

We were rousted out of the sack this morning at a cruel 0500 hours and told to pack all our gear because we're moving out. Our new home is still a mystery. Top said to be sure to bring sleeping bags, so we assume we're headed north…DMZ? Mountains? I don't understand why the military always has to keep us in the dark… Security? The rumors are intense and the anxiety high. We were just getting used to this place. All the flight crews feel like we're getting enough action here. A move is undoubtedly going to put us into a hotter area to help put a choke-hold on Charlie.

We're to tear down the tents first thing tomorrow morning, get the LZ cleaned up and then fly to LZ Dog to rendezvous for the move to our mystery LZ. We're hoping we won't have to move to another remote area that will require us to build new revetments and bunkers…we really don't need more work!

Time to fly.
Love, Bill

CHAPTER 16

WAIT A MINUTE

"I have seen Death blast out suddenly
From a clear blue summer sky;
I have slain like Cain with a blazing brain,
I have heard the wounded cry."

John Oxenham

30 September, 1967
Gilligan's Island

It's a sultry ninety six degrees at 0430 hours when the CQ wakes me from a fitful sleep. I lay in a puddle of sweat on top of my mosquito-netted cot.

Waking earlier for the first mortar attack at 2300 hours, I slept through the second at 0215 hours. Having flown fifteen hours yesterday and thirteen the previous day, my body collapsed into a deep sleep mode.

Thirty minutes remain before the preflight briefing, so I drag myself to the edge of my cot, slip on a clean pair of socks (the only frill I'll allow myself today), and dump the roaches from my muddy, reeking jungle boots. I'm already dressed because I was too tired to strip down when I crawled into the bunk last night. Giving my poncho liner a good morning shake, I see a couple of multi-legged creatures fall to the ground. My mind flashes back to college. Why didn't I apply myself there and try to fit in? I didn't have to wear boots there, and never had to go through the morning ritual of chasing away the critters (except perhaps for a few potato chip roaches).

Collecting my steel pot, shaving kit, towel, and M16 after donning my poncho, I head out the door of the tent into the steady drizzle that began about ten hours ago. Walking over to the Listre bag for a helmet full of water and placing it on top of a row of sandbags encircling another tent, I begin cleaning up. The entire camp has been rationing water. Charlie has blown up our water purification plant again. We don't have enough spare water for a real shower, but after having worn my fatigues for the ninth day, even a G.I. shower feels like a gift from heaven above. Mom would croak. Thankfully, the CQ had fired up the heater in the fifty five gallon drum so there is hot water for my shave. What a luxury!

The mess tent is only fifty feet away, so I have time to grab a bit of breakfast before game time. Even though I'm a full-blooded Swede, I never did enjoy the taste of coffee, but this morning I need the caffeine if I'm to stay awake through the first mission. Adding a dash of coffee to a three quarter cup of powdered milk and three healthy scoops of sugar, I head for the chow line. Two scoops of powdered eggs and a couple chunks of fried Spam are chased down with two glasses of Tang. Thank the good Lord for the space program!

The hope that the weather would be too ugly to fly with decreased visibility and low-lying clouds crossed my mind. I'd welcome a reprieve from so many back-to-back grueling, dirty, hot, and bloody missions in the past several days. This thought is punctuated by the loss of several buddies in two crashes resulting from enemy fire during their first mission yesterday morning.

After such a fine meal, it's time to walk off my indigestion on the way to the Flight Ops tent to see what we have in store for Charlie today…or what he has in store for us. It's just a short hike up the hill near the flight line.

Groggily wiping the sleep from their eyes, the selected crews for the morning mission are moving around the compound, completing whatever they need to do before going to the briefing. Some carrying flashlights partly covered by one hand, lit up their faces just enough to see their concerned looks. The anxiety could be blamed on the fact that we all knew today would be a challenging mission.

The tent flaps are closed to keep the rain out and also to keep snipers from taking a pot shot into the lighted tent. Sneaking quickly through the door, I'm greeted by a musty smelling, hot, humid, and smokey ops room. Several of the crews have already arrived and most are talking quietly and either clutching a cup of coffee, a cigarette, or both. Some discuss yesterday's morning mission, others are wondering aloud what today's flights might bring. Still others talk about home, girlfriends, wives, and family.

Several bulletin boards on easels line the inside walls of the operations tent. There are a couple of desks, several radios, wooden benches made from ammo crates, a few pinup gals, and a large easel in front holding a flight chart of our area of operations. The map is marked with several colors indicating friendly areas, known enemy and gun positions, anti-aircraft, .50 caliber, .51 caliber and other crew-served weapons.

At precisely 0500 hours, a curl of cigar smoke rises on a slight breeze as a hulk of a man, who looks like he eats railroad tracks for breakfast, walks through the tent door. Major Johnson, our company commander whose chiseled face is clean-shaven, demands respect due to his sheer size of six two and two hundred and twenty five pounds.

The major removes his poncho, re-lights his morning cigar, and walks to the briefing easel. We all take our seats and the room quiets.

Formalities, such as saluting and coming to attention when a superior officer enters the room, are all but forgotten in our outfit. The simple fact is that enemy snipers who have stalked close to our perimeter are always on the lookout for such acts of respect. They zero in on the saluted officer and thereby claim a real trophy.

The men seat themselves with no concern for protocol and the accustomed hierarchy of rank. Here we all work together as a team. Except for a few die-hards, we're all equal…enlisted and officers alike.

The C.O. looks slowly around the room. His steel-gray eyes have the look of a man who is about to lose a child to a deadly disease. I feel a chill run down my spine.

"Good morning, gentlemen."

"First I would like to commend each and every one of you on the great job you did on the morning mission yesterday. I'm extremely proud of you for working so well together under such adverse conditions. Your performance was super, and you worked hard from way before daylight until late into the night. Regrettably three of our men were killed and several others injured in two crashes."

"I'd like to inform you that of the six men who were injured, two will be back on line within a few days. The other four are critical and will be evacuated to Japan as soon as possible."

"The area we'll be assaulting at first light this morning has enough room in the village square to land three choppers in trail. We'll be utilizing nine lift ships with an escort of four gunships. We'll fly at an altitude of twenty five hundred feet to attempt avoiding ground fire."

"When Yellow One is three minutes out, you'll break into three separate formations in trail, the first continuing to the LZ. The other two formations will hold in a racetrack pattern one mile out until Yellow One calls "short final" At that time, Red Flight will approach the LZ, with White Flight to follow, as soon as Red One is on final."

"Intelligence tells us this village, though previously friendly, has been heavily infiltrated with VC. They're well entrenched. Men, this will be a very hot LZ. Before we arrive, Arty will do a three-minute "hot massage" of the village with their big guns. Approaching the LZ and the village, anyone and anything you see moving in or around the village will be considered a target. I don't care if that target is a man, woman, child, water buffalo, pig or chicken…you are to fire for effect…shoot to kill!"

Wait a minute!! I came here to fight a war! I feel like I'm prepared to kill a male enemy soldier who is shooting at me. But I didn't come here to shoot innocent women and children. I wasn't told this in Basic Training or in Crew Chief School. I will do my part to be a responsible player on this mission. I will protect my comrades as well as myself, but if I see women and children, I intend to hold my fire!

Approaching final, many of the grunts are cheering and letting out war whoops as they psych themselves to hit the ground. The veterans of hot aerial combat assaults remove their helmets and sit on them, to protect what they feel is more important than their heads. The new guys can't quite figure out this ritual. The radio chatter intensifies as the gunships identify the location of heavy ground fire for the rest of the flight, even as they continue to pulverize the LZ with minigun fire. My heart's in overdrive and feels like it's going to explode. It sounds like the inside of a popcorn popper as enemy tracers stream toward us and we take enemy fire from all sides on short final.

The new guys are now sitting on their steel pots too! Fast learners!

The LZ and surrounding village is filled with residual smoke from the artillery barrage and gunship prep that continues. Hootches are on fire in the village and there are secondary explosions as enemy ammunition caches are licked by flames and hit by rounds from the air.

The shouting of the grunts intensifies, and with all the machine-gun fire, the enemy's as well as our own, I'm riveted. I spot two young boys shooting at our flight with AK47s! I hear the rounds hit our aircraft...tick, tick...tick. Instinctively, I cut them down.

Oh Lord, what have I done!

My instinct to live has taken over, but I feel like I am going to lose my cookies.

I can't believe what I've just done! Did I just kill two boys who didn't look more than ten years old? Would they really have killed someone in our flight...maybe even me...or perhaps caused one or more of our choppers to crash, killing everyone on board? Or was their fire harmless, causing a few bullet holes in my ship? I can't believe that I didn't even think before returning their fire...or did I? How did I react so swiftly? Why couldn't I have missed my mark? Is this an indication of what the rest of my tour will be like? I can't handle this! I want to go home!

Born and raised in the Upper Peninsula of Michigan, I had hunted since about the age of nine. My father had given me careful instruction in gun safety, and let me shoot tin cans with first a pellet rifle, and then a .22. Graduating to the .22 was a proud moment for me. Now I knew that Dad fully trusted me to know my target prior to even putting the rifle to my shoulder. He also prided himself in the fact that due to his instruction, and my many enjoyable hours of plinking tin cans, I was a pretty fair shot. As a boy, my thoughts never brought me to the possibility that I would someday carry a gun and actually shoot at people. I couldn't even imagine pointing a gun at a person, let alone a woman or child.

How things have changed in the nineteenth year of my life!

4 October, 1967
Gilligan's Island

Dear Mom and Dad,

This is the first opportunity I have had to write since our relocation.

When we left LZ Dog, we flew out to the coast, then low level all the way up to our new destination. Our new base is called Gilligan's Island. After refueling at Chu Lai, we depart to the north and can see this tropical island a couple of miles ahead. Am I dreaming? Leaning out over my machine gun, my camera captures what appears to be paradise!

Gilligan's Island stretches along the South China Sea for seven miles and is only a mile wide in the middle with both ends tapering off to the sea. This beautiful place is rimmed with snowy white sand beaches where we perch our fifty-plus aircraft.

During our approach, I can see a fairly small village on the west side of the island. Arriving at 1400 hours, the village fishermen are out in their six-foot round basket boats collecting dinner. Looking skyward in disgust, they watch while our gaggle converges on their once private beach. About seventy feet back from the beach edge, lush jungle swallows up the sand. Other than the beach, the only cleared area is in the fishing village. It looks like we'll have our work cut out for us, clearing an LZ and a space for our tents. We've been informed that we'll not be staying on the beach. I guess beach life is too good to add to our dream escape.

This island has never been occupied by American troops, so we have to start building our new LZ from scratch. Just after arriving, about half our ships are committed for a CA just to the west. Since I'm included in the mission, I don't have to help erect the tents and build bunkers. However, we took so much fire on this mission that I would gladly have been manning a shovel rather than my M60.

I'm not even sure what day it is…they're all running together!

We haven't had time to put up concertina wire around our new home yet, so the local Vietnamese are running around the place picking up anything they can that we're throwing away…like pound cake from the C rations that we've been living on. A few things in these cases of C's are just not very appetizing. The Seabees had some heavy equipment sling loaded over here with Flying Cranes and Chinooks. They're clearing an LZ for us and making fairly quick work of it with their dozers. The Gooks are busily gathering up the smaller stumps and branches for their cooking fires.

Sitting on our ship between missions yesterday, Dale and I were eating C rations for lunch with our gunners, when two little girls appeared from a nearby village. They were really cute and even spoke a little English. Nan Ky is nine years old, but I couldn't make out the name of the other, who was eight. They were both very petite in their black silk pajamas, with gorgeous dark eyes, high cheekbones, long silky black hair with bangs, and nickel sized dimples. They both wanted food, so we gave them each a box of C rations and a handful of bubble gum. Thrilled with their handout, they ran down the path toward the village and disappeared into the jungle.

Since we aren't far from the DMZ, our ships are getting well ventilated. It seems like the local VC are better marksmen than their buddies were down south. They haven't perforated my ship yet, but I have seen tracers come so close that I felt I could've reached out and touched them…not that I'd want to.

We lost three ships yesterday to ground fire…two totaled and one salvageable. The crews all made it out alive, but several were wounded.

All the LZs we've flown into have been very hot. The barrels on our machine guns are not having any trouble staying warm. The VC appear to be even more determined to ruin our day here than they were down south. Hopefully, we'll be successful at giving them a major attitude adjustment.

The rain has been pretty persistent since arriving here. Thanks for sending the rain jacket…it's extra large, but that's OK, it keeps more of me dry. Anything is an improvement over what we have been issued for shedding water. The Government Issue olive drab ponchos slide over your head and have a hood. They have lots of room and just hang loosely from your shoulders. You sort of look like you're wearing a skirt around your neck. They're extremely hot, but certainly better than no protection at all.

No mail for a while. It sounds like we won't be getting any for a couple weeks due to our move. It will take a while to catch up with us. Our appreciation will be greater when it does finally arrive.

Love ya,
Bill

CHAPTER 17

KILL OR BE KILLED

5 October, 1967
Gilligan's Island

As dawn peeks over the horizon, our nine slicks and four gunships are crewed and ready for departure. All eyes are on "Yellow One" when he gets the call from Flight Ops to crank. The Flight Leader's rotating beacon comes alive, signaling the rest of the flight. Yellow One's blades begin to rotate, and the other twelve ships press the start button. After a quick warm up, the choppers back out of their revetments one by one, come to a hover, and depart to the west for a short flight to LZ Dog where we'll pick up our passengers. When each ship clears the concertina wire, all beacons are turned off to decrease the chance of attracting ground fire. Climbing to twenty five hundred feet enroute to Dog, the takeoff is uneventful.

Darkness still clings to the land, so visual references are poor as we approach LZ Dog. Yellow One is on the radio to Vipire One (the platoon leader of the troops we're to transport). Approaching the LZ, our nine slicks line up in trail. The grunts are waiting on the side of the strip and board the choppers as soon as the ships settle to the dusty dirt strip. Each aircraft is loaded with eight warriors who are wearing eighty-pound packs. Departing to the north headed for the target, I wonder what is going through the minds of these men. They've been briefed by their Commander prior to our arrival on what to expect on this mission. The tension among all of us seems tighter than a banjo string during our climb to twenty five hundred feet above the jungle.

The cooler air at altitude combined with the breeze blowing through the open chopper doors offers a welcome reprieve from the stifling heat down below. The flight to our destination is only ten minutes, and as the gap closes, the radios begin crackling. The attack is about to begin.

Yellow One is talking with Eagle Eye flying over the village, gathering last minute intelligence. Eagle Eye leaves the area just seconds before to the artillery battery begins to pound the village.

After a three minute artillery prep, the last artillery round to hit the ground is a Willy Peter. Sending up a plume of white smoke it signals that Arty has finished the fire mission.

Immediately, the gunships roll in hot with rockets, 20mm cannon, minigun, and machine gun fire, raking the LZ and surrounding village. I'm the gunner in Yellow Two, the second ship carrying ground troops, and can't believe the intensity while the guns blaze past us on their assault. They make several round robin passes on the LZ as we slow our airspeed allowing them time to work their magic. We're on short final and the guns continue their noisy escort, flying right alongside us now, miniguns belching fire and smoke, with rockets screaming toward the LZ. When the "Guns" fly along side of us, we can hear the loud whoosh – whoosh whenever another rocket is punched off, and the whirrrrrrrrrrr-whirrrrrrrrrrrr of the miniguns belching fire on the enemy. Psyching themselves up to join the battle, the grunts are cheering. All radio frequencies are alive and super active. Some voices are unbelievably calm as they state their circumstances while others sound several octaves higher. The adrenaline in each of us has reached its peak!

It sounds like the inside of a popcorn popper. We watch the green enemy tracers stream toward us, hitting our ship. We're taking enemy fire on short final! Even though we can't see the enemy, my crew chief and I are suppressing the area with bursts from our M60s. Yellow flight slows and flares over the treetops for a landing in the village square. The enemy fire intensifies. We pour out more lead, with the grunts joining in unison with their M16s and M79 grenade launcher. The gunships continue to pound the edge of the LZ. This village, a known enemy stronghold, is ablaze with artillery and gunship rocket fire. Already there are secondary explosions on the ground. The raging hootch fires torch enemy caches of ammo, and the rounds begin cooking off, as the war accelerates. Additional helicopters add to the intensity as hits and enemy sightings are called in . Gunships identify enemy positions while continuing to rake the village with massive fangs of firepower. Everyone is talking at once on three different radio frequencies. The intense noise continues; incessant explosions, minigun, rocket, and machine gun fire are killing the enemy. Enemy dead, a flaming village, falling palm trees, pulverized ground…catastrophic destruction. Despite the devastation, many of the enemy remain alive, fiercely determined to knock us out of the sky. Enemy tracers fill the sky, screaming not just past our ships, but connecting all too often. The thought of never aiming a weapon at another person vanishes. It's time to kill or be killed. Perhaps both will happen!

My faith in God has never been stronger. Even while stitching the area with machine gun fire, I find myself praying silently, or maybe even audibly, to Him for His protection. I firmly believe that God has a time table for all of us. He knows when we will die and in what way. He brought us in...and will take us out...in His way.

Is this my time?

The LZ and surrounding village are filled with residual smoke from the artillery barrage and continuing gunship prep. The shouting of the grunts on board intensifies.

Despite heavy enemy resistance, we continue the mission. Under normal conditions, our pilots exercise a lot of finesse when landing the choppers. These are not normal conditions! Our Aircraft Commander flares radically to slow the ship, levels the skids, and we hit the ground with about a four-g thud while the grunts bail out, firing their weapons into the tree line. Immediately, the pilot pulls pitch departing the LZ to make room for the next approaching ship. Our bird takes several more hits. We're still warming the barrels of our 60s while climbing over the treetops. Now that our troops are on the ground, we're much more selective of our targets, careful to avoid hitting our own soldiers.

When all the men are off-loaded, our helicopters head back toward base. No semblance of a formation is attempted. Each crew is busily making assessments of their aircraft battle damage.

64

The flight leader, Yellow One, calls for a head count during the relatively quiet time while we're licking our wounds. Contacting the Aircraft Commander of each ship, first assuring that all his men are accounted for, he calls for a damage assessment. Even though several are heavily damaged, all are still flying.

Some of the pilots request that the aircraft alongside of them check for unseen damage. Eventually, before returning to base, all aircraft in the flight make half an attempt at a formation. Though some of our aircraft are severely shot up, Charlie hasn't beaten us, and we want to arrive back at our roost with pride.

There are more missions waiting on the board in flight operations. These will have to wait until the choppers have landed and shut down. After a thorough damage assessment is accomplished, we can determine which aircraft need to remain on the ground and how many are flight-worthy enough for another go around at Charlie.

Some of the damage is from bullet holes that have gone clean through the fuselage without hitting any components. Though some of these need to be stop-drilled where cracks may have appeared, others are clean holes and the ships are returned to service. The minor repairs can be delayed until the flight schedule permits them to be patched up.

CHAPTER 18

SLEEPING ON THE BEACH

9 October, 1967
Gilligan's Island

Dear Mom and Dad,

The past several days have been overflowing with mission requests, so we've had little time to erect our tents or get the LZ ready for our birds.

We did get our dreams fulfilled about sleeping on the beach though. The only place to park our ships on the island is on the beach, and we're sleeping in them.

It's great! Before crawling in, if we aren't too beat, we can take a quick dip in the tranquil waters of the South China Sea! We don't have any fresh water yet to take showers, but at least the salt water gets the big chunks off. It's even worth the salt itch that comes later.

I'm finally doing what I came here for. As of today, I've been assigned a ship of my own. I'll be crewing an H Model #770. It just came out of a one hundred hour inspection. Mr. Bauer, the maintenance pilot, had to do a test flight for an hour and asked if I wanted to fly as his co-pilot. I loved it! Even though we only had time to do a few basic maneuvers, I'm hooked! Now I wish I'd gone to flight school...maybe someday.

The forecast is for a major typhoon to hit tonight. Most of the choppers were ferried back to Chu Lai to weather the storm. A few of us have to stay on the island to guard whatever is left behind. Since my time in country is not real high, I am one of the guys whose hand was raised by the First Sergeant to "volunteer" to spend the night. It started to rain fiercely about an hour ago and the wind is SCREAMING! There isn't any way to tie the choppers down. They're beginning to rock pretty hard and the skids are settling into the soft sand. That's a plus because it'll help anchor them. Guess we'll have to worry about digging them out when the storm subsides. We're keeping three here on the beach overnight. That seems insane to me, but it wasn't my decision to make.

It's 0300 hours. The worst of the storm is over. I'm on break from guard duty, so I'll try to finish this by the glow of my penlight.

The winds were ferocious about an hour ago. I thought we'd lose the choppers, but they rode out the weather with only minor damage to cowlings. I think the plexiglass windshields probably suffered from the sandblasting. We'll find out after daylight.

Now at 0800 hours, it looks like we'll have to spend the morning polishing the windshields. They were badly crazed by the wind-driven sand last night.

The mess tent is just that…a mess, so although C-rations don't compare to Mom's Swedish pancakes, if you're really hungry they are better than nothing. The few tents that had been pitched were all flattened by the storm last night. There are a lot of trees down and the entire company area is under several inches of water. Fortunately, the island is all sand, so I think the water will soak in readily.

Time for work.
Love,
Bill

CHAPTER 19

NITE HUNTER

14 October, 1967
Gilligan's Island

The missions began at 0500 hours, so while completing my post flight inspection at 1830 hours this evening, I look forward to the rest of the night off to catch up on some much needed rest.

While buttoning up the cowling, Top walks up to inform me that my ship is assigned to a Nite Hunter Mission, with a pre-brief at 2230 hours. Rumor has it that these missions are where the action is and although I'm exhausted, it sounds intriguing. My good friend, Dale Erickson, will be my gunner for the night mission.

The rules of the game over here are much simpler after dark. Anything that moves is fair game. This is when Charlie relocates the bulk of their men and supplies. Nite Hunter Missions are designed to put a kink in their supply line.

These missions involve two slicks, Lightning Bug and Rabbit, assisted by two gunships, Venom One and Venom Two. The missions are conducted well after dark to allow the enemy to get comfortably into his evening escapades before we interrupt him.

Since I've just done a post flight inspection, it'll suffice as a preflight. When finished, I tie down the blades before leaving the flight line.

While carrying my gear to my tent, I take a few minutes to go to the listre bag to rinse off the days dust and grime before getting a bite to eat.

I can smell the Italian aroma of lasagna on the way to the mess tent. I have a big appetite tonight because it's been a long, long day. But, my gut churns. I hate Italian food! Mom always told me that if I ever got hungry enough, I'd eat anything. As usual, she was right.

At 2300 hours, Rabbit is in the lead over the treetops. Venom flight climbs to twenty five hundred feet, and my ship, Lightning Bug, heads for five thousand feet. Our AO for the night is between Chu Lai and the area fifteen miles to the northwest. This area consists of a mixture of rice paddies, rolling hills, and meandering streams. Chu Lai is located on the South China Sea.

Here's the scenario: Rabbit is armed with its usual two M60s along with a couple cases of frags and Willy Peter. Lying on the deck of the ship is a sniper with a starlight scope. Flying slowly over the treetops, along the river, with the lights out, the sniper searches for targets (sampans and troops). The Gooks know they are not to be out at night unless they want to put up with harassment from us. When the sniper spots a target, he marks it with tracers, while the crew chief and gunner open up with their 60s and drop grenades on the sampans. When the Venom flight sees the action from twenty five hundred feet, they roll in hot. If it is a real dark night or the action gets dicey, Lightning Bug drops aircraft flares from above to light up the area.

We have forty five flares stacked on the deck of the aircraft. The four-foot long magnesium flares are five inches in diameter and weigh in at fifty pounds each.

Only five minutes into the flight, the sniper on board Rabbit spots a sampan through the eerie green light of his scope. He fires tracers into the target and both door gunners open fire. Venom One and Two come in hot from the rear as they punch off four rockets each. From our altitude, we have a ringside seat and watch as enemy tracers stream toward the gunships. The muzzle flashes are easily visible in the ink black night and they're coming from the shoreline.

"Lightning Bug, Venom One is receiving fire from the east side of the river. How about lighting 'em up for us?"

"Roger, Venom One. We're watching the action and will begin the drop now."

We begin circling while I scoot the first flare out the door. Prior to takeoff, I had prepped the first flare by fastening one end of a 1/8" x 48" aircraft cable to a "D" ring in the floor of the chopper. The other end is fastened to the arming pin in the business end of the flare. When the pilot calls for a flare, the prepped one is pushed out the open door of the ship, with the pin being pulled free by the cable. The flare is now armed and begins to burn brightly as it descends slowly suspended from its parachute toward the jungle below.

To keep the aircraft load properly balanced, my gunner and I release the flares out alternate doors. When the first nears the ground, the next is released. This keeps the area well lit while Venom continues firing at targets that are now more easily seen.

Rabbit is flying a slightly wider pattern to avoid being struck by rounds from the Venom flight as the crew continues their search for more targets.

After forty five minutes of sporadic ground fire, followed by a couple of secondary explosions caused by the American fire finding its mark and hitting enemy munitions caches, I release another flare. The cable snags, causing the pin to be pulled before the flare exits the aircraft. The end of the flare blows off instantly! With ignition, the parachute shoots out through the opposite door barely missing my gunner. The magnesium is now burning ferociously in the cargo area! My left hand immediately goes numb. The crew is all momentarily blinded while I scramble to kick the burning canister out the door so it won't ignite the rest of our cargo and blow us all to bits.

We're all in a state of shock. The pilots and gunner ask if I'm OK. Just after I say that I think I am, I feel blood running down my left hand, and a sharp pain in my left arm and shoulder. My hand is burned and bleeding profusely.

With Dale applying bandages to my hand and wrist, the mission is aborted and we fly immediately to LZ Baldy, the closest medical facility. Rabbit and Venom One and Two follow in trail since the entire mission is now scrapped.

Calling ahead to alert the medical personnel at Baldy that we're inbound with an ambulatory injury, the pilot continues his course to the LZ. The medics run out of the tent that serves as a medical aid station while our chopper descends to the heli-pad.

After shutting down, the pilots are informed that I'll have to be admitted until I recover, so they are free to return to Chu Lai.

The Medics clean up the wounds and stitch up the gashes in my wrist, hand, thumb and forefinger. The molten magnesium has caused second and third degree burns on my hand and wrist and I have some pretty good bruises. It looks like I'll be here for a few days. I'm thankful the accident wasn't any worse.

CHAPTER 20

HANG 'EM HIGH

31 October, 1967
Gilligan's Island

We arrive back on the island in time for supper - a rare treat - after a long day of flying re-supply missions and a couple of medivacs. We're told that one of our crews picked up a projector and a movie today from the mainland. The show starts at 2200 hours!

Not knowing just how to act, since we've not had the privilege of watching a movie since we've been over here, we all gather in the company area under the beautiful palm trees between the tents and the flight line, just prior to show time. Setting up our lawn chairs, footlockers and steel pots to sit on, we're ready for the flick. The beer and coke flow freely. The only thing missing is popcorn.

Half way through Hang 'Em High, several of us notice a very familiar smell...rotten fish...like the breath of the Vietnamese. We're sitting downwind of the village, so assume the odor is coming from there. Ignoring the smell, we continue watching Clint Eastwood at his best.

The minute the movie begins to run the credits, mortars and rockets precede a full-scale ground attack. While many run for the cover of the foxholes, several of the crews make it to the flight line. Most are too late. Their ships already destroyed by satchel charges placed by the VC who have penetrated our defenses. Dale's ship and mine are parked side by side. While running toward them, we find his ship consumed by fire, and continue to my aircraft. It appears to be unscathed…so far. Two pilots are running down the flight line looking for a flyable ship. We yell to them to come and fly ours. Charles Callahan takes the Aircraft Commander's seat, while his co-pilot jumps into the other. Hastily starting up the turbine, while machine gun fire is zipping all around, Callahan gets the rotors up to speed and we're off. Upset that they have not destroyed all the ships on the island, the Gooks open up on us just as we're clearing the trees. Though we take a few rounds, we're still flying.

Notifying the Flight Ops bunker that we're in the air, they ask us to fly to Chu Lai, just across the bay, to get a load of aircraft flares and keep the island lit up the rest of the night. A couple of gunships join us from the mainland. Throughout the night we continue to drop flares as well as refuel and reload flares back at Chu Lai when necessary.

The ground attack lasts only fifteen minutes. Most of the helicopters on the ground are destroyed or so badly damaged they are disabled.

Following the attack, action is pretty slow until 0300 hours when we spot two sampans making a run for the mainland. They don't stay afloat long. As soon as the gunships get our call, the sampans are blown to bits with rockets and minigun fire. Quite a sight in the middle of the night!

At daybreak, we buzz all the sampans that are out…mostly fishermen. One sampan has a straw hat lying in the water next to it. Further investigation reveals that the VC boat is moored in three feet of water. We see the suspected owner of the hat, floating face down about fifty feet away.

Approaching another boat, the two men aboard run to the bow and quickly cover up their cargo. Circling overhead with our guns trained on them, we make a call for assistance. A few minutes later another chopper arrives with several grunts on board. Herding the sampan to shore with the chopper guns trained on the suspects, several weapons are discovered under the cover. The two "fishermen" are taken prisoner.

When the excitement is over, we return to the flight line. On our approach we see six enemy bodies clad in black pajamas laying across the concertina wire. We also see that everyone is busily cleaning up the company area and flight line.

The report is that six Gooks were captured during the night and our unit had killed between eight and twelve enemy. We have five men injured, four ships demolished, and all but mine and two other choppers are heavily damaged. I have only one hole to patch from a piece of shrapnel that hit my ship. It appeared to come from the explosion when Dale's aircraft was hit.

According to intelligence, this attack was done by fifty men. After the strike, the Gooks were to head for the north end of the island to board waiting sampans and escape to the mainland to hide out. The boat that the gunships sunk was apparently one of those.

Yesterday, a little boy wandered onto the flight line and told one of the crew chiefs that there are a lot of VC on the island. The word was passed up to battalion headquarters where the colonel's only response was, "We'll watch them and see if they try anything." I guess the Old Man didn't take his education to heart last night!

CHAPTER 21

SILVER DAGGER

2 November, 1967
Gilligan's Island

When we identify the driver of the jeep from Flight Ops, my watch shows 1945 hours. Captain Nelson asks us to go on an emergency ammo re-supply mission into an area where we have never been. The unit requesting the ammo has been engaged in a fire fight all afternoon, using up the majority of their ammunition.

The situation is bleak. The company under attack requested an emergency re-supply over two hours ago saying that their situation is critical. The VC have them surrounded on three sides. Until now, the situation has been too hot to risk sending in a chopper even though over one hundred men's lives are at stake. If ammo isn't received soon, the American position will surely be overrun. Though not likely, the enemy pressure may slack off when the sky darkens. This is nothing more than a dream! Darkness is the enemy's friend. After several hours of battle, we all believe the attack will only become more ferocious as nightfall continues. A lot, if not all, of our men will be lost if we don't at least attempt an ammo drop.

While sitting on the cargo deck of the chopper receiving our preflight briefing, we spread out the flight charts. With the two flashlights that we've hung on the ceiling and a couple of pen lights, we plot our course to the battle-torn LZ.

Warrant Officer Callahan marks the coordinates on the map. Warrant Officer Jewitt, the aircraft commander, asks each of us if we're willing to risk our lives to save these guys. We all give him a hearty thumbs up! We're then advised that when we hover over to the ammo dump to pick up our load of munitions, there will be two men who have volunteered to go along. Their job is to off-load the precious cargo as quickly as possible enabling Eddie Hoklotubbe, my gunner, and I to stay on our guns to engage the enemy…not if, but when it's needed. This is beginning to sound a bit dicey.

But hey, we'll be under the cover of darkness…in the mountains…very dark, overcast night…looking and feeling like rain…black out conditions…an angry, unknown enemy concentration below us. Is this really what I came for?

I'm glad to have Eddie with me tonight. He's been my gunner since the first part of October, and we work well together. If things get tough, I know I can count on this Choctaw Indian to do whatever it takes to help get us out of a corner. "Chief" is a very aggressive gunner and deadly accurate. He's always loaded for bear with his arsenal consisting of an M16, M60, M79, several canisters of smoke, a couple Willy Peters, and enough frags to make him someone that Charlie really doesn't want to mess with. He's built like he could take on five or six Gooks at once and come out on top, and would willingly do so, if it wouldn't mess up his hairdo. He carries a comb in his ammo box.

After we're briefed on the frequency and call sign to use while contacting the engaged unit, the Flight Ops captain wishes us luck and assures us that we will return to a hot meal; he knows it's been a long day.

While hover-taxiing over to the loading area next to the ammo dump, the mission pre-brief runs rapidly through my mind.

How could I possibly have been in my right mind when I volunteered for this? Flying in Vietnam on a daily basis is hazardous enough. All the odds are against me on this one. Do I have a death wish that I didn't know was there? I don't need to be a hero! I have a family and girlfriend to go home to. What would they think if they knew what I'm about to do? Well, I'm committed now. Will God see me through this, even though I feel like I've made a reckless mistake? But…I had to help save those men out there!

God has sustained me for over three months in Vietnam. There are times that I honestly didn't think I would come out of the ruckus alive. White Robe Six is the reverent call sign that the flight crews have created for God. This is just one more assignment for WR6. Surely He will protect us one more time on this mission of mercy.

At the re-arming area, six guys quickly load our ship with ammo for M16, M60, and M79 grenade launchers. There are cases of mortar rounds and boxes of frag grenades in the mix too, along with flares, claymores and .12 gauge buckshot for close range work. Two of the loaders who are built like gorillas climb aboard, strapping themselves in to the jump seats. They're the crazy ones who volunteered to help. These men are both armed with M16s. Bandoleers of ammo drape their flak vests. They look like they mean business. Neither have shaven for several days and their jungle fatigues are ratty and torn. They look like they have a beef to settle with Charlie...just the kind of guys we want with us if we get in a tight spot!

Prior to departure, we all cinch up our seat harnesses. For some reason, this seems to give us a warm fuzzy feeling. Our ship is given clearance by the tower for a departure to the west. Unfortunately, this mission does not include gunship support. They're all committed to another mission. Did I say this looked dicey?

Clearing the perimeter fence, the co-pilot douses all exterior lights and turns the red cockpit lighting down to enable the crew to get accustomed to the blackness of the night. At this point, the pilots are essentially flying by reference to the cockpit instruments with no visible horizon on which they can rely. It's a nasty night!

My skin is feeling very prickly!

We fly northwest toward the coordinates of death and are able to contact Cat Claw at our target when we're four miles out.

"Cat Claw, this is Silver Dagger, over."

Heard over the staccato of gunfire, in a voice that sounds like his undies are in a wad, "Silver Dagger, we read you five by five, over."

"Cat Claw, we're four miles out with your boxes of cookies. Give me a ten count."

Keying his mike, the radio operator counts down from ten, so we can home in on his signal to give us a positive fix on which direction to fly to arrive at his position.

The location that we have marked on the map is at twenty five hundred feet in the mountains. Looking toward our destination, we have it pinpointed. Red and green tracers are wildly exchanging places.

"Cat Claw we see tracers coming from your position now."

Our drop off point is not an LZ, so we'll have to hover over the treetops while the munitions are booted out the doors.

"Cat Claw, what is your SITREP, over?"

Again over the sounds of sporadic gunfire, "We've been taking small arms and automatic weapons fire from all quadrants, but the bulk of it has been from up the mountain south of our present location. Enemy fire has dropped off substantially. We're nearly out of supplies and suggest you approach from the north. Fire has been lightest from that quadrant over the past hour. We have seven WIA and five KIA. Will you be able to transport? Wind is light. Over."

"We're unable to pick up wounded as we understand you have no LZ. Is that affirmative? Over."

In a louder voice to be heard above the intensifying gunfire, "Silver Dagger, there's a bomb crater down slope from our position, but within our perimeter. If you can make your approach to the edge of that and hover, we'd like to load four criticals, over."

"Cat Claw, we'll do our best. Have a ground guide on the south side of the crater with a flashlight to guide us. We're blacked out. Put down all the covering fire you can for us starting now. Over."

Turning a half-mile final, we see tracers sporadically going out as well as coming in to our drop-off point. Still no flashlight. Suddenly...

"Cat Claw, we have your light!"

We're in the popcorn machine and the enemy tracers begin arcing toward the sky in our general direction. The Gooks can hear us, but with the ink black sky and no lights on our ship, they haven't spotted us yet.

Approaching one hundred yards from our target, the altimeter shows we're a hundred feet above ground. Making a steep approach we can now make out some tree silhouettes below.

"Lookin' good, Silver Dagger."

Tick, tick...tick............tick.....tick. Rounds begin penetrating our chopper! No warning lights yet. We continue.

Eddie and I cut loose with the 60s and douse the area just outside the perimeter. We can clearly see where the enemy tracers are coming from.

"Silver Dagger's takin' hits…You guys better be quick!"

Unless things get a lot worse, we must continue the mission. We're the only hope for these brave young men to survive the night.

Coming into a low hover over the crater, we take several more rounds. The pilot places the left skid on the ground with a thud while the other skid hangs out over the crater. The rotor blades are barely clearing the trees on the left and off the nose of the helicopter. Eddie and I stay on the guns while our volunteer gorillas kick the ammo out the doors and into the crater as fast as they can, while several grunts help from the left side. More grunts are now running toward us with four of the most critically wounded.

The excitement intensifies. One of the wounded men can be heard screaming above the noise of the turbine engine mixed with that of incoming and outgoing fire. With the covering fire going out of the perimeter, you wouldn't think these men were almost out of ammo. But then, they know our primary mission is to drop off enough ammo to last them until daybreak when another supply ship will likely be ordered. Picking up the wounded is our secondary mission. We're glad to do it. Hopefully, they'll all avoid the Grim Reaper.

The emergency cargo is out and the wounded are loaded. From the bomb crater, we climb vertically to be sure our aircraft clears the trees that we're unable to see clearly due to the darkness and the flickering tracers that play havoc with our night vision. We're still drawing fire and taking hits during our climb while Eddie and I continue to hose down the area to our flanks in an attempt to keep the enemy at bay. The pilot pulls pitch and moves the cyclic stick as far forward as he can to produce a nose low attitude. This causes the aircraft to gain life-saving airspeed as rapidly as possible.

"Silver Dagger, you guys are angels! We can't thank you enough. We owe you big-time, over."

"Our pleasure Cat Claw. We know you guys would do the same for us if we were in a scrape. Glad to be of help. Best of luck tonight."

It's a fifteen-minute flight to the hospital pad at Chu Lai. We climb to fifteen hundred feet to get out of the range of small arms fire, enabling Eddie and I to crawl forward to see if we can help the guys we just picked up.

I turn the cabin lights on low to see what we're dealing with. They're all badly wounded. Though all wounds are bandaged, it's obvious that these guys were patched up during the heat of battle with very little time spent on the dressings. One severely injured has lost his left leg just below the knee, and his left arm is in a sling in an attempt to keep it attached to a bit of muscle and bone shards just below his armpit. He's staring into space...the effects of morphine and shock.

The second man is rolling on the deck of the chopper and screaming in pain. Half of his belly is blown away and there are numerous cuts on his face. It looks like he tangled with a grenade or mortar round.

A bullet passed through the right wrist of the third soldier. The wrist bones are shattered.

The fourth soldier has his eyes bandaged and a couple of bullet holes in his left arm. His left ear is hanging on by a thin shred of skin.

Why can't man settle his disputes in a more humane way than trying to kill each other? I hate this job!

When we're ten minutes out, Mr. Callahan calls in to alert the medical crew that we're inbound with four WIA.

Landing at the medivac pad, we're met by several attendants with stretchers. Unloading the four unlucky men onto stretchers, we wish them well. They'll need it! They'll get immediate care by men and women who seldom rest. The medical personnel over here are very dedicated and efficient. I'm sure they must have horrible nightmares over the ungodly amounts of blood and guts they see. They just continue on with whatever treatments they can offer the men who have sacrificed so much.

Flying back to put our bird to bed after a long day, we're very grateful to have been a part of this last mission. Though risky, it was very rewarding to be able to give the four wounded a chance to live. We can only hope and pray that the ammo we dropped off on that mountainside gives the rest of that unit the same opportunity.

It appears that our missions are complete for the day. Retreating to our company revetment, the pilots and gunner help me post-flight the ship. With our flashlights, we're able to find only seven bullet holes. None of them seem serious enough to warrant grounding the ship for the morning missions. I'll do a more thorough inspection at first light.

CHAPTER 22

HE DIED IN MY ARMS

4 November, 1967
Gilligan's Island

Dear Mom and Dad,
    Yesterday morning I went to get a malaria smear test. Even though I had all the symptoms…cold sweat, chills, severe headache, and fever with aching muscles, it proved negative. The Doc sent me back to my company, where I slept all afternoon in my sleeping bag with the outside temp at 105…and I was still cold!
    I went back for more tests after our missions this morning, and they decided to hospitalize me for a couple days of observation.
    Time for another siesta. At least maybe I'll get caught up on some sleep, if these guys ever quit sticking me with needles!
    After my nap, I'm told that I have Amoebic Dysentery.

6 November, 1967

    A few days ago, my ship was on a Charlie-Charlie. The colonel we had aboard was directing a massive ground attack. We were circling out of the range of ground fire while looking for enemy bunkers in the area and watching to see if any of the Gooks were trying to evade our advancing troops.
    We saw four Gooks working in a nearby rice paddy and flew low overhead to check them out. Two of the men looked to be in their early twenties and the other two were fairly old. It is very

82

uncommon to see young men working the fields. They're generally in the military on one side or the other. When they saw us coming, the younger ones made a dash for a path through the jungle that led to the village. The colonel wanted me to keep them in the paddy with my machine gun until we could call in some grunts to take them prisoners. One dove into a spider hole before my rounds even hit the ground, while the other kept going as fast as his bare feet would allow…until I shortened his toenails. He stopped abruptly, stripping off his shirt to show he had no weapons, and threw up his hands. We called in a gunship to keep him cornered so we could go to refuel. Before our replacement was able to get on station, our suspect made a beeline for a bunker. We swooped down on him and I cut loose. The colonel was screaming for me to kill him if I had to. My tracers were going between his legs when he got the message and threw his hands up again. By then, a load of grunts had landed and captured the slippery little guy.

The colonel congratulated me on my shooting and said he was glad that I didn't kill the Gook. Our men wanted him captured for interrogation. I was glad too, until that afternoon when we medivaced three Marines whose three-quarter ton truck hit a booby-trapped white phosphorous round on a bridge. When we picked these guys up, I was ready to kill any VC or NVA!

Approaching to land in a rice paddy next to the bridge, we received sniper fire. The second we landed, four men carried two of the wounded to our bird in filthy poncho liners, and the third hobbled aboard with one and one half legs. One man had his stomach and intestines hanging out. They were still smoking from the explosion. The other Marine was bleeding profusely from a one-inch diameter hole in the top of his head. None of these poor guys had any hair left…it had all been burned off. Their skin was ashen gray with splotches of red and black from the burns they received. On departure, we received a few more rounds of small arms fire, but fortunately, the enemy in this location couldn't shoot worth a darn.

I had one bandage large enough to stop the bleeding on the head wound, but the guy looked extremely pale. I think he had already lost more blood than he could spare. While I bandaged his wound, he died in my arms. Rivulets of tears streamed down my cheeks…I didn't even know this boy. I thought I was beyond that by now because I have seen so much of this. Perhaps I've seen too much. My emotions are totally frazzled. Without any more bandages on board that were large enough to do these guys any good, we felt very helpless on the eight-minute flight to LZ Baldy where we delivered these men to the field hospital.

So now, maybe you understand why I'm growing bitter and looking for revenge. Dad, I feel like I may have overstepped my bounds by telling you these graphic details. I'm sorry. I just had to tell someone. I'm overwhelmed. Why can't the politicians back in the world wake up and see how many men they are wasting over here…Americans as well as Vietnamese, Australians, Canadians, Koreans…what a heart breaker this war is!

I guess I better hit the rack and cool down.

I sure miss you all! Write soon!!

Love,

Bill

CHAPTER 23

DEATH VALLEY

7 November, 1967
Chu Lai

Our neighbors began to get rude with the fireworks and attacked us nightly on the island, so we elected to move to Chu Lai, just a couple miles across the bay. This is a much more secure base and almost like stateside. No flush johns, but we do have real faucets and even clean water - a real treat! We even live in hootches rather than tents. Most of them are built up on stilts, with wooden frames. The bottom four feet are sided with plywood, while the upper half is covered with mosquito netting. Plywood floors and a metal roof top it off. Spartan, yes. However, it's a lot more comfortable than the tents we've been living in.

Our company area is up on a fairly high ridge overlooking the flight line and the sea. It's a typical base with few trees, but well laid out with Navy, Marines, Air Force, and of course the Army on the same plot of ground. The majority of the living quarters are on the side hill and ridge, with the airstrip and various chopper flight lines near the shoreline. The large peninsula stretches out into the gorgeous South China Sea. The surrounding area is a lush emerald green and looks like pictures I've seen of Hawaii. This is one beautiful country! It's a shame that we are ruining it with bomb craters, agent orange and burned out villages.

There is even a PX here, so if I ever get some time off, I'll wander over there and see what I've been doing without.

We'll see how long it will be before the Brass makes the decision to move us again. I'm sure they won't want to spoil us!

8 November, 1967

Army intelligence has discovered at least three NVA regiments in an area west of here called "Death Valley." A couple of days ago, we began missions there with an eighteen ship CA. On the initial insertion, we lost five ships. Several of my buddies were shot down, but all crews miraculously escaped with only minor injuries. At any rate, we received fire every time we flew into our various LZ's in the valley. I guess it was properly named…
"Death Valley."

Most of our aircraft took several hits, mine included. My ship still holds water with only a couple minor holes that I need to patch. After getting shot up, it takes almost more time to inspect the aircraft than it does to repair bullet holes. Even though it's usually obvious where the bullets go in, it's very important to check in all the inspection holes of the fuselage to see what else the rounds may have hit. Inspection holes are cut in the aircraft during manufacture and covered with removable panels to enable maintenance people to inspect and adjust critical areas of the ship. Once they hit the outside skin, the bullet often shreds into multiple pieces and the resulting shrapnel may ricochet and do additional damage to hydraulics, controls, control cables, or fuel and oil reservoirs. Helicopters are very prone to vibration. If everything in the controls and main and tail rotor blades are not absolutely perfect, a vibration can result and cause severe damage, often resulting in a catastrophic crash without much, if any, warning. A thorough inspection is cheap insurance. Many say that a chopper is a pile of parts all trying to go in opposite directions. They are certainly cantankerous, but overall, if maintained properly, they are very reliable and a super asset in this war.

We flew all day today and I was feeling poorly the whole time. We began flying at 0530 hours and were supposed to be released at 1600 hours. We actually quit flying three and a half hours after that.

While the gunner and I are prepping the aircraft for the next morning's flight, we hear a jeep approaching. Our entire crew has a sick feeling. Another mission. We're wiped out and need rest. What flight could possibly be required at this time of day?

CHAPTER 24

UNDER FIRE

9 November, 1967
Chu Lai

Flying just above the treetops and snaking up the river at 2200 hours, we're navigating by the light of the moon reflecting off the water. It's a beautiful scene with the jungle quiet below. Only the whop, whop, whop of the big Huey blades can be heard. Carrying an urgently needed load of ammo, we're pretty heavy, causing the popping of the blades to be louder while our aircraft makes the tight turns along the stream toward our destination.

Our quick briefing instructed us to fly up the river about three miles, until we either spotted a firefight on the west side of the river, or until the unit under attack contacted us. They have our freq and have been told we would attempt a delivery of life saving cargo ASAP.

After only a couple of miles, we can see a glow in the sky a mile or so upstream. Another river bend and tracers are reaching toward the moon.

Calling in for a SITREP, we're not surprised to confirm our suspicions. The company we are to resupply has been under attack most of the day. The enemy is relentlessly continuing the onslaught from all quadrants. The American supply of ammo is all but expended. They're pleading for more so they can have hopes of surviving the night.

After discussion amongst the crew, the unanimous decision is made. We'll continue the mission. The grunt on the radio is told

88

that we'll continue directly toward their LZ. The destination is obvious by all the incoming and outgoing fire.

We're told that all members of our friendly unit are on the perimeter. The small clearing they're trying to defend is void of personnel. The LZ lies on a two hundred foot ridge right along the river according to the radioman.

Still lying low over the river, we're flying at ninety knots. Our plan is to surprise the enemy. If we try maneuvering around for a decent approach, Charlie will have us pinpointed against the fully lit sky. We'll be toast!

Gaining a little speed to make the two hundred foot climb up the ridge with the lights out, we're in good shape with no tracers coming our way. Just as we arrive over the tight LZ, our Aircraft Commander almost stands the Huey on it's tail as he does a quick stop, bringing the chopper to a hesitant hover. Eddie and I have already crawled up to the cargo area and are tossing the ammo out the doors as fast as we can move. After a couple crates of ammo hit the ground, the enemy fire begins to creep our way slowly. With our adrenaline pumping wildly, we get the load off in seconds and jump back in our seats to man our guns while the pilots pull pitch and rapidly move the cyclic forward to gain speed. Heading back down the ridge, the Indian and I hammer away at the source of the tracers heading our way like a swarm of angry hornets! We hear several rounds hit the aircraft, but are soon out of range of the communist gunners. Flying back down the river at low level, the aircraft is at full speed. We're all scared beyond words. It's much like being chased by a big dog, you not only run fast, but further than you need to. No one is chasing us, but fright has our entire crew charged up.

Arriving back on the flight line, we survey the damage by flashlight. Finding several bullet holes in the blades and fuselage, we ground the ship until first light, when we can do a more thorough inspection.

We've cheated death again. Hopefully, we delivered life to our men on the ground.

In just four days, another one of our crews will be less fortunate.

CHAPTER 25

MIA OR KIA

13 November, 1967
Chu Lai

Dear Mom and Dad,

During the time I was in the hospital with dysentery, I meant to tell you that I met several grunts who told me how much they appreciate the whirly bird crews. Their praise was enough to make all of the missions I've been on worthwhile.

We just received word that LZ Baldy is under attack. Three of our ships were shot down and two of our men were wounded. I'm on standby to fly tonight, so I better get ready to go.

Will try to write more later.

Love,
Bill

17 November, 1967
Chu Lai

A couple of days ago while crewing Yellow Three on a CA, we were taking heavy automatic weapons fire when the Charlie Charlie ship, flying above the battle, took several hits from automatic weapons and .50 cal. and crashed. All on board were killed including the crew of four, a colonel and two majors. The crew chief, gunner and aircraft commander were all close friends. The co-pilot was new in our company, so I didn't know him well.

The gunner's name was Paul Johnson. He bunked in our crew chief tent even though he had just begun to be a gunner. He slept just two bunks down from me and was a very soft-spoken grunt with a great personality...just a super nice guy. He was tired of being in an infantry platoon and asked to be transferred to our unit to be a gunner.

It was tough to watch as these guys went down. Even though there was a chance they would all survive, when they're heading down in a disabled aircraft toward enemy infested territory, the odds aren't favorable. The feeling of helplessness was overwhelming as soon as they were hit. There was nothing we could do except attempt a rescue.

Landing alongside of them, and finding most of them dead except for the gunner, was awful. In the few short months that I've been in this unit, I've made some very close friends...maybe too close.

The story unfolds below as it happened.

Making a high approach to the LZ on the edge of a village for a CA, we are descending out of one thousand feet. The reason for the higher than normal approach is because of the expected unfriendly territory below. The first ship in our gaggle of six plus two gunships has landed, unloaded and departed. We've all received fairly heavy resistance. Now on short final, our flight is receiving sporadic fire when the co-pilot of the Charlie-Charlie aircraft calls...

"Mayday, Mayday, Mayday...Charlie-Charlie is hit. We have a fire light. Going down!"

There's not much time to carry on a conversation. The crew is very busy...and very scared, judging by the sound of the co-pilot's voice.

"Yellow Two has a visual on you. You're on fire, better get it down as fast as you can! We'll follow you down, Buddy."

"Roger, Yellow Two. We're going to attempt an autorotation into the rice paddy ahead."

"We haven't dropped our grunts yet, so will insert them to secure your LZ. We're right behind you. Good luck!"

The ground fire intensifies. The Gooks know they've made a score. They can see the smoke trail coming from the crippled chopper.

The troubled ship and our aircraft are still taking enemy fire. Tick…tick…tick…tick…tick…tick. We're low and slow enough now to make for an easier target.

With an even higher pitch to his voice, "We've lost hydraulics! Losing control!"

Within a few very short seconds, "We're goin' in!"

On short final to the small rice paddy, it's obvious that this ship is struggling. They've lost too much rotor rpm now, and their smokey final descent is much too rapid for a safe arrival. Landing in the far end of the paddy, the skids collapse from the extremely hard crash. The aircraft lurches forward in the stinking muck, causing the main rotor blade disc to tip rearward, chopping off the tail boom just in front of the vertical stabilizer. This sends pieces of the tail and rotor blades scattering in all directions while the ship burns ferociously. The main rotor mast is twisted from the impact and the weight from the mast head causes the mast to fall over the back of Paul, pinning him against his machine gun mount.

Landing within thirty yards of the burning chopper, seconds after they hit the ground, our grunts bail out into the mud to set up a protective perimeter while Eddie and I make a run for the downed aircraft with our ship's fire extinguisher. The heat from the burning magnesium is hotter than hell itself, and no match for our small extinguisher! We're only able to get to the Colonel at the open doorway of the cargo area, release his seat belt, and pull his lifeless body from the wreckage. He's already badly burned. Both Eddie and I grab him by the forearms. The skin on his right arm slides off in Eddie's gloves...a gruesome site!

There's no sign of movement. It appears that everyone has perished from the impact. Running from the heat, expecting an explosion at any time, one last look back, and we see that Paul is still moving, though pinned between the mast and his machine gun. Returning to the inferno, we have to try to save our buddy! Attempting to free him from the weight of the rotor mast, we find the weight of the mast, rotor head and the broken ends of the blades to be too great for us to even budge. Retreating from the heat and looking back, Paul's clothing is now engulfed in flames. Stepping back in anguish, we watch while his body writhes in pain. His eyes have an eerie look of appreciation for our failed attempt to save his life, and even though he's within seconds of death, his gaze also appears peaceful.

Further rescue attempts are impossible. The smells of burning flesh and hair mixed with that of the flaming aircraft, fuel, magnesium, engine oil, and hydraulic fluid are unforgettable. Grabbing one of the passengers by the arms and legs, we carry him back to our running aircraft, and as soon as we're on board, Mr. Jewitt pulls pitch. Just clearing the tree line and beginning a right turn, we hear the explosion as the destroyed aircraft takes five good men to their fiery grave.

While our aircraft reaches for a safe altitude, I cry out to White Robe Six.

"Why must good men die such horrific deaths Lord?"

You always told me that life isn't fair Dad, but this is beyond my comprehension! I've seen a lot of aircraft shot down and have lost several good friends. I thought I was being hardened and getting used to death, but this one hit me really hard. I will certainly miss Paul, even tonight. He was not only a close friend, but my bunk mate.

With five men still in the charred aircraft, the grunts stayed in position to guard what was left of the bodies until the remains could be collected. If the site had been abandoned, the Gooks would have taken great pleasure in scraping up what was left. They successfully count on their barbarism to be a real morale breaker.

This terrible accident happened at 0700 hours. We were unable to collect any dog tags other than from the Colonel and the passenger, who we freed from the wreckage. We had a mission in the afternoon to the crash site with a team of three from Graves Registration. Their job was to sift through the ashes looking for dog tags. We left them there for two hours and picked them up an hour before dark. No dog tags…Therefore, military policy are to list all these men as MIA!

Our entire crew argued with Flight Operations and the Old Man over that decision. Our crew and passengers witnessed not only the fatal crash, but also the fact that there were absolutely no survivors, and told them that the military is being dishonest when they know beyond a shadow of a doubt that all these good men were killed in action for their country. This is their policy and apparently always has been. It stinks.

93

Dad, I have a good notion to write to the families myself and tell them what happened, but I would probably be court-martialed! (I later did write to one of the families.)

The Battalion Chaplain held a memorial service for these brave men that evening after dark. All of us who weren't out on a mission attended, and I didn't witness a dry eye in the tent... including mine. What a sad occasion.

I love you Dad,
Bill

Though I lost a lot of good friends while in Vietnam, the way the deaths were handled by the military bothered me for months. When the crash on 13 November, 1967 took place, all the men who we were unable to free from the wreckage were considered MIAs rather than KIAs. Initially, that really stuck in my craw. I thought this to be very deceitful on the part of the military. I understand their reasoning a bit more now. The last thing they would want is to notify the next of kin that their loved one has been killed in combat, unless the military was absolutely positive. But at the time, I thought their decision was unfair to the families of the deceased.

Having known the gunner so well, his death put a real emotional strain on me. I saw a lot of buddies die in this nonsensical war. That has always bothered me, however, having to watch Paul being burned to death, really took it's toll on me.

CHAPTER 26

BROWN ARC

19 November, 1967
Chu Lai

Dear Family,
    A couple days ago I found two bearings and two damper tubes in the main rotor head assembly excessively worn on my ship. Since we have so many ships down due to battle damage, the Maintenance Officer decided we had to get three flyable by morning. So all crew chiefs went to work at 1830 hours, and I worked until 0100 hours. This was after having flown eleven hours already yesterday! I rolled into bed and slept for five hours before the CQ woke me up for a re-supply mission at 0630 hours. I flew until 1600 hours, had a short nap, and then flew Nite Hunter after supper until midnight. I feel like a walking zombie, but too tired to sleep. It would be nice if Uncle Sam paid us by the hour. We'd get plenty of overtime!
    Thanks so much for the letters. I got several from the family today, including an eight pager from Bruce...large writing. Barb's cookies arrived a few days ago and disappeared as fast as we (I had help) could get the package open. MJ sent some apples that arrived smelling like "fresh squeezins" but they hit the spot.
    Dad, you asked if I'm getting more excitement than I had hoped for. I'll have to say that the pucker factor is way up in the brown arc on most days. There are a lot of days when I'm exhausted and frustrated with the way they force us to fight this war, and on those days I would like to pack up and head for home. On the other

hand, when I realize how much the choppers and crews, both in short supply, are needed here (often around the clock). I probably wouldn't go home now if I had the chance. I signed on for a full year and feel I owe that commitment to the guys we support. I actually feel like I'm doing some good. But every time I have a few minutes to think of home, I miss you all terribly. Being lonesome seems to be high on the list of pains I could do without. You can bet that when August 11 comes along, I'll be fighting my way aboard that 707 for my return home!

I'm still working on getting a .38 and a flight jacket from the supply sergeant. It looks like I'll have to figure out a way to bribe him. He's tighter than the bung on a whiskey barrel! He treats all this Government Issue stuff like he paid for it out of his pocket.

We all got a charge out of the article you sent about the NVA moving into our area ...during the "lull in fighting." Although it's true that the NVA are moving in, the "lull" that the reporters are talking about doesn't exist. They should come ride with us one day and then rewrite the article. If the truth were told about what goes on here, this war would come to an end and we could all go home and stop this horrible loss of lives!

Have a great week...and keep the letters coming. Thanks for being so faithful in writing.

Love,
Bill

20 November, 1967
Chu Lai

There are obviously a lot of hazards in a war zone. Facing the enemy is bad enough, but sometimes facing ourselves can be just as dangerous. We always do hot refueling, meaning that we do not shut down the aircraft. Reasons for this are that the fueling area is continually used by all aircraft and can be a very congested area. In addition, helicopter crews are generally in a hurry to get back to their missions. Today, while we were refueling between missions at LZ Baldy, an OH-13 (Bell 47) observation helicopter landed to refuel at an Av gas bladder nearby. The crew was apparently in a hurry because when they finished refueling, they mistakenly left the fuel hose draped across the skids of the helicopter. The aircraft lifted off hooking the fuel hose on the tips of the skid tubes. When the hose tightened up, the ship crashed. Fortunately, both pilot and crew chief escaped with only minor injuries.

Major Johnson, our battalion chaplain was bored yesterday, so asked if he could ride along as my gunner for the day. We were scheduled for re-supply missions, a fairly safe day. The only action we saw was just before lift-off after dropping off supplies at a remote LZ, when a rocket landed just in front of our ship. The only damage was a shrapnel hole in the chin bubble about the size of a baseball. Still, I don't think the chaplain will ask to ride with us again.

CHAPTER 27

JAMMED MACHINE GUN

26 November, 1967
Chu Lai

Making our approach to one of the most picturesque villages I've seen from the air, all is quiet and peaceful except for the popping sound of the Huey's blades and the chatter on the radio. If it weren't for all the smoke rising from the village following the artillery and gunship prep, this small hamlet looks like something you would see on the cover of a travel magazine. It's nestled down between two mountains that rise about four thousand feet on either side. The lush emerald green rice paddies take up whatever land is not covered with banana and coconut trees. Foot trails along the edge of the village lead to a stream that is about thirty yards wide, cascading down the mountain into an inviting frothy pool.

We have several loads of grunts to insert this morning. The mission briefing says this "should" be a cold LZ. This is our drop off point. From here the grunts will do a search in an area a short distance away. The village is surrounded by heavy jungle and is the closest spot with a clearing large enough to drop off our men.

We're in a nine plus two gaggle (nine slicks and two gunships). Our mission is to transport two battalions into three different LZs in the mountainous terrain near the border between Vietnam and Laos, and we're close enough to spit on Laos.

The Gooks at the first two supposedly cold LZs peppered our birds with machine gun fire. We've just touched down in our third LZ, a small rice paddy next to the village, and everything comes unglued. The second we land four choppers in the LZ, we find that intelligence was wrong again!

Dale's machine gun jams after he fires just a few rounds. His ship is taking intense fire from a hootch just thirty yards outside his door. The side of his chopper is being raked by enemy AK47 fire. He's frantically trying to get his M60 operating again. The grunts are bailing out the doors of his ship and diving for cover behind a rice paddy dike while they attempt to silence the '47 fire. The infantry is running for the security of another rice paddy dike. When my load is out, I'm tempted to fire through the open door of Dale's ship. But remembering that Dale is a bundle of nerves on his best day, and with safety in mind, my instinct tells me this is not wise. I can see the Gook's upper torso through the window of the hut as he peppers the side of my buddy's ship. Seconds seem to turn into several minutes as our grunts off-load and we're again airborne. Dale's ship departs just prior to ours, and when our pilot pulls pitch, adding lift to the massive Huey rotor blades, the sucking rice paddy muck releases the skids and we shoot skyward. At about ten feet of altitude, I'm able to get a clear shot of the rifleman and take him out.

While one of our gunships makes a pass along the perimeter from where the grunts are taking heavy fire, it flies into a volley of enemy fire.

"Mayday, Mayday, Mayday…Bandit Two is going in!"

"Roger, Bandit Two. Red Three has you in sight. We'll follow you down buddy."

Departing the LZ, we're still taking sporadic fire, even though the men on the ground are giving us covering fire.

"Bandit Two has lost hydraulics! We'll try to limp home. Red three, if you could follow us, we'd appreciate it."

"Red Three is on your six. We're in this together man."

The airlift continues uneventfully, other than occasional small arms fire. Have we scared the enemy off, or just educated them enough to keep their heads down?

Most of our slicks took a lot of hits, but White Robe Six was looking after us again and we all escaped with no injuries.

28 November, 1967
Chu Lai

Dear Dad,

As you can see by the enclosed menu, we didn't have C rations for supper, but a full course turkey dinner for Thanksgiving. This was a total surprise! We spent most of the day hauling turkey dinners in thermal boxes to a lot of the units in the field. We started "serving" at 1000 hours and did the same thing over and over all day until 1800 hours. We even got the rest of the night off! The most amazing thing is that for all the flying we did today, we didn't get shot at even once...a real Thanksgiving!

The mail call was great yesterday - I got five packages! They included goodies from the young peoples group at church, a package from Grandma and Grandpa Johnson, Grandma Peterson, one from Karen, Dan, Joan and Dave, and a Swiss Army Knife from Dick and Harriet. Wow! If I can find a place to hide all the food, it may last a week or so.

Headquarters was supposed to show the film "The Ten Commandments" this evening. Entertainment is rare here, so most of us who weren't on a mission attended. The film was so old and brittle that we didn't get to see it. When I went back to the tent, I met a new guy who transferred from an engineer battalion to join the Cav to be a gunner. Dan Bowman is a Spec 5 from Las Vegas. His hobbies are hunting and fishing, so needless to say, we really hit it off. We talked for three and a half hours before turning in. I showed him all the hunting and fishing pictures that you sent me from home...says he's ready to move there.

Speaking of hunting, in your last letter, you said that Lin just shot a ten pointer and showed up Bruce's eight pointer. Congratulations to both of you! I must say, not being home for deer season makes me even more homesick. But, deer season will be even more fun next year after spending a year here.

My ship had a high EGT, so after doing an inspection, we're pulling the engine out. It will be down for two or three days.

Morning will be here soon. Goodnight.

Love,

Bill

CHAPTER 28

SILENT NIGHT

15 December, 1967
Chu Lai

Dear Mom and Dad,

Please forgive me for not having written for a while.

My ship is still grounded. The maintenance department doesn't have the necessary parts to get it back in the air. We're short three hangar bearings and three special washers. With all the ships in this country and the parts available, I've been told we're waiting for the parts to arrive from the States! Isn't that just like the government? Stop the war…at least a small portion of it, until the parts arrive! I'm anxious to get back in the air. I offered to be Dale's gunner, but the maintenance officer is making me work on my ship while it's down.

The humidity is rather high right now - about knee deep! The skies have been emptying since yesterday afternoon, and it doesn't look like it will let up until March. The temperature is actually down to about forty-five tonight. I had no idea it could get that cold here!

I received nine Christmas cards yesterday, including a card from the third grade class from home. All the students signed it. That was really special and appreciated. I need to write them a thank you.

I just found out that I've been promoted to Spec. 4. That will increase my salary by a whopping $50.00 per month!

It's time to crawl into my sleeping bag. I usually sleep on top of it, but the inside will feel good tonight.

Talk to you later.
Bill

21 December, 1967
Chu Lai

Yesterday several of us were given a few hours off - for good behavior - I guess, and told we could go see the Bob Hope Christmas Show here at Chu Lai. What a surprise! We went early and were able to get a pretty good perch on top of some sand bags near a drainage ditch. With binoculars we could see fairly well. The only problem we had was arguing over who got the field glasses when the girls were on the stage. Miss World (can't remember her name, but I sure remember what she looked like!), Raquel Welch, Barbara McNair and one other good lookin' specimen were in the show. The rain held off for the entire show, although it was really hot. The last song they did was Silent Night. There wasn't a dry eye in the place! I can't imagine why anyone would want to spend Christmas in a war zone, but we sure appreciate the efforts of the USO and all the people who give so freely of their time.

The Commander of the First Cav, General Tolson, popped in this afternoon for a barracks inspection. So we had to pick up all the dead rats under our bunks and do some general house cleaning. We even threw away all the fruit cakes that were beginning to mildew since no one is eating them.

When we finished with the General, we actually had a little free time and went over to the USO club for a snack. They had letters written from kids all over the US to G.I.s in general. I read several of them. They were mostly thanking us for serving our country and they asked a lot of questions. I took two of them that I plan to answer.

The First Sergeant said that my entire crew was recommended for Distinguished Flying Crosses for rescuing those Marines awhile back who were under intense fire. Unfortunately, the Old Man put his foot in the spokes and so now only the pilots will get DFC's and my gunner and I will get Air Medals with valor. The officers always come out with the best stuff even though we were a crew. Without each other we would be nothing. Bureaucracies suck!

Dad, you asked about our AO. It spreads from about fifteen miles south of Chu Lai to Da Nang and from the coast to the Laotian border. That's just for our company, not the whole Cav. Death Valley is located thirty five miles northeast of Chu Lai, just a few miles northeast of Tam Ky.

CHRISTMAS DAY

We had most of the day off today. I would rather have flown. The day would have gone by so much more quickly, and I wouldn't have had my heart torn apart with loneliness. I did get a package from you today as well as one from Cindi…great timing!
I spent most of the day reading old letters and outdoor magazines. When I wasn't reading, I was catching up on some much needed rest. One of the other crew chiefs woke me for Christmas dinner. It was excellent! It sure beat SOS!

29 December, 1967

Last night after a Nite Hunter mission, I grounded my ship because the pilots complained of the tail rotor pedals binding. I spent all day re-rigging it and then went on three test flights with Mr. Bauer, the current maintenance officer. He even let me do most of the flying…kind of like trying to thread a needle while riding a wild bronc! But, I finally learned to relax, and things smoothed out a bit. What a blast! Wish I had gone to flight school!

Dale, my crew chief buddy from Tulare, S. Dakota asked me to be in his wedding. We'll be leaving this God-forsaken place at the same time. His wedding is being planned for two weeks after we get home.

Sorry for taking so long to get this long overdue letter out. I'll try to do better.
    I love you all,
    Bill

CHAPTER 29

DELIVERY

1 January, 1968
Chu Lai

The Gooks gave us a New Year's party this morning from 0100 hours to 0600 hours. They hit our perimeter with mortars and rockets and tried to overrun an ARVN post right next to us. We killed over sixty enemy, but we all came out unscathed.

Today I flew log runs and CAs. On one run we evacuated refugees from a village near the Laotian border. Every aircraft was overloaded - nineteen on my ship, plus our crew. Every one of them looked scared to death. I can't blame them. They've had to leave their home after being harassed for years by the enemy, not knowing if or when they would be killed. Their lives are in total disarray. It makes me want to cry out for each of them!

Did I mention that one of the passengers was VERY pregnant? We were fifteen minutes from the refugee camp...too long a flight. Just after lifting off, guess who decided to give birth? This girl was on the floor screaming and hemorrhaging... really making a scene, with all the other villagers staring blankly. The pilots wanted to know what was happening, so I filled them in. Mr. Jewitt, the aircraft commander, quickly made a command decision.

"Pete, get in there and help her!"

Following orders, I forced myself among the refugees, got on my knees and found that the head was already out! This was not in my contract! Anyway, I grabbed that little bitty head, and eased that tiny fella out like I had done it hundreds of times. What a miracle!

Shortly after, we landed and let the medics take over. Although it scared me silly, it was really kind of neat! After having to deal with death on an almost daily basis, the gift of life was more than welcome. It sort of amazes me that with war all around, people are still interested in raising a family!

Tomorrow, life will not matter.

CHAPTER 30

DAY OF DEATH

2 January, 1968
Chu Lai

It's early, only 0200 hours, and it promises to be a day of death for both sides in this "Police Action."

Four of the major LZ's in our AO are simultaneously being hit with mortar and rocket fire. The second that the last mortar hits the ground, the Gooks are climbing under, over and through the concertina. The defenders are doing their best to repel the attacks, but they're massive and vicious with hand to hand combat the norm in a bloody battle.

Within minutes, the radio crackles with cries for help. As soon as one call is answered with promises to assist, several other LZ's call in with frantic pleas for aerial assistance.

All crews are awakened and scrambled to Flight Ops for a briefing. Our company already has one aircraft on station over LZ Baldy, dropping flares. Intelligence was correct for once and an attack was expected on Baldy tonight, sometime after midnight. However, LZ Leslie, Colt and Ross are also in big trouble.

The decision is to scramble nine of our slicks. All the crews work together along with several volunteers to load three of the ships with flares. After departing, they each fly a course to three separate LZs and arrive on station at 0300 hours. The other six, loaded with medical supplies and one medic each, depart and fly in pairs with a gunship escort to each of the LZs. By the time we arrive, the attack has broken off at LZ Baldy, with the others still receiving mortar rounds. It appears that the Gooks have given up on the ground attacks, at least for the moment.

Our two ships are assigned to fly the evacuations from LZ Leslie. We make our approach under the umbrella of flares being dropped from overhead by our sister ship. On final approach to this mountaintop LZ, we can see mortar and rocket rounds exploding and begin to receive small arms, automatic weapons and .50 caliber fire. The gunships do their utmost to keep the enemy at bay. My gunner and I are also pumping rounds at any visible muzzle flashes, but the little beasts are too numerous. It appears that the entire LZ is surrounded judging by the intense fire we're experiencing. Crossing the concertina wire perimeter, we cease-fire and prepare to load the WIAs.

The most severely wounded have been carried to the edge of the LZ in ponchos, doubling now as liters. The liters are covered with red clay from the recent heavy rains, but much of the red clay is not visible due to the massive spattering of blood all over them. Even before touchdown, the comrades of the fallen are scrambling toward the chopper carrying the less fortunate. As the first man is loaded, the medic on board frantically begins his efforts to stop the bleeding. While he works, Eddie, my gunner, and I help pull five others on board. A couple of mortars drop in and explode within fifty yards of us, so the power is kept to full RPM while the AC keeps our bird light on the skids for an immediate take-off the moment all of our precious cargo is loaded. When the last of the wounded is aboard, the ship lifts off, barely clears the concertina and dives down the mountainside to stay over the tree tops and gain as much speed as possible in an attempt to avoid the tentacles of enemy fire streaming toward us. Two gunships are escorting us and pouring out volumes of fire in addition to that of our M60s. Once we're outbound a half-mile or so, the tracers that have missed us so far cease and we seem to be in the clear.

As the crew breaths a sigh of relief, the co-pilot plots a course to Chu Lai while the aircraft commander pulls all the power he can to get our wounded to the medivac pad as quickly as possible.

After several more sorties our job is complete. We've transported only the seriously wounded.

The next morning our first mission was to go in to the same LZ to haul two loads of KIAs who were to be delivered to Graves Registration.

Landing in the now quiet LZ, our crew could smell the dead men who were laid out in rows. A few were in body bags, some of the others were wrapped in ponchos, but the rest were just added to the pile with no covering. There was a shortage of body bags.

As soon as we arrived the grunts began to load the dead on our ship. They were all laid sideways, door to door, on the deck of the Huey. We transported ten on the first trip.

The second trip was the same as the first. We took the last nine KIAs. The ship was already covered with blood from the first trip. After about five or six minutes into the flight, all was going well. It was actually a very peaceful ride...no radio chatter, no shooting...very quiet. Suddenly, one of the "dead" men sat up from under the pile! He just sat up in the pile of dead soldiers in the middle of the ship! I climbed outside of the aircraft to get around my seat post and crawled around to the cargo area to help this guy. He had been shot in the head. I wrestled him over to a jump seat and strapped him in before bandaging his forehead. He never said a word, not a murmur. This poor Grunt was in shock...his eyes staring off into space. The pilots wanted to know what all the commotion was all about. When I explained what had just happened, we made our first stop at a medivac pad. The second stop was the last helicopter ride for the remaining eight young soldiers.

It was a very tough night for these units. It'll be even tougher when the Department of the Army notifies the loved ones.

Unfortunately,the aircraft assigned to the other LZs had close to the same number of missions.

The military will have to notify more next of kin after tomorrow's mission.

CHAPTER 31

BLOOD-SOAKED FATIGUES

"We are the dead
Short days ago we lived,
Felt dawn, saw sunsets glow,
And now, we lie in Flanders Field."
From: "Flanders Fields"
By: John McCrae

3 January, 1968
Chu Lai

Stowing my machine gun, I look down to see how much ammo I have left. Out of the corner of my eye, I see liquid streaming toward my boot. My flashlight confirms that the liquid is blood. It runs freely from the cabin of the chopper. It's flowing out the open doors, catching in the slipstream, covering the lower legs of my jungle fatigues, and splattering all over my machine gun. I tentatively peak into the cabin to see where all the blood is coming from. It appears to be pooled from the two men lying on the aluminum deck of the aircraft. They have serious wounds from the firefight they experienced just moments ago. A thicker, pinkish liquid is mixed with the blood. In amazement my mouth drops open. I taste the lifeblood of my comrades as the bloody mists catch the wind and hit me in the face. Shocked, my mind is barely able to grasp what is happening, though I sense the sweet taste and spit it out. Somehow tasting the blood of another person isn't as repulsive as it might be if I weren't in the thick of a deadly war.

The young man lying on the floor just ahead of my crew chief seat is horribly shattered. His blood-soaked fatigues shredded with holes, reveal bone chips, marrow and mangled flesh. A very ragged patch of skin and shard of shoulder bone are all that remain of his left arm. His left leg appears to be held on by just a couple of tendons just below the knee. The blood-soaked tourniquet applied at the LZ is no longer beneficial to this soldier. A portion of his skull is missing and what appears to be brain matter is oozing out onto the deck of the helicopter. I trace the flow and find that it's the source of the pinkish substance mixed with blood that is splattering my legs. He made the ultimate sacrifice!

The man next to him, who appears to be about eighteen years old, is missing the majority of both legs and both arms. His right leg is a ragged stump below the knee with the left leg torn off at mid-thigh. His shattered femur juts grotesquely from a wound that looks like it was carelessly cut by a chain saw. Ribbons of muscle and flesh hang loosely from the bone. His left arm is completely severed at the shoulder. The other is a bandaged stub above the elbow. The bandages on the left side of his face are now drenched with fresh blood.

I chance a look at this man. His tear-filled eyes stare blankly up at me. He's in shock. Who wouldn't be! I feel totally helpless. Fighting the tears now streaming down my face, I manage a weak smile. His horrible fear is transparent through his blood-washed tears. I have to look away, yet can't help but steal fleeting glances into this warrior's eyes. He'll be going home in pieces. How will his loved ones bear the news? How will he cope with his drastically altered body…assuming he survives?

On short final to the medivac pad, one man begins screaming. Pain and reality have set in.

We work continuously evacuating the many wounded from our time of arrival at 0330 hours until 0600 hours. Charlie has raised havoc with massive ground attacks at several LZ's. There are enough wounded at each LZ to fill our three ships each time we arrive for another load. The KIA will have to wait until the wounded are taken care of. They are in no hurry. Their duty to their country is sadly complete.

We're so busy flying these missions of mercy under the umbrella of flares being dropped from our circling sister ship five thousand feet above, we quickly lose count of the sorties back to Chu Lai. Almost every time we near the LZ's, we're greeted with . 50 cal., automatic weapons, mortar and rocket fire. Approaching the LZ's, we return fire that ceases when we cross the perimeter concertina. Gunships continue to hose down the outside of the LZ with minigun and rocket fire between sorties.

On each approach, it's good to see the enemy bodies lying about within the LZ...sappers who have also completed their duty for their country. As I think about how happy I am to see the enemy dead, I feel guilty. Those men have left behind parents, widows, girlfriends, children and other loved ones, just as the American men have. I guess it's sweet revenge when I'm so conscious of all of our own men who are maimed and killed because of the attacks. I always felt as though I were a compassionate young man...before coming to this war.

What's happening to me?

I believe the emotional stress is taking its toll on me.

The majority of the wounded met their fate at LZ Leslie, perched atop a mountain ridge. At first light, we complete our bloody runs and now begin CA's all around the base of the ridge below Leslie in an attempt to encircle the enemy. Two ships are assigned to re-supply the men that are left atop LZ Leslie. They've had a long, grueling night and have expended most of their ammo.

The week is far from over...

CHAPTER 32

FIRST SHOOTDOWN

4 January, 1968
Chu Lai

After several sorties to the mountaintop hauling ammo, water and hot breakfast for the war-torn troopers, we begin inserting replacement men for those killed and wounded over the past several hours.

On the second turn around, my ship is flying White One, the fifth ship in our gaggle. After dropping our load of grunts on the LZ, we bank right just after takeoff and climb to one thousand feet at ninety knots when suddenly the aircraft shudders violently. Sparks, shrapnel, and pieces of the aircraft are flying throughout the ship from the explosion. An air burst from an enemy .37mm anti-aircraft emplacement on the mountainside to our right has found its mark. The instrument panel lights up like a Christmas tree, and the low rotor RPM horn is beeping loudly...not a good sign! The round went right by Eddie's head and hit the transmission.

The pilot reacts automatically in this emergency and is entering an autorotation while the co-pilot calls out, "Mayday, Mayday, Mayday...White One has been hit! We've lost hydraulics and are headed for a rice paddy at our twelve o'clock. Receiving automatic weapons fire from all quadrants!"

Our popcorn popper starts again while more rounds strike our aircraft. Pop...pop...pop...pop...pop...

"White One, White Two has you in sight. You're on fire! We're close behind you."

A split second later the unmistakable, dreaded sound, slower than normal machine gun fire, the measured cadence of larger rounds joins the battle. While we're trying to suppress the heavy ground fire with our 60s, the .50 cal rips off our tail rotor. Things are not looking good. Our riddled ship does five or six spins to the left. The pilots have lost directional control! With our hydraulics shot out, control is extremely difficult.

While returning fire, my mind is racing.

This one is going to kill us. I've managed to stay alive for five months here. That's longer than many of my buddies. Will we all die in the crash? Will we be captured, wounded? I was beginning to think I was invincible. I guess that myth is about to come to an end. How will my family be told, and what will they be told. How will they tell Cindi? How will they all react? I've had a great life, can't complain, God has been gracious. I love my family and Cindi dearly. They probably expected this would happen to me.

"God, please uphold my loved ones through the ordeal they are about to face. Wrap your loving arms around them, and let them know I love them. Amen"

Suddenly old 770 hits the rice paddy nose first and rolls over on its right side. The main rotor blades chop off the tail boom and there are other Bell Helicopter parts being scattered all over the ground. I find myself looking skyward. I'm now lying on my back while in my seat, firmly strapped in with two thousand rounds of unspent ammo on top of me. I smell smoke and hear automatic weapons fire pinging on the aircraft. Great incentive for getting out of this coffin! I feel like a turtle on his back while struggling out from under the rubble. Crawling out the door that is now the top of the ship, a stream of AK47 fire whizzes past my ear. Diving back inside, I hoist myself out the pilot's top window that's been shattered in the crash and faces away from the source of the AK fire. Both pilots and Eddie are already out of the ship. We make a frantic dash toward a rice paddy dike for cover while bullets splash in the mud all around us. Just a few weeks prior, I had my Dad send the 9mm Browning pistol that he had purchased for me prior to leaving the States. It felt comforting in my hand right now. With the ship burning, there wasn't time to grab the M60s off the ship. The Gooks are running at us from all sides and are within fifty yards of us when

White Two lands next to us as promised and we all dive on board, while the gunners lace the attackers with machine gun fire.

The rescue ship departs while our gunship cover is ripping the enemy with minigun, 20mm and rocket fire. Sweet revenge!

After getting back to camp, we're ordered to go see the flight surgeon who pronounces us all intact, though shaken up. We got banged up a bit and got a few scratches, but White Robe Six protected us from serious harm. For that we are most grateful.

CHAPTER 33

FEAR AND TREMBLING

7 January, 1968
Chu Lai

Three days after my first shoot down, whether or not to remain on flight status was something I was really struggling with. I didn't feel I could discuss this with my family, since I had not told them the entire truth about all my close calls. However, my cousin and very good friend, Gerry Goffin, is a person I could always confide in. Following are excerpts from a letter I sent him.

Dear Gerry:

On Friday morning my aircraft was shot down by enemy fire. While descending for a crash landing, none of our crew of four thought we would escape alive. Things looked rather grim. As soon as we crashed, we were surrounded by V.C. who were firing at us with automatic weapons while advancing toward our crash site. Fortunately, the crew of another Huey rescued us immediately. Though none of us were injured seriously, we were all shaken up, when we realized just how near death we had come.

Three more of our aircraft were shot down in the same place that same afternoon. While there were several injuries, a gunner and one of our pilots were killed. Both were great friends.

Yesterday, I thought I was calmed down enough to fly, but felt terrified. I went to the flight surgeon who suggested I take a couple days off.

One of the ships belonging to my buddy was shot up yesterday while unloading supplies in an LZ near where our ship was shot down. Two infantrymen were killed and four were wounded. We also had five other ships shot down yesterday. Six men are missing. We believe they were captured.

Our division captured more documents and two Chinese advisors this week. According to intelligence, Charlie's orders from Hanoi are to wipe out the entire third brigade at all costs. That happens to be our brigade! They've certainly been working overtime to achieve that goal lately. They've been pounding our LZ's with mortars, rockets, automatic weapons, sniper fire and ground attacks ever since Christmas, and steadily for the past five days.

Though I never thought it would happen, I have a real fear of flying. Since it is hazardous duty, the First Sergeant said I can resign from flight status if I wish, but as I told him, crewing a chopper is my job, the infantry needs support and after all, what am I here for? But still, I'm a nervous wreck. I plan on leaving for R&R the twenty fifth and hope that will help, but I doubt that it will.

I feel as close to you as a brother, Gerry. If you can give me any suggestions, I'd really appreciate it. Part of me wants to take a leave from flight status, but the last thing I want to do is to let down my comrades.

Anxiously awaiting your reply,
Bill

Within three weeks I received the following letter from Gerry.

Dear Bill,

Though your letter was very disturbing, I can certainly understand where you're coming from. It takes guts to admit your fear. It's much better to admit it than to try to hold it in. My guess would be that most, if not all, of your buddies go through the same fear on a daily basis. There is nothing wrong with that.

After all the stress you have gone through, it amazes me that you continue to fly, especially when you have lost so many friends who were doing the same thing at their time of death.

You've already shown your guts more than most have done, including myself. Though I commend you for not wanting to let

116

your friends down, you should feel proud of all you've done and maybe let someone else take your ship, at least for a little while. I hope you'll take me up on that suggestion, and survive, so we can take a lot more canoe trips when you return home.

Behind you all the way,
Gerry

CHAPTER 34

HELICOPTERS DON'T GET SHOT DOWN

11 January, 1968
Chu Lai

Since 770 is history, I've been given another ship to crew temporarily. The crew chief has completed his twelve months tour and is going home tomorrow. New ships will be arriving soon. When those come in, one has my name on it and this older aircraft will go to a new crew chief who has just been assigned to our company. Seniority is nice!

Today is the third day I've flown missions since our shoot down. We flew log runs into LZ Leslie all day. Enemy activity there is still dicey, so we take a different route in on every flight at tree top level. Keeping the skids in the treetops and hopping over mountain ridges is a pretty good adrenaline rush at one hundred twenty knots. After one of the flights, Dale wanted to show me something on his ship. He said that his pilot is really nuts and proved it by showing me the leaves stuck in his M60 gun sight! That's a bit too low!

We lost a ship and crew a couple days ago. They were flying low level over a small rice paddy surrounded by trees. They hit a wire stretched between trees that had a claymore attached. Gotta give Charlie credit for ingenuity!

Since my M16 was lost in the crash, a new one was issued to me. I zeroed it in today. One of the gunners, Twiggy, from

Connecticut, was with me and had an AK47 that we had hauled in yesterday while on a re-supply mission. The unit we were supplying had found a large cache of weapons. He also had plenty of ammo, compliments of Charlie, so we had a blast wasting it. As far as I'm concerned, the AK is superior to the M16. The action is very sloppy, and not machined to close tolerances like the M16, but no matter what you do to the AK, it keeps on firing. This is a great weapon for the filthy conditions over here. I believe you could drag these through the mud all day and still fire them without missing a round…unlike the M16. Case in point; after firing a couple of magazines, we field-stripped the AK. It had a half-cup of rice in the action! Apparently it had been buried in a cache of rice.

Today, the intelligence report stated that the NVA get 10,000 piasters (less than $100.00) for every chopper they shoot down. Guess that's why we draw so much fire!

Speaking with an Army Reporter today, he told me that some colonel in Saigon must approve his stories before they're released. Twenty-two of his twenty-six stories written last week were rejected because they were too true to life! The colonel wrote this guy a letter stating, "Helicopters don't get shot down, nor do they receive fire." That's just one example of his stupid remarks. I would call his remarks uninformed, but that's not the case. He knows perfectly well what goes on here daily. But, if he were truly not informed, I'd love to invite him to ride along with us on a typical day. Maybe that would change his mind…if he comes back.

One of our ships was shot down three days ago just after dropping off a load of ammo. The aircraft commander, crew chief and gunner were all killed in the crash in a very remote area. The co-pilot found a stream and floated downstream until dark, when he dug a hole in the stream bank where he spent the night. He said there were NVA searching all around the area for him. In the morning, he crawled out of his hole, killed a Gook with his knife, stole his PJs, and found his way to a village. On the edge of the village, he encountered a little boy who offered to go get help. The help turned out to be several NVA. When he saw them coming, he outran them and was lucky enough to finally find an American patrol. But remember, according to some colonel, "Helicopters don't get shot down."

I'm getting terribly homesick, but almost over the halfway point, two hundred and twelve days and a wake-up!

16 January, 1968
Chu Lai

For the past two days "Flame" and I have been working on remodeling our hootch with rocket crates. "Flame" is the crew chief who was shot down a couple days ago. They went down in a ball of fire, hence the nickname. The pilots were injured seriously, but "Flame," Jeff Madsen from New Jersey, and his gunner walked away.

I'm not sure why we're remodeling; something to do between flights, I guess. Word is that we may be moving again soon.

We took an NBC photographer into LZ Leslie yesterday. The enemy fire we received before getting there didn't seem to bother him. Guess he's been shot at before.

"Swede" and "Rabbit" (Dale Rabine) just raided the mess hall and came back with a bag of walnuts and three lemons. Guess we'll have lemonade and walnuts for a snack.

25 January, 1968
Chu Lai

While flying a log run today, Dale was shot down by friendly fire! The EOD team was in the process of blowing up several seven hundred and fifty pound bombs near the LZ that we were servicing. These were bombs that hadn't detonated during a recent B52 strike. They stopped detonations when we called them to tell them our aircraft were about to fly overhead. But, some poor private messed up and lit one off when Dale's ship was directly overhead at two hundred feet! Our ship was just behind his and saw his tail boom take a bad hit. They fell to the ground pretty hard, totaling the aircraft, but fortunately, no one was hurt. We picked the crew up and flew them back to Chu Lai, so they could get another ship. They were not as shaken up as they might have been if the enemy had shot them down. I guess that's psychological. But were they ever angry!

We just received word that our company is moving north again…tomorrow. This time we'll by flying to an unnamed place between DaNang and Hue. The Marines are in trouble and we've been asked to go bail them out.

I'll be leaving for An Khe either this afternoon or in the morning on my way to R&R. Still don't know what country I'll be heading to, but I sure feel ready for a few days away from this place!

CHAPTER 35

R&R CONCERNS

30 January, 1968
Hong Kong

After sleeping for almost the entire duration of the flight, I have finally arrived in Hong Kong. Most of the other countries that were available for R&R have been booked. I just needed a break from Vietnam, so took what I could get. It's a beautiful country, and after the hustle of clearing customs and being briefed, our planeload of weary G.I. s is ready for some relaxation.

The first order of business is to buy some civvies, followed directly by finding a good restaurant. After a great steak dinner, a cab takes me to the hotel. My eyes are drooping while I'm checking in. Exhaustion overtakes my body. After lying down, however, my mind replays the previous missions I've been on. I realize how fortunate I've been to be under God's care since leaving my family and friends back in the States. Reliving every mission in great detail while they march through my head makes sleep impossible. Sitting and staring out the window after crawling out of bed, daydreams fill my mind and a feeling of uneasiness interrupts my thoughts.

Having promised to call my folks and Cindi while on R&R, I wonder what I should say after not seeing them for so long. After experiencing daily dangers, seeing close friends getting shot down, wounded and dying, I've lived a totally different life. I've been away six months. How difficult will the calls be?

After hours of contemplation, the first call is to my folks. At first, it seems awkward, with tears being shed on both ends of the connection. It's great to hear the voices of my family again! After catching up on some small talk, they naturally express their concern for my safety, and I assure them once again that I'll be fine and plan to return to them in August...unscathed. Though it's easy to say these reassuring words, I feel as though I'm not telling the truth. I feel like I won't make it home alive, on the one hand, and on the other, I realize how God has protected me for this long. His grace is sufficient.

But, what about my buddies?

After close to an hour, it's time to quit lining the pockets of Ma Bell, and we say our good-byes. This is very difficult for each of us. Somehow, I feel like Mom and Dad are also wondering if I will return to them in a casket.

Spending a good half hour sobbing in loneliness after calling my family, it's time to give Cindi a call. Disappointment takes over when her college roommate answers the phone. She reassures me that my girlfriend is down in the TV Room, and she'll get her to the phone immediately.

When Cindi answers, she's giddy with excitement. It's so good to hear her voice! I know this conversation will make me even more lonesome, but I enjoy it while it lasts. After thirty minutes or so, we regretfully have to say goodbye. This conversation has given me a new desire to stay alive. Maybe I'll leave Vietnam in good health after all. But, one thing for sure...I know I've changed a lot. I feel much more serious. I wonder if I'll ever laugh as easily as I used to. It's a scary thought.

Have I aged that much in just a few months? What will I be like when I finish my tour?

Spending my days sleeping and sightseeing, overall it's a relaxing time. I've ridden cabs all over the city, saw a John Wayne western in Chinese of all things, and I rode the tram up to the top of the mountain for a spectacular view of the harbor. Seeing all the sampans and junks brought Vietnam right back in my face. The only difference here is that the harbor is extremely busy, and there hardly seems room to maneuver the boats for all the craft that are jockeying for position to sell their goods at the open market. It's a hectic place.

I'm impressed by all the preparation the locals are involved in to get ready for the Chinese New Year on January 31. Floats are being made right on the streets while other folks are hanging colorful decorations along the parade route. Then it happens; on my last night in this country the fireworks for the New Year celebration kick in. After about an hour of steady explosions, telling myself that this is indeed friendly fire and I don't need to take cover, I begin to settle down. Watching the activity from my hotel room overlooking one of the main streets, I have no desire to get out in the crowd.

For the most part, my R&R in Hong Kong is a good break. I try to put the war out of my mind. Impossible! The haunting thoughts are glued in my memory! I can't shake them.

How are my buddies getting along back in Vietnam? They're constantly on my mind. Though we all get an R&R, I can't help but feel guilty for being gone. A sense of urgency overwhelms me...I should be there helping my comrades. Are they in trouble? Have good buddies been wounded? Did more friends go back to the world in body bags to be grieved by their loved ones? How can I relax while I'm supposedly on vacation?

CHAPTER 36

THE TET OFFENSIVE

30 January, 1968
Chu Lai

Unfortunately, when the following mission took place, I was still in Hong Kong on R&R. A good friend, crew chief Jack Etzle related the following two missions (chapters) to me.

Our company was in the process of moving from the base at Chu Lai to Camp Evans, not far from the DMZ and Hue. Our first order of business was to relieve the Marines who were under siege at the Khe Sahn fire base south of the DMZ.

While enroute to Evans, the flight leader of the initial ten birds received a message stating that the Marines currently based at our future home, haven't totally abandoned the LZ.

Consequently our flight was asked to split up. Five birds diverted to DaNang and the other five were ordered to land at Phu Bai where they waited for further instructions. The flight leader of the second flight of five radioed the Seabee base at Phu Bai, asking for permission to spend the night. Five choppers need a sizable place to land, and with the available space occupied at the main base, Charlie Company birds were asked to use the soccer field. Imagine...a soccer field in the middle of a war zone!

Though American intelligence is very good, there are times when we underestimate the Wiley enemy that we face every day. The past several days had been unusually quiet. What was the other side up to?

After securing the ships for the night, the crews were told they could either sleep on the choppers or in several smaller tents that had been made available.

The Chinese New Year began the next day, and unknown to the Americans, the enemy had amassed troops and supplies near all the major cities and American bases in South Vietnam. The enemy hds synchronized their watches. At about 0230 hours on January 31, the peaceful chirping of the crickets and croaking of the frogs in the rice paddies came to an abrupt halt. This generally indicates that they've been disturbed by something...or someone. Within thirty minutes, the silence was rudely interrupted by sudden explosions throughout the encampments and cities across the country. The TET Offensive had begun!

Many of the bases, both small and large, including LZs and Vietnamese cities throughout South Vietnam were attacked simultaneously. The countrywide attacks were fierce and ugly, killing and maiming brave American, South Vietnamese, and other allied soldiers in addition to many South Vietnamese civilians. Our response was swift as usual, but we had no idea how firmly the enemy was entrenched within so much of our American-held territory.

The grogginess of sleep was quickly replaced by a rush of adrenaline as the crews scrambled for their ships in an attempt to get airborne before the enemy gunners scored direct hits on the ships encamped on the soccer field.

Warrant Officer Mel Canon, sleeping in his jungle fatigue pants, rolled out of the sack and ran to his assigned ship as fast as his bare feet would carry him. The rest of his crew arrived at the same time and worked rapidly as a team, getting the ship airborne in record time.

Luckily, all ships were up and flying before any were hit. In the air, the crews were assigned various missions. One was assigned a flare mission to light up the area in an attempt to discourage enemy attack. Others were asked to scout the vicinity in search of flashes from the enemy gunner's mortar tubes. The ships were flying with all exterior lights blacked out in an attempt to avoid ground fire. While circling, flares were dispersed into the night sky as needed in the Phu Bai area, making it tough on the enemy's concealment.

The radio communications in the underground TOC looked like an ant farm during a major storm. Those present were extremely busy pouring over local maps in an attempt to figure out the next line of defense. Others were talking on numerous radios giving and receiving SITREPS. Incessant explosions transform the night sky into intermittent daylight.

By daybreak, all five aircraft were flying on fumes and returned to Phu Bai. The Khe Sahn mission was scrubbed. There were numerous places that needed more immediate attention.

One of these was Hue, also under siege. Apparently, the enemy was dug in right in the middle of the Citadel, the heart of this beautiful city, a cultural center of the country and home of the University of Hue. Already, many South Vietnamese civilians and soldiers have died. The outlook was grim. The City of Hue was among those hardest hit during the night

After intelligence briefings throughout the night and into the morning, plans were made to do a recon mission over Hue late in the morning. Hopefully, by then, some of the enemy pressure would abate.

Dale's ship was chosen to fly the recon mission over Hue in an attempt to ascertain enemy positions, layout of the city, and to determine where an American assault might be executed based on the current situation. Fred Parsons and Company Commander Jim Wolfe would fly the aircraft. Bob Oliver would man the gunner's seat.

As they arrived over Hue, searching for clues on how best to plan the assault, Dale recalled having his last aircraft shot out from under him just two weeks previously by friendly fire. Suddenly, the recon bird was severely jolted by anti-aircraft, .50 caliber, and automatic weapons fire from the area of the Citadel. While the crew chief and gunner returned fire, American blood was splattered throughout the cabin as the aircraft was peppered with automatic weapons fire. Several of the rounds entered the cabin and killed three of the four passengers. The fourth passenger, a high-ranking NCO was severely wounded.

They entered an autorotation, while a Mayday was called in with the ship's location and dire situation. The enemy fire intensified. Fully aware of the immense buildup of NVA and VC, the ship was headed for an enemy beehive.

There was a small rice paddy straight ahead…a good target for a landing. The aircraft made a hard landing, squeezing in between a thick hedgerow and rows of concertina wire. Fortunately, the wire encircles an ARVN compound. Unfortunately, the hedgerow is highly infested with enemy!

Erickson and Oliver unbuckled and bailed out to help the pilots escape the ship. While the pilots ran for the safety of the ARVN compound, Dale and Bob take a look in the cabin. All four passengers were still buckled in their jump seats and appeared to be dead. Still taking fire, the crew chief and gunner ran back to their seats, pulled the quick disconnect pins on their machine guns, grabbed a bundle of ammo and ran for cover. Together they wound up on the right side of the ship and dove into the rank rice paddy muck to avoid intense enemy machine gun fire intent on cutting them to ribbons.

Tension continued to build with the unrelenting VC fire. An enemy mortar whistled overhead and exploded right next to the two men. They were both critically wounded. Dale was hit in the legs and back and was bleeding profusely. Bob was hit in the back and his right arm was mangled. Blood squirting into the mud turned the water an eerie purplish color. Both were knocked unconscious.

The ARVNs in the compound on the other side of the downed aircraft assumed Dale and Bob were dead.

CHAPTER 37

MEDAL OF HONOR

31 January, 1968
Camp Evans

Warrant Officer and aircraft commander, Fred Ferguson, and his crew, co-pilot Captain Buc Anderson, crew chief Jack Etzle and gunner James Cole, had been flying a flare ship mission all night during the attack on Phu Bai. Landing at daybreak, Jack did the daily maintenance on his ship so it would be ready for whatever the next mission might be. During breakfast in the mess hall at 0730 hours, enemy rockets began dropping in again. Scrambling to their helicopter, the crew spent most of the morning flying recon missions while the enemy continued it's assault.

Late in the morning, the crew was refueling at a POL dump just north of Phu Bai when Ferguson received word that one of our Charlie company ships had been shot down near Hue. While Jack finished topping the aircraft off, Ferguson called the aircraft commander of another ship that was taking on fuel to explain the situation and asked if he would join them as wing man to help with the rescue of the downed crew. The crew of Mel Canon's aircraft quickly agreed and the two ships immediately departed for the scene of the shoot down. Hue was only about a five-minute helicopter flight from their current position.

Flying as wing man on Ferguson's ship, Canon would back up the first aircraft. In the event the first aircraft went down for any reason, whether due to a maintenance problem or having been shot down, the wing man's job was to continue the mission if possible. If the number one ship had to divert for maintenance and the problem wouldn't cause an imminent crash, the second ship would go in and complete the rescue. If the problem were more serious, he would fly "wing" on the ship in trouble and rescue that crew if need be.

Arriving over Hue, the two slicks surveyed the situation from an altitude of about fifteen hundred feet in an attempt to stay out of the range of small arms fire while talking to the ARVN Commander in their compound just south of the Perfume River. The ARVNs stated that two pilots were now in their camp and the rest of the crew and passengers had been killed. The ARVNs were still receiving sporadic enemy fire.

Ferguson then switched over to intercom and, after briefing the crew on the situation, asked them individually if they were willing to risk the rescue. They were unanimous in their decision to go for it. It was standard practice in our unit to brief the crew on the situation at hand and to ask if everyone was willing to risk their lives for the mission. I don't recall a time when any of us refused a mission, regardless of the situation. We all knew that if we were the crew on the ground, there would always be at least one crew or more that would risk their lives to save ours. On numerous occasions, several lives were lost to save just one.

After waiting several minutes for the necessary gunship support to increase the likelihood of a successful mission, the rescue ship dropped below the cloud deck and flew low-level over the river, taking enemy fire from nearby buildings. The bullets punched numerous holes in the aircraft. In an attempt to protect the ship, the crew chief and gunner blazed away with their M60s while the gunship escort followed suit, unleashing their rockets, minigun and 20mm canon fire. The crew in the wing man position overhead could see pieces flying off the ship while it was literally being shot to bits. Flying near the Citadel, Jack watched several NVA soldiers raising their flag, giving him yet another target. While on final approach to the compound, Ferguson yelled that they were receiving heavy machine gun fire from a tower in the middle of the river. The gunships flew alongside and silenced the gun with a couple of well-placed rockets.

Over-flying a bridge, the pilot noted several uniformed soldiers positioned on one knee, shooting at the flight. Overjoyed at a great opportunity, the crews of the gunships opened up with their miniguns, tossing the lifeless bodies like rag dolls into the river.

On short final, the pilots could see that the ARVN compound was going to be a tight fit. Squeezing into the space available, the bird hit the ground while the crew chief and gunner jumped out to rescue the pilots from Dale's ship who had escaped the crash for the relative safety of the ARVN compound. Suddenly, mortars started dropping and it was time to leave. Jack jumped back on board and manned his gun, assuming that his gunner had done the same. Departing the LZ, the crew chief had expended his ammo and returned fire with an M-2 carbine that he had on board as a back-up weapon.

On climb-out, Ferguson radioed his wing man, Mel Canon, that the LZ was hot, but there were still wounded in the compound. He suggested that if another rescue was attempted, it had to be done quickly and at low level.

After gaining the necessary altitude to get out of the enemy fire, Jack crawled over to check on Cole since he hadn't heard him returning fire. The gunner was missing! He had not been able to get back on board prior to the helicopter departing. Sadly, the compound was too hot to attempt another rescue.

Unknown to the crew at the time, one of the incoming mortars had landed right in front of gunner Cole while he leaned over to pick up another wounded man. Though he was severely wounded, Cole's chicken plate took the brunt of the explosion and saved his life.

Canon decided that a low level rescue was too risky. He didn't like the odds. He elected to make a steep approach into the compound. Positioning the ship for an autorotation the aircraft glided out of the sky from about thirty five hundred feet, while receiving fire all the way. Canon flared and increased collective pitch to decrease the descent rate while settling into the tight LZ. The moment the aircraft landed, the crew chief and gunner dashed into several buildings looking for wounded. The enemy fire was intense enough to keep the ARVNs busy returning fire. Not finding anyone, the crew again jumped on board and returned fire, while their ship departed into a hailstorm of enemy bullets. Apparently the Americans they were attempting to rescue were in a different building and unable to scramble out to the ship.

131

The aircraft took a couple direct hits and the crew was told by the gunships that they were trailing smoke. The crew chief leaned out the door to check the damage and confirmed that they were indeed smoking and needed to get on the ground. Canon said he would try to make it back to friendly territory before landing due to the high enemy concentration below. Limping back to Phu Bai, and safely clearing the concertina wire, the damaged ship landed. Upon inspection by the crew chief, it was found that one of the rounds had clipped a fuel line, causing fuel to spray on the hot section of the engine. Amazingly, God protected them from a fiery crash.

Late in the afternoon, Dale regained consciousness. Still lying in the mud and weak from having lost a large volume of blood, he looked over to see his gunner lying just a few feet away, covered with blood. Dale managed to crawl over to Oliver, assuming he was dead, Dale shook him and his gunner regained consciousness. Though both were in severe pain, Dale low crawled to the side door of the ship to retrieve the first aid kit fastened to the inside door-jamb of the aircraft, just behind the pilot's seat. Since the helicopter had sunk to it's belly in the rice paddy, Dale's movements went unnoticed by the enemy. Quickly grabbing the first aid kit, he heard someone inside the cabin moan. Though seeing no movement, he was now aware one of the passengers was still alive. Desperately in need of morphine and weak from severe blood loss, he crawled back to his gunner to administer morphine to each of them. Shocked to see the morphine missing from the kit, they resigned themselves to enduring the extreme pain until they could get more help.

The enemy could be heard talking softly among themselves while approaching the chopper from the opposite side. Dale and Oliver listened as two of them boarded the ship. Another moan was heard from the dying man strapped in the seat. With horror, the crew heard the sound of the North Vietnamese triangular bayonet being thrust into the only living passenger. After a gurgling sound…the moaning ended. Assuming the crew chief and gunner were dead, the NVA didn't even take time to strip the ship. They would have been spotted by the ARVN troops and killed, so they quickly disappeared back into the enemy infested hedgerow to join their comrades.

The NVA continued firing at the compound. After several more minutes, two A1E Skyraiders made a low pass while strafing the hedgerow and dropped napalm on the jungle adjacent to the disabled aircraft and wounded crew. The heat was almost unbearable for the men lying in the mud and they knew they had to get the attention of the fighters. On the next pass, Dale gathered up enough energy to wave at the pilot about to make his drop. The Skyraider pilot pulled out of his dive and radioed the ARVN compound that there was still someone alive next to the chopper.

With the aid of cover fire from the compound, Dale and Oliver helped each other as they slowly made their way across the rice paddy on their bellies. Dale still had two good arms that he could use to pull himself along the ground using stalks of rice as anchors. While dragging his mangled leg and pushing with his good one, he helped his buddy along, who had only one arm intact…the other dragging uselessly in the muck alongside his body. As they reached the edge of the South Vietnamese compound, they were pulled over the earthen berm by the ARVNS to relative safety.

Both men were administered first aid by the ARVN's and placed in a small building with other injured men, including James Cole, the gunner who had been mistakenly left behind. There were also wounded ARVNs who had been injured while defending the outpost. Apparently, during the second rescue attempt, there had not been time to check this building for wounded due to the intense enemy attack.

A French Catholic Priest, who was in the compound, said he would attempt to get them across the Perfume River during the night and into a Catholic hospital where they would be safer. Due to repeated heavy attacks day and night, that never happened. Several days later, it was learned that the NVA had performed yet another unspeakable atrocity. They entered the Catholic Hospital, and massacred the entire staff and all the patients.

Three days later, another C/227th helicopter courageously came in under heavy fire and rescued the crew chief, two gunners, and several of the ARVN wounded. Quickly boarding the choppers with the aid of the South Vietnamese soldiers, the injured passengers cringed while bullets flew toward their targeted helicopter. Though taking several hits, the Huey delivered its precious cargo to a field hospital. All three Americans were soon evacuated to Japan and then to the US for further intensive care.

For the heroic efforts of the crew for the first rescue attempt, Chief Warrant Officer Ferguson was awarded the Medal of Honor.

Captain Anderson, SP5 Etzle and SP4 Cole were awarded the DFC and Silver Star. In addition, Cole was awarded the Purple Heart.

CHAPTER 38

HAUNTING MEMORIES

1 February, 1968
An Khe

Dear Dad,

It was so good to talk to you and Mom and the rest of the family a couple nights ago. I wish we could have stayed on the phone longer, but I know what that must cost. Thanks so much for picking up the tab on that. We still have a lot to catch up on, but I guess it's going to have to wait until August.

Just a note to say I'm back "home" again. I only got to spend three days in Hong Kong, but loved every minute of it! It was such a nice change from Vietnam...still hot and humid, and even though I couldn't put the war out of my mind, it was very relaxing just to get away from the noises, irritations, smells and hazards of war for a while. Fortunate enough to be there during the Chinese New Year, there were a lot of festivities and everyone seemed to be having a great time. I was jittery over the fireworks for a while, but after a half hour of trying to convince myself it wasn't incoming, I was all right.

After arriving in Cam Rahn Bay yesterday afternoon, it was time to process back "in-country". And after being held over night, I'm in An Khe today. By the looks of things, I won't be able to get to the field for a few days, depending on Charlie. The Tet Offensive took place while I was gone. It sounds like I missed out on a lot of excitement. Everything is still in a state of turmoil.

The NVA have taken over Hue and are pretty well set up. Looks like they plan to stay for a while. From all reports, our company is flying more than ever.

Until I go back to the field, I have to pull guard duty at night because a bunch of NVA came through the wire two nights ago and killed eight guards. Apparently, they were all asleep.

Two nights ago, Charlie mortared the Cav Headquarters here in An Khe, destroying a lot of helicopters, including two brand new Huey Cobras. The Cobras are much faster than the old "B" model Huey gunships. They're only thirty six inches wide and carry two pilots. A mortar round landed on one of the hootches, killing one man who was scheduled to go back home in only six days. There were also six other men wounded. The attack lasted only a little over an hour, though everyone was up all night on red alert.

Love ya,
Bill

12 February, 1968
An Khe

The past eight days have seemed like four months.

I'm bored to tears! I don't know how the guys can stand it back here in the rear. Absolutely NO excitement! Spending the day reading, sleeping, throwing darts and dreaming of home gets old fast. Too much free time on my hands. I hate it; I just want to get back in the air! Yesterday, while playing darts with our new supply sergeant (trying to get in good with him, so I can get a flight jacket), I found out that he was stationed in Fort Greeley, Alaska, before his assignment to Nam. He was a mountain ski instructor and taught climbing and river rafting. Now that sounds like my kind of duty!

One of the guys had a small stove and talked the mess sergeant out of a loaf of bread and some cheese. We were craving cheese sandwiches. We then discovered that we didn't have a pan and sarge wouldn't let us use any of his. So we fried them up on a handsaw held over the fire.

15 February, 1968
Camp Evans

Only 178 days to go!

A Huey came into An Khe for a supply run and they had room for one body, so I jumped on board for the trip to my new home at Camp Evans. It's great to finally be back with my unit.

Our new LZ is located twenty miles northwest of Hue. The camp is perched on top of a ridge with rolling hills on three sides and a mountain with an elevation of about two thousand feet to the west. There's a sign in a nearby village that reads: "Hanoi – six hundred twenty three kilometers".

Having been away from my unit for so long coupled with our big move, I haven't received mail for quite sometime. But, today five letters caught up with me. I feel so honored to have a family, girlfriend and other friends who write to me on a regular basis. Several of the guys in our outfit never get any mail. I'm sure that must make for a much longer year! I feel richly blessed.

The Huey that's supposed to replace the one we had shot out from under us still isn't here, but expected soon. While I await its arrival, I'm spending my time putting up tents, building bunkers, piling sandbags for new bunkers and pulling guard duty. Whenever a gunner is needed, I volunteer just to get my adrenaline pumping again, not to mention getting out of boring duties back at Evans.

A Mig17 was spotted over Hue two days ago. Another was shot down a bit north of Hue. It was chasing an F4 that was escorting a B52.

There are no showers set up yet. Not only that, but we have a shortage of water…plenty to drink, but no extra. The flies love it… everyone's getting pretty rank!

Since Dale was medivaced to Japan, his replacement has already arrived and now resides in Dale's space next to me. Jeff is from Oregon and seems to be an OK guy but I dearly miss my best buddy, Dale. That's a real tough loss. We went through a lot together, beginning with Basic, helicopter training, and then half a year attempting to dodge lead. It's almost getting to the point that I don't want to get to know anyone else for fear of losing them, too. It's a feeling that's very difficult to describe. I guess I feel like I've been on too many emotional roller coaster rides since arriving in country six months ago. My stomach is in knots over the loss of a dear friend, not to mention several other buddies killed or wounded. I don't feel as though I can take a lot more of that.

Whenever I have a little time to myself, I begin to think back on the past six months since I've been in Vietnam. All the missions run like a continuous movie in the back of my mind. I can recall every little detail, including the looks on the faces of so many young men who have been severely wounded. The pale faces of the dead who have been loaded on my helicopter in remote LZs also haunt me. Grueling attacks often cause units to run short of body bags, and the only helicopter re-supply has been to deliver ammo, food, water, and replacements for men lost. Body bags are not necessary, but are sure appreciated by the helicopter crews and the medical crews. They save a lot of grief on our part…not to have to look into the face of another dead comrade, let alone a whole shipload of them. But then, why should we be saved from the horror of death at the hands of the enemy? When I think of the infantry on the ground, and how they live from day to day…the almost continual contact with the enemy, and the pain they suffer when they vainly attempt to save the lives of others only to see them get blown away, I get a big lump in my throat. Not only do these men have to go through all of this grief, but then have to live in the jungle with these dead friends, lying in plain sight while they're fighting for their own lives. Undoubtedly they're wondering if they will be joining these brave men in the next split second. Watching the millions of flies swarm over their friends...the smell of rotting flesh...How many more of these brave men will lie on the floor of my chopper before I return to the States? How do any of us stay sane?

CHAPTER 39

NEW CHOPPER

19 February, 1968
Camp Evans

Dear Dad,

My belated mail came yesterday. I got several letters and a couple of packages. There were 4 letters that had apparently been dropped in a mud hole and run over. They were unreadable...I couldn't even tell who they were from. Cindi sent a birthday cake that came just in time for my birthday. She did say she was sending one a while back. She told me that it was chocolate with white frosting. The package was somewhat crushed with a couple holes in it. The frosting was green rather than white, but it was still moist. After what we eat here on a regular basis, we figured a little mold wouldn't hurt us.

Having turned twenty today, I feel like an old man. Compared to a lot of the guys here, twenty is old.

I spent all day working on getting my new ship ready...in the rain. You can now watch for tail number 17092 on the news. Eddie helped me mount the machine gun brackets and put supplies on board. We got it all greased and ready for tomorrow's missions. What a great birthday present!

Two nights ago we had a red alert. We spent all night in the foxhole during a hard rain. Intelligence reports said that we were to be rocketed at 0300 hours. Wrong again...real intelligence!

Our platoon sergeant has completed his tour. His replacement is a Sergeant Stone. So far, he hasn't impressed anyone. He complains about having to build bunkers because he's an NCO! He doesn't stick up for his men either. So, we took him in the tent tonight and had a heart to heart talk, telling him he had better shape up. We explained to him that we've all been in country longer than he, making every attempt to work as a team, and need him to join us in that effort. I think he's now on board.

20 February, 1968
Camp Evans

Our co-pilot was flying our first mission this morning. We were flying low-level convoy cover. He was not looking where he was flying, and WHAMO! He hit the top of a tree! My brand new bird! I told him to land on the road so I could check out the damage. He wiped out the chin bubble and scratched up the belly. The left side, tail boom, and elevator were all dented. Momentarily, I "forgot" he was an officer and told him how irresponsible he was and that I don't ever want him piloting my ship again. He's a hazard! We had to fly back to Evans where I spent the rest of the day doing the necessary repairs.

A letter came from Dale yesterday. He's in Okinawa and in pretty bad shape. His leg, back, nerves and muscles are all screwed up. The Doc is still digging shrapnel out of his body. Scheduled to leave for home when I do in August, he'll be getting home prematurely. He has done more than his share. He said it's not that bad in Okinawa: hot and cold running water, flush toilets, good chow and nurses that wait on him as if he were the only soldier in the place. The military nurses are superb!

22 February, 1968
Camp Evans

We flew 25 sorties for the 1/7 Cav yesterday and drew fire on every one! The 1/7 are voracious fighters. They have to be. It seems like every time we work with them, they get into horrendous battles. They have an incredible team!

A couple of times Charlie lobbed mortars into the LZ just as we were about to land, so we had to abort, circle and try again as soon as the rounds stopped exploding. In the afternoon, the mortars stopped and 122mm rockets were coming in. I guess the Gooks ran out of mortars. Immediately following a rocket attack, we swooped in to pick up wounded. Trees were down everywhere, craters littered the landscape, and everything was either burning or shattered beyond recognition. The stench of spent gunpowder filled the humid air. There were wounded and dead G.I.s littering the LZ. This is the worst battlefield I've ever seen.

Miss you,
Bill

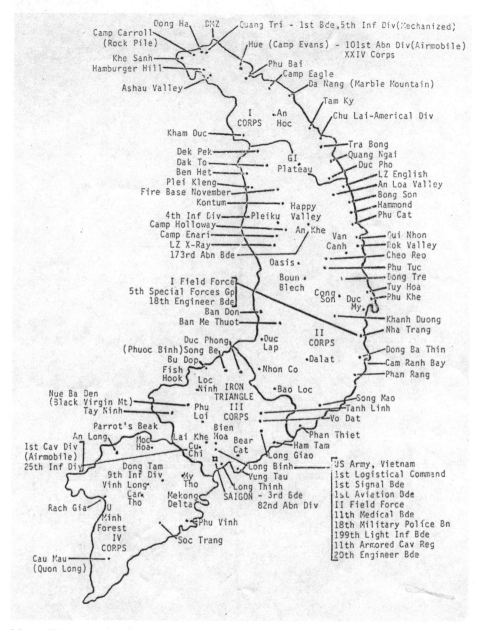

Map of Vietnam 1967.

Author's adrenaline pumping home for 3600 hours.

Crew chief seat.

Mortar attack LZ Uplift.

Mad minute - LZ Uplift.

Mortar attack LZ Uplift.

Combat assault.

Tree strike damage. Author on the left.

Author loading ammo tray for the next mission.

Willy Peter prior to assault.

Waiting out the weather.

Prep for Khe Sahn assault.

1st Lt. talking to his unit during an assault.

Refugees just evacuated from their village that is occupied by the VC.

Eddie Hoklotubbe listening in on an assault on a PRC-25.

Pilots W.O. Ide and Jewitt enroute to combat assault.

Crew chief Roberts burning sweetheart's love letters in the rain the day after ammo dump explosion at Camp Evans had burned most of Charlie Company's tents to the ground.

.50 caliber damage to aircraft wiring harness.

Commendation by General John J. Tolson to author for "White Robe 6" tract.

"White Robe 6!
White Robe 6!
    This is Yellow One
    calling White Robe 6.
    Come in, please!"

A stranger or a newcomer to South Viet Nam hearing this radio call might be greatly puzzled that no answer is ever returned--at least, not an audible answer.

It is common practice to assign radio code names to military units and aircraft to enable the caller and the called to identify each other while hiding their identity from the enemy. One would search in vain through all known code books for the identity of White Robe 6. But the men of the First Air Cavalry understand that White Robe 6 is a special designation for God.

No one knows where the code name originated, or when. But it has become familiar through frequent use, in letters home, in personal conversation, in radio communications. It is not used casually or irreverently, but in tones of deepest respect, of personal acquaintance, of devout worship. The name has special meaning to the helicopter crew who flew their chopper to 10,000 feet, far above normal operating altitude, to feel nearer to White Robe 6. And to the wounded Cavalryman whose clenched teeth muffle cries of pain while his lips move in confident prayer. And to the grateful men who rest in safety after a courageous flight to rescue buddies downed behind enemy positions where success depended as much on the help of White Robe 6 as on their skill and nerve.

'White Robe 6 calling
Yellow One...over.'

This is the same God they have known through boyhood days; of whom they learned in home and church; to whom they prayed in less trying days than these. This is the God whose word of promise, giving assurance to those who trust in Him they have believed: "When he calls to me, I will answer him; I will be with him in trouble" (Psalm 91:15).

White Robe 6 does answer when men call upon Him. Not as a voice audible on radio circuits, but in the inmost recesses of the soul. "For thus says the high and lofty One who inhabits eternity, whose name is Holy: I dwell in the high and holy place, and also with him who is of a contrite and humble spirit" (Isaiah 57:15). He speaks through His eternal Word, the Bible, giving a message of salvation, of hope, of comfort and encouragement. To men engaged in the grim business of war, facing daily the basic issues of life and death, comes His word of assurance, "As your days, so shall your strength be" (Deuteronomy 33:25). And to men who are weary of bloodshed and conflict, physically tired, mentally, emotionally and spiritually drained by the awful tension and fear, the almost unbearable horror and destruction, the unresolved struggle between moral principle and painful duty, comes the ageless word of the Living Savior, "Come to me, all who labor and are heavy laden, and I will give you rest" (Matthew 11:28).

The voice of White Robe 6 is heard, too, in the message of the man of God, your chaplain, who ministers the Word of the Living God to men in every situation and trying circumstance. By word and deed and by his very presence with them he speaks for White Robe 6, assuring men who call upon their God in the hour of trial and need that their cry is heard as they call in faith and trust: "Thou dost keep him in perfect peace, whose mind is stayed on thee, because he trusts in thee" (Isaiah 26:3).

You cannot hear it unless you are tuned to the proper wavelength, but the voice of White Robe 6 is unmistakably heard in answer to the call of the trusting heart: "Yellow One, this is

White Robe 6. I read you loud and clear. How do you read me? 'Have you not known? Have you not heard? The Lord is the everlasting God, the Creator of the ends of the earth. He does not faint or grow weary, his understanding is unsearchable. He gives power to the faint, and to him who has no might he increases strength. Even youths shall faint and be weary, and young men shall fall exhausted; but they who wait for the Lord shall renew their strength, they shall mount up with wings like eagles, they shall run and not be weary, they shall walk and not faint'" (Isaiah 40:28-31).

This was inspired by letters home from Bill Peterson, Crew Chief with C Co, 227th Avn Bn, 1st AIR CAV DIV. whose home is Carney, Michigan.

Perfume River winding through Hue.

Author on break prior to insertion on LZ Stud.

Combat assault on hot LZ in Ashau Valley

Chief Hoklotubbe cleaning M-60 on deck of chopper.

Mud hole was deeper than we thought in Phu Bai. Old man's jeep.

Evening over Giligan's Island just north of Chu Lai.

Company clown crew chief Roberts.

Gunner Tregellis "Twiggy" serenading the troops.

PZ for the initial assault on Khe Sahn.

Loading up for the assault on Hue. Note the ropes for scaling the citadel walls.

Enroute to Khe Sanh to relieve marines.

Crew chief Roberts taking a break before initial assault on Ashua Valley.

Tree strike during Ashua Valley initial assault. Author's ship "770".

Charlie Company's illustrious pilots.

Dale Erickson reading a letter from home.

"SSSHH SH SH WHOOMP!"

INCOMMINNNNLLL......

Cartoon by author's brother-in-law, Jim Worden.

CHAPTER 40

NUDE IN THE BUNKER

24 February, 1968
Camp Evans

Last night I had planned on accomplishing so much. The plan was to write letters, take a shower...the first for 17 days, have a pizza party with the pizza mix that Fran sent, clean my weapons, and repair my flight helmet.

We finally have sufficient water to bathe. For a couple of weeks, we've only had enough for drinking. We not only have enough water now, but we've even built a new shower. Of course, it's very spartan, but at 1900 hours, I decided it was time to try it out in the quietness of the evening. No need to dress for the occasion...helmet, bar of soap, a towel, and of course my ever-present weapon. After taking the eighty yard walk to chip off almost three weeks of grime, I took great pleasure in rinsing off and then soaping down. It felt wonderful! At 1910 hours I was reaching for the rope to turn the shower back on to rinse off, when I could hear the all too familiar sound of incoming rockets. Ssshhhh...wwwooooocrump... "INCOMINGGGGG!!!" I grabbed my steel pot and M16 while I made a soapy dash, barefooted through the garbage pit and mud for the bunker next to our tent. By the time I got there, the rest of my buddies were already under cover. No one was smiling. The rockets were dropping everywhere and were very close. However, when I came sliding in the door dressed only in my steel pot and soapsuds, the place erupted in laughter! I'm glad my comrades have a sense of humor! So far, I know of only two men injured in the attack, and I didn't get any shrapnel holes in my clothes.

After the rockets stopped falling, Top wanted us all out to the flight line at the crack of dawn to build more revetments for the aircraft before our 0830 hours departure time.

One of the gunners asked when we would have time to work on our bunkers and was told by the CO, "You men can be replaced. The protection of those helicopters takes precedence over your personal bunkers." He's not a real popular guy!

During our Charlie-Charlie flight this afternoon, the colonel wants us to haul ropes out to his men at Hue, so they can scale the walls of the Citadel. The city is extremely well fortified. We're taking a small amount of ground at a time and leveling a lot of surrounding villages. What a sad sight. The problem is, there are no front lines in this war. The enemy is a master of camouflage, never dressed the same, and when we do see him, it's difficult to distinguish him from the friendly villagers. It's an impossible situation.

The 1/7 found a huge weapons cache yesterday about four clicks northwest of Hue. Our ship hauled them all back to Evans. I now have an AK47, five thirty-round magazines, and a semi-automatic M21.

Yesterday, while on an ammo resupply, Charlie popped smoke right near one of our LZs. The enemy smoke was released before our guys popped theirs. Usually, the pilot verifies the color of smoke just because of this situation. The lead pilot thought the smoke had been released by our men and made its approach to that area. Their ship was shot full of holes. We aborted and called in two Cobras to teach them a lesson.

CHAPTER 41

VENTILATED AGAIN

24 February, 1968
Phu Bai

Dear Dad,

I'll be in Phu Bai for the next several days, after arriving yesterday. This base has a much more complete maintenance shop than Evans.

Four days ago while flying Charlie-Charlie for 1/7, we spent most of the morning reconning an area just north of Hue where they were to make their next assault.

The assault was made late in the morning. In the middle of the afternoon, we were called on to fly a single ship re-supply. When we established radio contact with the unit, to tell them we were one minute out, we were told that the LZ was green. Flaring for the landing, the Gooks opened up from behind every bush. Taking several hits, we were able to push the ammo out and depart with no injuries.

At 1650 hours we were scheduled to go out to the same area to pick up Red Baron Six. This major is the CO of the 1/7. Supposedly, he was about two miles northwest of Hue. As we circled low-level over the area trying to establish radio contact, we heard the all too familiar chatter of machine gun fire, and old 092 was shot full of holes for the second time in the past couple of hours. This time the AC took an AK round in the right thigh, after the bullet went through the floor and center console, knocking out all of our radios. We returned plenty of fire, but as is often the case, we

173

don't know if we did any damage to the gunners below. We flew back to PK 17, the closest LZ, to check out the pilot and ship. The pilot is OK, but the ship took thirteen hits after only six this morning. After returning to Camp Evans, I grounded the ship, after closer inspection.

The next morning the maintenance pilot flew the aircraft to Phu Bai for repairs. I was asked to fly left seat, but elected to fly to Phu Bai on another ship. I knew how bad off my ship was and didn't care to try to cheat death again. There were holes in the fuel cell, and a bad one through the main rotor blade. Other areas that were well ventilated included the doors, windows, cargo compartment, tail boom, engine deck, mast and head. The one that got most of my attention was one that came through the left engine cowling from the rear and through the firewall, lodging against the soundproofing by my head. It's beginning to look like it may be time to go home!

Intelligence reports state that the enemy has literally been found chained to recoilless rifles, and .50 cals. in and around Hue. They've been ordered to kill or be killed. The morale of the enemy is low with a lack of dedication, but the determination of their commanders is high and they apparently want to hold Hue at all costs. It's amazing how barbaric and inconsiderate the Communists are! They have no regard for human lives…not even those of their own men who are just young boys more often than not. We assume their losses have been so great that they'll recruit anyone that can hold and fire a gun. Age is not a factor.

Love,
Bill

CHAPTER 42

OLD MAN'S JEEP

27 February, 1968
Phu Bai

Certain pleasures are derived from having your helicopter shot full of holes while out on a mission. Number one, of course, is to not find yourself peering at the wrong side of a body bag. Losing control of your ship is also a poor option because if you draw fire from below, it's not too hard to imagine who may be lurking in the jungles below. Being killed, seriously wounded, or fried to a crisp in the ensuing crash are very real fears to all of us who fly these missions. But after battling it out with the enemy, being captured always seemed like an even poorer option.

It's always a great feeling of accomplishment after drawing enemy fire to find everyone on board has escaped new holes in their uniforms. Holes are bad enough, but those with liquid running out are always an adrenaline rush that none of us look forward to. It's gratifying to beat Charlie at his own game.

As a crew chief, it's often a pleasure to receive a lot of battle damage. Though it's really tough on the nerves, in our outfit, it means a mini-vacation. Providing the aircraft is unsafe for further missions, it's either flown or sling loaded to Phu Bai for repair. The crew chief is required to go along to help with the patchwork. During any time off while away from our unit, we're on our own at a base with a real PX, nightly movies, and even a few round-eyed girls to gawk at. The guys in these rear areas really have it made!

After having received sixty seven hits on a troop insertion, it's been decided that our ship is indeed ready for the Band-Aid factory. The aircraft assigned to Eric, one of my buddies, has also been shot up pretty bad. They are both unsafe for missions but still flyable, so we make the flight to Phu Bai, a repair depot that has a lot more maintenance capabilities than we have at Evans.

We've spent a very wet couple of days working on our ships and are walking to lunch at one of the clubs on the base when we happen to spot a jeep sitting all alone in an unloading zone. Now that's very tempting for two guys who have been walking through knee-deep mud. Seeing no one else around, we decide to investigate. The temptation is too great after reading the lettering on the jeep. This particular set of wheels belongs to our company commander. What a coincidence...it belongs to us! Well, at least it belongs to our company.

Eric has a very mischievous nature, and I'm tired of muddy socks. The Old Man's jeep is prepped with a sling and ready to be sling loaded to Evans, probably that same day, so we have to work fast. Removing the sling gear, we fire this baby up, and drive to lunch in style. This is perfectly harmless. After all, the Old Man has managed without his personal jeep for the past three weeks, has no idea where it is, and has a helicopter at his disposal anytime he wants to travel. Besides, the military seems to have plenty of jeeps. It doesn't take us long to get accustomed to riding instead of walking through the mud, so the decision is unanimous...this will be our wheels during our stay at Phu Bai.

Both Eric and I have been in country for nine months and feel strongly that we deserve a little fun. We don't even feel like we're stealing from the government because we are government property just like the jeep. Besides, we'll only borrow the vehicle as long as we're in Phu Bai and that will probably be not more than a week or so. After that time we'll return it to the loading zone from where we have "purchased" it. It's a foregone conclusion that this delivery will occur under the cover of darkness. We're keenly aware of government covert operations. Uncle Sam himself would be proud.

Since Eric and I are such loyal government employees, we work and sweat for long hours over the repair of our helicopters for the next couple of weeks. Yes, it takes longer than we had anticipated. It stands to reason that hard work should be rewarded, so in our spare time, we feel compelled to see just how good army jeeps are. Our CO seems to have a bug up his rear over enlisted personnel, so we elected to treat our newly acquired jeep as if it were a rental car. This was a great antidote for our time away from "home."

We're successful! Taking turns, we always try to outdo the other guy in the depth of the mud holes we can get through, the depth of the streams we can ford, and the hills we can climb. Normally, these jeeps are great at hill climbing, but during the monsoon season it can get a little dicey.

After two weeks our choppers are ready, and so is the jeep. We feel like we have fulfilled our goal of making the jeep impossible to recognize to the untrained eye. We return the wheels to the same place where we had picked it up, covered from top to bottom in about a half ton of mud. After enough mud had been scraped off by the shipping crew to decide where to send it, it did turn up at our company shortly after we returned with our aircraft.

As could be expected, very shortly after the Old Man discovered the return of his jeep, he was rather suspicious that someone under his command might know something of the incident. He heatedly addressed the troops that evening. Now Eric and I are very honest soldiers, but since we were not addressed directly, we offered no information. However, there were a couple of guys in our company that were always in trouble and they were away on R&R at the time of the great mud slinging, so of course they had the pleasure of cleaning up the jeep. Eric and I felt bad for them, but we sure had no desire to be pulled off flight status, followed by a month of KP and guard duty, so we were easily able to keep a secret.

CHAPTER 43

BIG MISTAKE

1 March, 1968
Phu Bai

Dear Dad,

    While waiting on parts for my aircraft, I'm still here in Phu Bai patching bullet holes from my last mission. Since I've been here, two other company ships were shot up too, so Eric and I have a couple crew chief buddies who have joined us.

    Today, one of our company ships stopped in and brought our mail to us. I had two letters from you and six from Cindi. So, it was a great day! Mail from home is the highlight of any day over here... when it comes. Thanks so much for being so faithful in your letter writing. I know it takes a lot of your time, but it means everything!

    Yesterday there was a chaplain here, so Rob, another crew chief from Ohio, and I went to a service. They even had communion. I guess I never expected to see communion offered in a war zone. Maybe that's what made it extra special. The service lasted about forty five minutes and was really good. Afterwards, walking back to our ships, Rob said, "Ya know Pete, that's the first time I've been to church in fourteen months. I used to get attendance pins for attending Sunday school back home and seldom missed a Sunday." He's a Baptist, though denomination seems to matter very little here. We're all pretty much thrown into a big pot. It seems that an awful lot of guys are fairly open about their faith, or lack of it, in this place. There's a lot of foxhole religion going around. I think a lot of it is for real. When God taps on your shoulder over here, you'd best pay attention!

Your idea of a gospel tract written by Uncle Oliver, based on my letters home, was a great idea. By the way, I got the proof for the White Robe Six tract today. Everything looks great! Let's go with it! I'm excited to see it in print and distributed here! I think it will be well received.

Talk to you soon.

Bill

8 March, 1968
Camp Evans

Dear Dad,

My ship is covered with metal band-aids and I've finally returned to Camp Evans. It will be nice to get back in the air. My buddies tell me things are heating up and our unit has begun to see and engage tanks and truck convoys in the past several days.

As soon as I got back "home" I asked about Dale. He's been flown back to the States for more hospitalization and therapy. He can't walk and may never be able to again! I'm glad he's back stateside, but saddened that he had to leave under such circumstances. If you will recall, Dale had asked me to be in his wedding as soon as we got home. I wonder how his wounds will affect those plans. I'm having a difficult time accepting the fact that Dale is in such bad shape. Though I see this stuff happen every day, when it happens to someone you're so close to, it's very hard to come to grips with.

Two days ago, a very good friend of mine, Lt. Shy from Ohio, was shot down in his Cobra and killed while on a Nite Hunter mission. I met him awhile back during a break between missions. We had landed in a rice paddy just outside a village to have lunch. While dining on C rations, we got talking about fishing and hunting and quickly became good friends. It seems strange how rapidly friends are made in a war zone…and how suddenly they can be lost. When I volunteered for this duty, I truly believed in this war - thought it was necessary to help stamp out Communism, protect our freedoms, and all that stuff. Anymore, I think America has made a big mistake by coming here in the first place. I'm losing friends as fast as I make them! Are we Americans that expendable? Was World War II, or any other war that way? What is our purpose here?

Discouraged,
Bill

12 March, 1968
Camp Evans

I was stunned to get a letter from Dale today, complete with a wedding invitation! He sent it to me, "for all the guys in Charlie Company." He's back home and getting married March 16! I wish him the best. He certainly deserves it!

Another lucky day today. Due to avionics problems, my ship is knocked out of the Yellow One slot and is flying White Two instead. At 1815 hours we're flying a re-supply mission in support of the 101st Airborne about one and a half miles east of Hue. Snipers open up from the front and left flank while we make our approach to an emerald green colored LZ. Eddie and I kick the ammo and chow off before our chopper makes an immediate departure. Charlie is almost on top of the grunts. They're so close that we can't return the fire and risk hitting our own men!

On the way back to Evans to lick our wounds, we stay low over the rice paddies and tree lines. The area is saturated with enemy and we want to make for a tough target. The flying pilot has the aircraft red-lined, going as fast as the chopper can safely fly according to the manufacturer. We're sailing just above the water over a narrow rice paddy in an exhilarating flight when, "KAROOOOM!!" Charlie messed up and led our ship by too much! Fortunately for us, his RPG round explodes ten yards in front of us. With lightning speed, the pilot veers sharply to the right, climbs a hundred feet to just barely clear the trees, and we continue on. The co-pilot calls Flight Ops to report the enemy position that will be marked on the charts. It's a free-fire zone, so a Scout and a team of gunships will be called in to troll for fire and destroy the target, or the area will get hammered by artillery…all just a phone call away. Time for an undie change!

Though it is easy to take the organization of the military in a war zone for granted, it constantly amazes me how well all the branches of services work together. Our teams help each other out of trouble on a daily basis. From the Seabees who clear land for LZs and build bridges, to the Navy who give all of us tremendous aircraft support with their fighters and bombers, along with the support of their gun line that often gives us artillery support for our missions...incredible firepower! The Marines are running their own missions on the ground and in the air, but they also work together with the rest of us to defeat the enemy. Then there is the Air Force who give us more aerial support with not only fighters and bombers, but with smaller aircraft flying FAC missions to help gather intelligence and engage in other missions searching for the enemy...low and slow with their butts hanging out for Charlie to blow away. The B52 support they fly for us is indescribable! When these guys fly an Arc Light mission, the area they bomb looks like a huge pig pasture filled with huge holes. Everything is pulverized. Enormous trees are now toothpicks, shattered beyond belief. And the enemy? If still alive, their ears will never be the same!

In addition, the Air Force flies Ranch Hand Missions. Using C130s they do aerial spraying of jungled areas with a herbicide, Agent Orange. This defoliant turns a triple canopy jungle into a leafless, horrible-looking mess within hours. The purpose is to deny the enemy cover and to be able to see the ground, revealing countless trails, bunkers, enemy trucks and anti-aircraft emplacements. This is a real boon to all of us fighting this ungodly war...we can now see the ground where previously the enemy had the advantage. However, it's a shame to see beautiful, lush jungle turned into a bleak winter landscape (without the snow) in such a short time. Often, our missions are flown right after the aircraft fly the spray missions. The mist is still in the air and the rotor blades stir it up. It even comes in the doors. I'm not too concerned at age twenty.

We weren't warned of the health dangers of this stuff. What do you suppose this is doing to the water in the streams where the grunts are filling their canteens? This was is all paid for in later years by many of us. Though we all knew this was an extremely powerful chemical, we did not know that Agent Orange would cause skin diseases, diabetes, many types of cancer and numerous other severe problems. Many of us who were fortunate enough to live through Vietnam would later die as a result of exposure to this nasty chemical.

13 March, 1968
Camp Evans

Dear Dad,

Charles did it again. Between 2430 hours and 0130 hours we received a steady barrage of 122mm rocket and 81mm mortar fire. They hit the ammo and fuel dumps, and three ships on our line. One aircraft was totaled. A rocket landed right next to our NCO bunker, crumbling part of one wall and making a hole six feet deep. These rockets are just over eight feet long and 122mm in diameter, so they tend to leave quite an impression. To my knowledge, no one was injured, but three NVA Forward Observers were killed by the perimeter patrol.

A box of cookies and nuts was waiting for me when I finished flying today.

I'll be sending you a couple rolls of black and white film and should have another before long. We made an initial assault into some mountains that had not been breached by Americans until this afternoon. I think I got some great photos.

To answer some of your questions:

We're about thirteen miles south of Khe Sahn and are expecting to give air support to the Marines that are dug in up there if they need it.

A "click" equals one thousand meters.

Some of the LZ's we work are: Sharon, Ann, Carol, Jeanie, Jane, Nola, High-Low, PK17, Phu Bai, Hue and Sally.

One hundred forty nine days! Can't wait to get home!

Love ya,

Bill

CHAPTER 44

TOMORROW'S MISSION

14 March, 1968
Camp Evans

After the missions for the day are completed about 2030 hours, all crews are summoned to the flight operations tent for another mission briefing.

"Gentlemen, we've been asked to do an insert for the Special Operations Group first thing in the morning. This mission is very important to gain further intelligence on what the Gooks are up to in Laos. Yes, we'll actually be landing in Laos, but that didn't come from me. Laos has been an enemy stronghold for too long, and through the information gathered by SOG, we'll hopefully gain some insight into how to deal with Charlie before he reaches Vietnam."

There's a stirring amongst those of us seated on the benches. We all look at each other in amazement!

All right! We're finally going to hit the NVA in their hidden sanctuaries!

"This important mission has been requested by the top brass and is highly classified. We over flew the area this morning at altitude and with the help of the Green Beret Commander, we've selected three LZs. Two of them will actually be dummy LZs to confuse the enemy. Two ships each will actually make approaches to all three LZs, landing, and departing immediately. Each flight of two slicks will have a double gunship escort, just in case things get dicey. Only one of the LZs will have a special forces team inserted.

Immediately after insertion, all aircraft will return to Evans."

"I don't mind telling you that this mission will be extremely dangerous. Added to the fact that it will take place in an area that is totally unfamiliar to us, is the fact that Charlie has no clue that we're coming. It will be a complete surprise to him. It's called a "Sneaky Pete" mission. On this mission, even though we could meet heavy enemy resistance, I've been told that under no circumstances are we to return fire. I know, you'll have your weapons and gunship support, but again, you are ordered to not return fire. We don't want an international incident over this."

"If you volunteer to be a crew member tonight, I want you crew chiefs and gunners to go out to your ships after the briefing and tape over all exterior numbers on your aircraft. Also tape over US Army. In addition, you are to take the logbooks out of the aircraft. In the event of an accident, we don't want Charlie to know who owns the aircraft. (*Did you ever think the enemy might remove the tape, sir?*) One more thing, you will be required to leave all identification, including your dog tags back here at Evans. In the morning briefing, those of you who want to volunteer will be shown on the charts exactly where we are headed, the location of the LZs, and the location of the nearest friendlies…all across the border in Vietnam, of course. If you should go down and survive, you'll have knowledge of the best route back to safety. This is very rugged country, so if you are shot down, the going will be tough at best."

"Now, though this is an extremely important and sensitive mission, I want each of you to know that it is strictly voluntary. You won't get any pressure from me if you refuse to go. I feel like there are enough of you that'll volunteer, and I'm counting on that."

Surprisingly, enough of us volunteer to fulfill the mission request…Yes, even me.

CHAPTER 45

MORNING BRIEFING

15 March, 1968
Camp Evans
0600 Hours Briefing: Flight Ops

"Good morning gentlemen. I want to thank all of you for stepping forward to join us on today's mission. Again, I remind you that this Delta Mission is strictly voluntary. Those of you who go on the mission today will be expected to return for the extraction, with date and time to be determined. Likely that will be within ten days or less. If, for any reason, after thinking it over during the night, you wish to be removed from the flight, you are welcome to do so at this time. As it turned out, several more men came to me after the briefing last evening and asked to be included. Since we already had enough to fill the request, they're on a standby list if you should change your mind, but you must do so at this time."

An eerie quietness fills the room. Each man's thoughts are the same. *Did I make the right choice last night? There is still time to back out. It's now or never! Not a hand goes up. We're in.*

After a brief, quiet pause, "I'm proud of each and every one of you. You're a real credit to our unit. Remember, you'll be inserting a Special Forces team along with their Montagnard counterparts. The LZ is deep in the mountains, a known NVA stronghold, where American forces have never set foot. The target for this mission is about twenty five miles northwest of Hue, just inside the Laotian border...and remember, you didn't hear that location from me. It's just north of a known camouflaged NVA airstrip."

"There are several known .50 cal positions and plenty of NVA in the general area. Hopefully, our insertion will be about three miles from where the enemy is located, according to intelligence we've received. The Green Beanies will hoof it in to do their operation from where we drop them off. Several truck and tank convoys have been spotted in the area. If you go down, no one will be in to pick you up. Get all weapons, ammo, first aid kits and survival kits out, then destroy the aircraft. If you go down after crossing the river shown on this chart, strike out on a due east course until you come to the river. From there, follow the river north until you get to the fork in the river. Hide and camouflage yourself well. You are to wait there. The Air Force will try to pick you up at that point, but it may be awhile."

"Crew chiefs and gunners…if you draw fire, you are not to return it. (*RIGHT!!*) Pop smoke on the location. The gunships are to roll in on your smoke."

The question is then asked by another crew chief: "Sir, what's the difference who returns the fire?"

"The job of your slicks is to get these men on the ground and depart as quickly as possible. The gun team will handle the dirty work."

"You'll crank one hour from now and pick up your team at precisely 0730 hours. Time now is 0612 hours."

What have I gotten myself into today? I have second thoughts. I was asked if I wanted to volunteer for this mission after being told first how important it was, followed by how dangerous it could be. After all I've been through to date, I feel like it's just a matter of time before I go home in a body bag. I have over four months left. Will my luck run out? If I'm going to die in a helicopter crash or by an enemy bullet, why not go out with a bang and volunteer for a mission that's a lot more hazardous? This one is bound to be exciting by the sound of it…a super adrenaline pumper! Though I really don't think I have a death wish, I admit to enjoying the rush, even though it usually scares me beyond belief! This seems very contradictory!

Every mission that I am involved in that puts my pucker factor in the brown arc (I couldn't suck a pea up my butt) puts me one step closer to going home. I desperately look forward to that, but I realize that these missions could just as easily put me in a body bag and send me home...or, I could be captured. It is difficult to explain, but once a hairy mission is completed, there is an extreme sense of accomplishment and for whatever strange reason, a desire to go back and do it again. A lot of that desire comes from wanting desperately to help those guys in the field. We, as flight crews, feel safer knowing that our team will help protect us and rescue us if need be. Though I don't feel invincible, that's a huge factor.

CHAPTER 46

SNEAKY PETE INSERTION

15 March, 1968
Camp Evans

After a long, hard look at the map of the area we're about to attack, we have a good idea of where to head in case we're shot down. Not a real pleasant thought!

Our twelve slicks are loaded and ready to go at 0720 hours. Prior to cranking our engines, Yellow One makes a call to Delta Company, our sister company. They'll supply our gunship escort.

"Gunslinger One, Yellow One. Are you up?"

"Yellow One, Gunslinger One, go."

"Roger, Gunslinger. Is your flight ready to go?"

"That's a rog, Gunslinger flight standing by."

"Yellow One cranking. Give us a call when you're ready for departure."

"Roger."

The odor of kerosene fills the air. It's the smell of another battle about to begin. Nervously, I recheck all my gear, and confirm that my six extra ammo boxes are within easy reach under my seat. Ammo tray is full, M16 fastened to the bulkhead on my left, ten additional M16 clips hanging on the bulkhead in my magazine pouch above my M16, assortment of grenades…smoke, frags, and Willy Peter. My Randall knife, compass and chicken plate are all strapped on.

I know, we've been ordered not to return fire if we're fired upon, but I have this uneasy feeling…I want to be fully prepared.

A tremendous dust storm develops while the pilots bring the six slicks to operating RPM. After requesting a flak vest ever since arriving in country, and being told it was not standard issue for helicopter crew members, I have one on board today. I "requisitioned" it from a grunt a few days ago. He was dead. Another grunt had thrown his bloody flak vest on my ship after the body was loaded. Unfortunately, he doesn't have need for it anymore. I am now sitting on the vest with plans to swap it for my heavy chicken plate if we go down. It will lighten my load substantially if I have to escape.

"Yellow One, Gunslinger flight's ready when you are."

"Roger. Yellow One's ready."

"Tower, this is Yellow One. Flight of sixteen from the 227th Charlie and Delta revetments. Requesting departure to the northwest."

"Roger, Yellow One. You're flight of sixteen is cleared to depart northwest. No reported traffic in the area. Have a safe flight."

"We're cleared to the northwest. Thanks."

Reality sets in when I realize the high percentage of gunships to slicks. This could be more exciting than I had initially thought.

Charlie Company clears the revetments first in a wild flurry of red dust, with Delta Company close behind. The mission is on. Each of us is privately considering what adventure may lie ahead.

From the briefing, we know that it's probable that we will meet up with a lot of resistance to our insertion. Judging from the reported known weapons sights, it's likely that we will not only draw heavy fire, but some of us may not return today…if at all. For the SOG teams, this is old hat.

All flight crew members are volunteers. Many of us are certainly having second thoughts. In most cases, our machismo is rapidly dwindling, but it's too late now. We're on our way…time to buck up, stay alert, and do our utmost to stay alive.

Since Charlie is not supposed to know we're invading his territory today, an artillery prep is not on the agenda. We're to arrive without warning.

The Green Berets and their Montagnard counterparts stand beside the runway while our flight lands in another dust bowl. The twelve team members are split into two groups. The first climbs

189

aboard Yellow One and the second boards Yellow Two. These guys are well prepared in their tiger stripe jungle fatigues. All bare skin has been painted green, brown and black. Their camouflaged boonie hats are pulled down tightly to keep them from blowing off while they ride seated on the available seats with the rest on the floor of the ship. There are three on each side. Weapons vary...some carry AR15s while others carry an assortment of grease guns, shotguns, an M60 and M79 grenade launcher. They all carry a sidearm of their choice. Being a Special Ops Group, the weapons they carry are chosen from a well supplied arsenal. Under a heavy pack, their web belts carry an assortment of ammo and various grenades. One of the men has two bandoliers of machine gun ammo slung across his chest. Each of these young men has a very solemn look about them. They've been on similar missions. Each of them has survived so far, but a lot of their buddies haven't been so lucky. They know the odds are nothing to bet on.

All Charlie company ships are flying in trail. The five gunships on either side space themselves to provide protective fire for the entire gaggle should it become necessary.

All is quiet except for the steady beating of the rotor blades. I can't help but take in the beautiful scenery. The area below is even void of the ever-present bomb craters and areas sprayed with defoliant. We have flown deep into Laos. A river falls over the rocky outcroppings, tumbling down the mountainside amidst the emerald green triple canopy jungle. What a paradise!

My emotions are mixed. My ship seems to be favored by Lt. Lawton, the flight leader, who gets his pick of aircraft and crews. So, once again, 092 has been requested for the number one position. He has flown a lot of missions with Eddie and me, knows we have always done a good job, and likes my ship. It seems to have plenty of power...more than some of the other aircraft. If things get messy we will need all the power we can get today.

My experience has been 50/50 on previous missions. If it's a cold LZ, Yellow One is generally pretty safe; it seems to take several ships before the locals wake up enough to start firing on the flight, if they do at all. If it's a hot LZ, enemy fire can be intense on the number one ship, or the Gooks may wait until more troops are on the ground in an attempt to inflict even heavier casualties. I've learned not to ever bet on the mood of the NVA.

Crossing a saddle in the sharp ridge line we dive down the other side and skim the treetops at one hundred twenty knots. Our proposed LZ is just ahead. It's a double bomb crater that was made a couple days ago. They must have fallen by "accident" from one of our fighters since we don't fight in Laos. In actuality, American air activity is present in Laos and selective targets have been hit. Yellow One and Two slow to approach speed, with two Gunslinger birds flying swiftly by on each side. The balance of the flight splits into two formations of two slicks with two gunships each. Each flight goes a different direction in an attempt to confuse the enemy that may be lurking below. Two of the slicks will make approaches to dummy LZs within a couple miles of us.

All I hear are the sounds of the rotors, but the hair on the back of my neck feels like it's pushing on my collar. The radios are silent with the crews thinking about how crazy they were to have volunteered for this mission. I feel like I'm at death's front door, and it's creaking open…in slow motion. Dad always taught me to keep my safety on and finger off the trigger until I had my quarry in sight and was ready to shoot. My target's not in sight yet, but my butt is tighter than the bung on a whiskey barrel. My safety is off with my fingers ready on the double triggers. I've fired many thousands of rounds through this machine gun and know it inside out. There is some play in the trigger mechanism. But, right now, my fingers curl more tightly and the play is non-existent. This is no man's land and I want to be ready for whatever might lie ahead.

The fact that our orders were to not return fire, even if fired upon, are forgotten. This will be a life or death situation and the Brass sitting in the rear chewing on cigars aren't the ones who have their butts on the line here. Normally, orders are followed precisely. But in this situation, we plan to use common sense to save our hides and those of our passengers. We all sense that we're about to go through the meat grinder and WILL respond with the firepower we have available.

We're slowed to five knots as we settle in just over the tree branches that have been ripped apart from the explosion of the bomb that formed our LZ. The AC smoothly lowers collective to begin our descent, and with aft cyclic to help slow our forward airspeed, right pedal is added to keep the aircraft in trim. As the descent is arrested, we come to a hover a few feet above the bottom of the crater in the shattered LZ. We can't descend any further for fear of entangling the tail rotor or main rotor blades in the downed trees and stumps scattered around the LZ. Immediately, the first two American Special Forces troops jump to the ground with enemy automatic weapons fire kicking up the dirt around them and the helicopter. The remainder of our load consists of very dedicated Montagnards. They follow closely behind the Americans, returning fire as they hit the ground running. This all happens in a matter of seconds. Immediately upon lifting off, we return fire over the heads of the troops we've just deposited into the thick of things. Our ship clears the tops of the trees amid a hail of gunfire.

Within a split second of lifting off, the second ship is dropping its troops with the same results. They also escape and tuck up behind our ship for the return flight to safety.

The gunships are laying out streams of minigun and rocket fire while they escort us out of this mess. With Lt. Lawton on the controls, the co-pilot is calling to the rest of the flight about the fire we received. Just as he begins to speak, a .50 cal. opens fire. It's a very distinct thump…thump…thump as Charlie tries to connect. Fortunately for us, he's out of practice, and White Robe Six is on our side again.

The enemy continues firing at us within a radius of a quarter mile of the LZ. Several more .50 cal. positions are called in, with a red smoke grenade dropped to mark their locations, so they can be pounded by the Gunslinger flight. They're happy to accommodate.

Crossing the previous ridge, we're joined by the rest of our aircraft. The timing is perfect. Lawton radios each chopper in succession to assess the damages. We've all taken hits, but none serious enough to have to land in Laos.

Miraculously, the team has been inserted and none of the crew members have been hit, even though several of our ships are well ventilated once again.

Upon returning to Evans, a report is made to the Company Commander that we did encounter plenty of enemy resistance. He was given coordinates of the enemy positions and told that the gunships did a fine job. He didn't ask about our company returning fire, and we didn't offer any information. Had he walked out to the flight line and examined our aircraft, he would have seen empty ammo boxes and spent casings lying all over the decks of the ships, in addition to more bullet holes. But he didn't...he knew what he would find.

Mission accomplished.

CHAPTER 47

A SORROWFUL PICK UP

21 March, 1968
Camp Evans and Laos

When we delivered the Special Forces team in the Laotian mountains, the agreement was to pick them up six days later. Today is the day.

In our briefings prior to the insert, the plan had been to meet these men at a pre-designated point on top of a mountain at precisely 1000 hours today. We have all been advised that timing is critical for the extraction. We don't want to hang around Laos any longer than is absolutely necessary. Either the team will be at the coordinates given in the briefing at the exact hour, or they will have to hoof their way back to Vietnam. We are to make only one attempt at recovering the team.

While enroute to the PZ this morning, the delivery of this brave team is still fresh in our minds. We recall the warm welcome by the NVA as we made the drop. The pick up will be made in an LZ about three miles away. Hopefully, the enemy gunners will be non-existent.

After entering Laos, we see the ridge perpendicular to our flight path that we had flown over six days before. Again crossing the ridge, we fly within a mile of the original LZ and continue on to the PZ situated on the next mountaintop. At tree top level, we're flying as fast as possible with our gunship escort, scanning the area for trouble. As before, the only sounds in the valley are those of our pick up ship, one rescue ship, two cobras and one B model gunship.

Though we're all ready for action, we'll be happy to keep our guns clean.

Closing the gap to the mountaintop, our feelings of uneasiness increase. Knowing that one of us will be a rescue bird in case one of the others is shot down is somewhat reassuring. But what if more than one of our aircraft go down?   Remembering that if we're shot down, we may have to escape and evade the enemy on our own...the rugged country below looks evil.

The PZ is just ahead, and slowing for the approach, we see several monkeys scurrying about in the treetops watching the unfamiliar creatures flying overhead. The aircraft settles quickly to the pinnacle. No one is in sight. Suddenly, two Americans and one Montagnards burst from the brush, jump on board, and signal the pilot to get out...NOW!

Lifting off with the three passengers aboard, we load the edge of the PZ with lead. Our Special Ops guys have been followed to this position by the enemy. While our bullets begin ripping the leaves off the trees, the enemy soldiers return fire and pepper holes in the side of the ship as we plummet down the mountainside in an attempt to escape the barrage. As soon as we're out of range, one of the camouflaged men crawls up to the cockpit console and explains to the pilots that the rest of the team has either been killed or captured. Sadly, there won't be any more men to pick up.

For the balance of the ten-minute flight over Laos on the way to Vietnam, our sorrow for the men we couldn't retrieve deepens. They died heroically for their country in a war within a war. What will their families be told?

Arriving back at Evans, we all attend the post flight briefing. We're told that the entire team was able to escape the original ambush at the drop zone six days ago. On the fifth day after having gathered a lot of valuable intelligence, including photos of a large NVA headquarters camp, they ran into a squad of soldiers and had a massive shootout. Enemy reinforce-ments joined the fight killing seven of our men and capturing two others. The remaining three were able to evade until the following morning when we picked them up. Two slicks went in to get them accompanied by two gunships. They had been followed to the PZ by the enemy. After lifting off and receiving fire again, the gunships wiped them out.

CHAPTER 48

PSYOPS MISSION

23 March, 1968
Camp Evans

Dear Dad,
    Today's mission is designed to convince the local populace that our purpose here is really humanitarian in nature. It's called a PSYOPS Mission.
    Eddie and I loaded a bank of loudspeakers onto my ship. A South Vietnamese interpreter boarded the chopper carrying a script that he would read over the loudspeakers while we flew at an altitude of fifteen hundred feet over the local area. The purpose of these flights is to attempt to re-educate the natives below. This is a poor altitude to fly, especially at slow airspeeds. If the Gooks choose to fire at us, we're easy targets at that altitude. However, our escort of four gunships seemed to deter the would-be marksmen below.
    Bird Dog was part of our flight. Its job was to drop leaflets explaining the position of the Americans in their area and was designed to try to convince any VC to defect.
    We had burned most of our usable fuel, after several passes over the area designated for our mission, when I spotted two Gooks who were running toward the tree line. I made an attempt to notify our pilots on the intercom, but it wasn't working! On the next pass, I saw nine uniformed men carrying weapons. They quickly disappeared into the brush.
    I yelled at the pilots to get their attention, but it was too late…all of our birds had to return to the fuel dump. While the

gunner fueled our chopper, I showed the pilots the location of the enemy on the nav chart. Our mission being over, they called dispatch to have a couple more gunships over-fly the area to see what they could find. But they came back empty handed.

After our PSYOPS Mission, we had to fly a re-supply mission. One of the units in the field is expecting a full-scale attack tonight according to intelligence, so we hauled a load of ammo out to their very tight LZ.

The mission was expected to be routine, so we took a new co-pilot along for his indoctrination flight. He did the flying. He got into the snug LZ OK, but on departure, Charlie fired a few rounds at us. Our new guy got excited, tightened up on the controls and struck a tree with the main rotor blades. The aircraft commander took over the controls and got us back to Evans, though we had a pretty bad vibration. Bottom line is, the maintenance crew will be joining me at daybreak to install a new set of blades.

Have a great day!
Bill

24 March, 1968
Camp Evans

Dear Dad,

Yesterday our birds dropped two companies into the area where I spotted the eleven NVA the day before. They were in heavy contact all day, and we pulled them out just before dark last night. During the battle yesterday, a couple of captured POWs spilled their guts. It turns out that there is an NVA regiment of two thousand men in this area, 11 clicks due east of Camp Evans. It sounds like our PSYOPS Mission wasted a lot of leaflets.

Talk to you soon.
Bill

26 March, 1968
Camp Evans

Dear Dad,

The mail has been very scarce lately. All of us look forward to mail call, some more than others. I really feel sorry for some of the guys who seldom, if ever, get any mail. I'm so thankful for a loving family who are so faithful in writing. I know you are writing often, but the carriers between the states and this God-forsaken place must be doing a poor job of keeping an even flow going. There are many days without mail from home, often several days in a row. And then, there is a flood of mail. At any rate, I guess loneliness is really setting in.

We were mortared again last night after midnight. There were six men killed over by the base post office. Maybe that's why the mail has been so screwed up. Our Nite Hunters spotted five enemy mortar tubes but there were friendlies in the area so the enemy gunners couldn't be fired upon.

Yesterday, just northwest of here, the 5/7th ran into a regiment of NVA tanks. Even though our men put up a good fight, there were several killed. As soon as the tanks were spotted, the Air Force was called in to bomb and strafe them beyond recognition.

The news this morning is that we're planning a major flight into Khe Sahn to relieve them in a couple of days. They've been getting pounded up there and need some relief. I went over to maintenance and told the crew that I really want my inspection finished so I can be on that mission. They're still waiting for parts and don't know when they'll be in, so we scrounged parts off of other non-flyable ships, worked all day, and should have mine back on the flight line in the morning.

I've been wanting a short survival weapon that I can depend on, so decided to saw the barrel and stock off of my AK47 this morning. After test firing it, I was very pleased with its performance. Nothing against US made weapons, but the AK is much more reliable than the M16.

Time for some sleep.

Hi to all, and keep those letters coming.

Bill

CHAPTER 49

APRIL FOOL'S DAY

2 April, 1968
Camp Evans

Dear Dad,

     The Marines have been taking a beating for quite some time up at Khe Sahn and are in desperate need of relief. There has been talk for several days that the Cav has been chosen to help them out. We made our initial assault yesterday…April Fool's Day.

     With over sixty Hueys involved in the assault, I'm sure Charlie must have been overwhelmed. In addition to the slicks, we had twelve to fifteen gunships, twelve ARA ships, two Cobras, two Charlie-Charlie aircraft with Pony Soldier Six (General Tolson) aboard one, and four crash recovery ships. We also had Tac Air and B52 strikes on standby if needed. According to intelligence, the Gooks are well entrenched and are expected to fight like tigers.

     Two of the four crash recovery birds on this mission came from our company. My ship, 092 was the lead bird, and 319 was the other ship from Charlie company. The four recovery ships were interspersed evenly throughout the flight to allow for the best coverage of any other aircraft that might be shot down. Each of the recovery birds had a jungle penetrator on a one hundred and fifty foot rope. In the event that an aircraft crashed in an area where we were unable to land, the penetrator would be used. Generally, these are used with winches. While the helicopter hovers above the trees, the device is lowered through the trees for the crash victims to grab onto, and then they're winched up to the waiting helicopter. None of us had winches, so the plan was to get the victim on the penetrator, raise him vertically through the trees with the Huey ascending straight up until the trees were cleared, and then sling load the victims to the nearest open friendly terrain. If the guys on the ground were unable to hold on, it was up to the gunner and crew chief to rappel down the rope to assist them. Leaving the guns unattended in a hovering helicopter where a ship was just shot down sounded like an idea designed in Washington!

We picked up the grunts at LZ Studd. We'd been advised that there could be anti-aircraft batteries in the area. Shortly after liftoff, that intelligence proved to be true when two air bursts exploded just off our nose! The flight received a few other rounds of AAA, but all the aircraft fulfilled the mission unscathed. We're planning another assault tomorrow that could be more interesting since Charlie knows we're on his doorstep.

Some of us heard part of LBJ's speech yesterday about his grand scheme to halt the bombing. What a fool! That's just what the North Vietnamese want so they can increase their supply runs to the south. Why can't our government understand that this "police action" is like a lopsided game of checkers…we make one move and then take a nap while the Commies clean the board! We have the firepower available to put an end to this war in short order. If the politics could be put aside, we could win this war, put an end to the loss of American lives, and go home!

3 April, 1968
Camp Evens

Another assault into the Khe Sahn area today with forty slicks plus all the support hardware. Only sporadic fire was received except for one of the LZs where the enemy was well entrenched. That hill had been pulverized by B52's last night, but the little buggers had quite a bunker and tunnel complex and it was still crawling with enemy. We abandoned the LZ while Phantoms were called in to light it up with napalm.

We're planning an assault west of Khe Sahn on the Laotian border in a couple days. After weeks of B52 and artillery strikes in the Khe Sahn area, there are plenty of bodies and body parts littered all over the valley. The local rats are having a feast and getting huge. From the air, they look like the size of Chihuahuas! Bubonic plague is rampant in the area, so we're getting our immunizations up to speed. The vast number of enemy soldiers that were killed by the arc light strikes are rotting in the sun. The stench while flying low level over these areas is horrid. When landing in some of the LZs the smell is overpowering!

I love you,
Bill

CHAPTER 50

STEEL TRAP

4 April, 1968
Camp Evans

During a re-supply mission for 5/7th between LZ Studd and Khe Sahn, after we have dropped off the requested supplies and are flying back to LZ Studd for another load, we hear a frantic call for an emergency medivac. An infantry unit is in contact and has several men critically wounded. There are three gunships on station already, but they're in desperate need of a slick to do the evacuation. Answering the call, the co-pilot plots a course toward their coordinates and asks for a SITREP while enroute to the bloody scene. The lieutenant on the radio answers with a great deal of excitement in his voice, several octaves above a normal man's voice.

"We were under heavy mortar and automatic weapons fire twenty minutes ago. We need to get five seriously wounded men out or they won't survive. Gunships and ARA have been pounding the area outside our perimeter and the enemy fire is just sporadic. Our LZ is on the mountainside and very tight. You'll have to make your approach from the south to the bomb crater in the middle of the LZ, over."

"Roger, we're two minutes to your northeast. We want all the cover fire you can afford. Pop smoke, over."

"Smoke's out."

"Roger, we have red smoke."

"Affirmative, red smoke. As soon as you hover, we'll get these guys on board and you're out of here, over."

We're now on a quarter mile circling approach to final and receiving sporadic small arms and automatic weapons fire. While the gunships and ARA are making passes, Eddie and I cut loose with our 60s. Approaching the treetops on the edge of the LZ, and not knowing where all the friendlies are located, we have to cease-fire. The gunships come alongside and while they bear down on the enemy, the grunts in the LZ open up with withering fire.

"Very tight" would be a great exaggeration of this LZ. The entire unit encircles a single eight foot deep bomb crater that is thirty feet across and surrounded by jagged stumps and broken trees. Just outside of the damaged trees, the LZ is ringed by triple canopy jungle. If this were a normal mission, we would abort until a larger LZ could be cut, but there are five comrades that will likely die without the aid of the helicopter. It's worth the risk. Continuing into what appears to be a steel trap about to spring, the aircraft commander brings the ship to an authoritative hover over the crater, and begins our vertical descent...we're sitting ducks. One of the idiosyncrasies of a helicopter is that a vertical descent needs to be less than three hundred feet per minute. A descent greater than that, and the ship can settle in its own down wash, increasing the rate of descent rapidly, and is all too often unrecoverable. In this super small LZ, if that happens, there is insufficient room to recover. We'll crash. High elevation, heat, humidity, wind, and weight of the aircraft are all contributing factors to the equation. The temptation to increase the rate of descent becomes much greater when the Gooks begin peppering the ship. We're taking rounds from all sides and can hear the AK slugs hitting the ship.

Our crew today has nerves of steel and we continue the rescue attempt, while gritting our teeth and praying that this rescue will be successful with no further loss of life. Though that may sound very heroic, we're all scared spit-less! But unless we get the wounded out, they don't stand much of a chance. The men we're trying to rescue, though strangers to us, are brothers. If our roles were reversed, they would also risk their lives for us. We're family. That's just the way things are in this war.

The aircraft comes to a hover right over the center of the crater, barely clearing the bomb-damaged trees. Appearing to be calm, the pilot rests the left skid on the edge of the crater to enable the wounded to be loaded. The wounded are carried in ponchos by two grunts each. The soldiers are running in a duck walk position in an attempt to avoid being hit by flying bullets and our rotor blades. Unbuckling my monkey harness, I lean out to pull the first of the wounded aboard, and then the second, when something hits me in the chest, right in the middle of my chicken plate. Immediately, another AK round hits the seat support post that I'm holding on to with my other hand. Shrapnel from the exploding bullet and post splatters into my arm and shoulder. Another round bounces off my gun support and enters behind my left kneecap. At the same time, I feel a well-spent round bounce off of my boot. The pilot immediately pulls pitch when I tell him that I'm hit, but ok. His reaction is so quick that I know he's looking out for his crew. He doesn't want to abort the mission anymore than the rest of us, but his crew comes first. As we clear the trees, I insist that I'm not seriously injured, and the decision is made to try another shot at rescuing our comrades.

Making our second attempt, another slick in the area heard our radio conversations and volunteers to take our place. Since our entire crew is tightly wound, and second attempts under these conditions of high stress are often fatal, we welcome the relief and apologize to the ground unit while we depart to lick our wounds.

Monitoring the same radio frequency, we learn that the second ship makes a successful recovery while only taking a few rounds with no additional injuries.

Returning to LZ Studd we survey the damages. My wounds are superficial and can wait to be attended to back at Evans. My ship has seventeen more holes, but is still flyable, so we head for home. While the blades are slowing to a halt after shutdown, I release the Velcro on my chicken plate and slide it over my head to set it down on the deck of the ship. Just before I set it down, an AK round falls out of the center chest pocket. This was the first round that hit me. Though I had felt the impact, the armor plating stopped the round from going any further. There is a dent in the chest protector just above the pocket. The tip of the slug bent over upon impact and then dropped into my pocket. This cool souvenir could have easily ended my life, had I elected not to wear my chicken plate today!

White Robe Six is watching over me...once again. He has been rather busy!

CHAPTER 51

READY REACTION FORCE

9 April, 1968
Phu Bai

Dear Dad,

  One of the pilots is supposed to come down here and claim me. Until he does, I'll get a quick note off.

  I've been here in Phu Bai for the last couple of days patching bullet holes again. My ship is ready to go back into action just as soon as a pilot is dropped off to fly it back to Camp Evans. Usually on these flights, the maintenance pilot is sent, so when Mr. Beyers shows up we'll take off for home. He usually lets me fly when we're together doing test flights or RTS flights. So, hopefully I'll get some more stick time. The RTS flights have been more numerous than I care to think about.

  Another one of our ships was shot up yesterday. When they flew that ship down here for another patchwork quilt job, the crew told me that the latest news from Charlie Company is that The Old Man, Major. Burkhalter, decided to go on a flight yesterday. It should have been a relatively safe mission - re-supply to an LZ near Khe Sahn. When he landed, he set the ship down on a land mine. Fortunately, the injuries were not serious. But the ship had to be sling-loaded out. It should be arriving here soon.

  Because of our new AO, our crews are averaging about twelve hours of flying every day. We often miss meals, so if you could send a box of snacks, including chocolate bars, I'd really appreciate it. Despite the extreme heat, if chocolate is well wrapped it seems to arrive intact.

I dug some more shrapnel out of my shoulder yesterday that had moved closer to the surface. The rest is still pretty well embedded, so I'll have to wait for it to work its way out.

Here comes my pilot. See ya.

12 April, 1968
Camp Evans

Dear Dad,

Well, Mr. Beyers let me fly all the way back to Evans. Flying over the treetops is a blast!

As soon as we landed, Top came out to tell me to gather up my overnight gear and a full supply of ammo and grenades. Our crew was drawn to spend the night stationed at LZ Studd to serve as RRF.

When we arrived at Studd, we were directed to a high knoll on the south end of the perimeter. There was just barely enough room for the Huey, let alone enough ground for us to stretch out under the stars that filled the otherwise black night sky. Mr. Clark and Eddie elected to sleep in the aircraft cabin. That left the top of the ship for Mr. Detuncq and me. The night was beautiful from up there and I saw every bit of it. I was so concerned about rolling off the top of my ship and down the hill that I didn't get any sleep!

There was a small firefight on the other end of the perimeter about 0200 hours, but it ended abruptly, so we didn't even crank.

After a breakfast at dawn with the Marines, we flew all day, extracting a brigade of Marines from Khe Sahn and moving them to LZ Sharon.

We flew for thirteen hours with just enough time to refuel between missions, no lunch, and a box of C rations at 2000 hours.

Upon our return to Studd, our ship and crew were chosen to be on standby for the nite hunter flare mission. Luckily, it rained hard all night so we weren't called for any missions. At daybreak we were told that we could go home. When we got to Flight Ops, they told us we could take a few hours to catch some sleep. Here I am, lying on my cot, too tired to sleep!

Our Khe Sahn operation was supposed to take sixty days. We finished it in ten days and are ready to move on to the next challenge. That will be Ashau Valley and it's expected to be pretty rough.

One hundred and twenty days to go!!
I love you,
Bill

15 April, 1968
Phu Bai

The last day and a half have been spent at Phu Bai. We're putting a new input quill in my ship's transmission. At least I'm not here to repair combat damage again!

We had to take a colonel up to Khe Sahn for a meeting a couple of days ago and had time to walk around a bit during a lull in the shelling. The best description of that place is that it looks and smells like the county dump! The Marines of course had been there and under heavy fire for months, with the enemy barrage often around the clock, so the Americans spent an awful lot of time underground. During my walk, I found two M16s just lying in the mud. There is various field gear scattered all around and shrapnel littering the ground amidst the rocket and mortar craters. One can only imagine how many American lives have been lost on this ground. The acreage surrounding the base looks just as rough, only with larger craters from the bomb and artillery strikes. Huge man-eating rats are everywhere! They are literally feeding on the bodies of the enemy dead that have been left behind. Looking at this horrid mess is enough to ruin your lunch. The stench is worse than anything I have ever smelled! What has America gotten involved in?

CHAPTER 52

ASHAU VALLEY

19 April, 1968
Camp Evans

After a restless night, the CQ opens the door of the tent flap an hour and a half before daybreak. He doesn't have to be selective this morning about which crews he awakens. We're all needed to make the initial assault on The Ashau Valley, "The Valley of Death."

2 Samuel 22: 4-7

4. Call to the Lord, who is worthy of praise, and I am saved from my enemies. 5. The waves of death swirled about me; the torrents of destruction overwhelmed me. 6. The cords of the grave coiled around me; the snares of death confronted me. 7. In my distress I called to the Lord; I called out to my God.

None of us have slept well, knowing what dangers and bloodshed will likely greet us this morning.

While I groggily dump the bugs out of my jungle boots, my heart is already racing in anticipation of this morning's initial flight. I stagger out to the listre bag to rinse the sleep out of my eyes, fill my steel pot with warm water from the immersion tank, and take a G.I. bath. After drying off, I can see the faint morning glow on the eastern horizon.

My thoughts are not on the mission, but on home, family and Cindi.

I have never felt this way prior to departing on a flight since arriving in Vietnam. Until now, though I haven't felt invincible, I never had a premonition like I do this morning. It's spooky and I have to work to control my nerves.

Maybe I've been at this too long. I've seen a lot of buddies killed not long before they were due to go home. Maybe I should go into Flight Ops and ask to be removed from flight status immediately and permanently. But no, if I do that I feel like I would be letting my buddies down. Someone else would have to go in my place. What if they should be killed or severely wounded. I couldn't live with myself.

I go back to the listre bag and rinse my face again, hoping to wash away the shame I feel for even thinking that I need to stay on the ground today.

What's happening here? Why do I feel this way? How will I die? Will my ship be shot out of the sky and crash into the mountains surrounding Ashau? Will it blow up in mid-air, or will I simply take the golden BB and everyone else aboard the aircraft survive?

I pray for God to protect us all on the flight today, even though I really don't feel like I'm praying with a lot of faith. I ask that if He chooses for me to be zipped into a body bag today, that my family and Cindi will understand, and get through the grieving process with as little heartache as possible.

What a strange feeling!

I'm drawn to the mess tent by the smell of strong coffee and reconstituted eggs. Even though I'm not a coffee drinker, I decide to try a cup this morning...I believe, my second cup of the war. It's very bitter, even when mixed with a strong dose of cream and sugar. My Swedish ancestors can have the stuff, in addition to Ludefisk. After switching back to Tang to chase the bitterness of the coffee away, I eat the rest of my instant eggs, bacon and toast.

For some reason, I feel that this may be my last meal, not just for the day, but...forever.

Again, I'm tempted to resign from flight status and I have to fight the urge. Flight status is strictly voluntary so I could quit anytime.

Do I have a death wish? I don't think so. I can take another chance. If I get through the day unscathed, perhaps I'll end my flight duties with the day's last mission.

It's almost 0600 hours when I gather up my flight gear and head for Flight Ops. Opening the tent flap, the smell of that awful coffee and the cloud of cigarette, cigar, and pipe smoke make me want to gasp for a breath of fresh air.

"Gentlemen...yesterday was a tough day. Today will likely be worse. Due to weather restrictions over the past several months, there have been no Americans in the Ashua Valley for a long while. Intelligence tells us to expect heavy resistance. We expect the presence of major supply depots, hospitals, training areas and staging areas. Men, this is where the Ho Chi Minh trail turns into a superhighway."

"The next few weeks are the transition period between the two monsoons, when the valley has a break from the incessant rains and cloud cover."

"Numerous anti-aircraft batteries are expected throughout the valley. Those weapons include: 37mm and 23mm guns, and 12.7mm, 14.5mm, and .50 cal machine guns. There are reported to be several regiments in the area, including armor elements and possible fixed-wing and helicopter battalions."

"Looking at the map over here, you can see that the known sites for enemy anti-aircraft and .50 cal have been marked. Be sure to copy these onto your charts. These are last known enemy positions, but reports are that there are likely a lot more that haven't been pinpointed."

"We'll be assaulting two LZs...LZ Tiger and LZ Vicki. More LZs will be established as the fighting continues."

"The supply routes are well camouflaged. In some cases, the tops of trees have been bent over and woven together, hiding the trails."

During the briefing by The Old Man, my feelings resurface when all the known gun positions are pointed out on the chart. Even though I've flown through a lot of anti-aircraft and .50 caliber fire before, my premonitions make my skin crawl.

How can I be foolish enough to volunteer to fly into such a well-fortified valley? I must be crazy! Do I really think God will protect me through all of this?

210

Looking around the briefing room and into the eyes of the rest of the crews, it's obvious that most are thinking the same things I am.

We're a team...I can't let these buddies down. I will fulfill my duties as crew chief. I feel good about my final decision, because I've fought alongside most of these men for months, and we have always done everything in our power to help anyone in trouble.

The camaraderie this morning seems especially strong.

"Men, I know I haven't painted a very pretty picture. I'm only giving you facts from the intelligence reports. This is extremely rugged country. Right now it belongs to Charles. By this afternoon, it'll be ours! The best of luck to each of you."

When the briefing is complete, the flight crews exit the tent as if they're leaving a funeral parlor. Rather than the normal noisy cockiness that has been so prevalent prior to most missions, there is total silence while we each wrestle with the thoughts passing through our minds

Walking to the flight line, Eddie and I make small talk, but the danger of the upcoming mission makes deep conversation impossible.

Arriving at the revetment where my ship 092 has spent the night, I'm reminded about all the missions my ship has brought me safely through. I can only hope and pray that she will do the same today.

As Eddie busies himself with mounting the machine guns, loading the ammo trays, and hanging smoke, frags and incendiary grenades in all the usual places by each of our seats, I do the preflight. All appears normal and after topping off the engine oil reservoir, the pilots show up with their arm-loads of flight gear. Mr. Jewitt is our aircraft commander today for which I am grateful. He and I have flown many missions together. He's one of my favorite Charlie company pilots, very competent with a good sense of humor and a good friend. Mr. Clark, also an excellent pilot will be the co-pilot today and, of course, Eddie will be my very capable gunner.

How can things go wrong with such a qualified crew?

Mr. Clark does his preflight to double check my work. Two sets of eyes are certainly better than one and we always like to find any problems while still on the ground. After checking the aircraft logbook for any previous write-ups by other pilots or the crew chief, he signs the aircraft off for flight…into the unknown.

According to the briefing, there will be forty slicks involved in the initial insertion just after daybreak. We'll have a heavy compliment of gunships, including B model Hueys and Cobras. There will also be plenty of TAC air and artillery supporting the mission. A couple of slicks with only flight crews are going to accompany the flight, their sole purpose…search and rescue. *A humbling thought.*

The slot assigned to 092 today is Yellow Five. At the appointed time of 0645 hours Yellow One cranks his turbine. In fairly close unison, the balance of the choppers posted in various places on the flight line do the same.

When Yellow One checks in on the radio, he calls for the rest of the flight to follow suit. When all are accounted for and a clearance is received from the tower, the flight departs to land on the Camp Evans airstrip where the grunts are waiting in anticipation. The grunts are very well organized and clustered in small groups along the edge of the airstrip, many of them having done this dozens of times before. The new guys just follow the old timers. Most are fearful of the unknown. Some don't realize what there is to be afraid of, but they'll find out soon enough. When all are loaded, the flight joins up in formation just outside the western edge of the perimeter. The orange ball on the horizon to the east confirms that we're on time. We're headed for LZ Tiger.

Just after our gaggle forms up, Yellow One contacts the FAC who is flying his O-1 Bird Dog in the area we're to attack.

The Bird Dog pilot, sounding very perky and alert, announces that the mountains we're to cross on the east side of the Ashau Valley are shrouded in dense fog. He gives Yellow One the coordinates for a large rice paddy just east of the mountains where we can land our birds while waiting for the fog to lift. He's been circling that area for the past hour and hasn't drawn any fire or seen anything out of the ordinary. He declares it a cold LZ.

Arriving over the rice paddy, our flight circles to the west to make its approach. All eyes are on the ground searching for any telltale traces of enemy. All appears normal and peaceful. The entire flight spreads out over the full length and width of the LZ and lands like a gaggle of geese arriving in a harvested cornfield for breakfast.

Yellow One commands the flight to shut down to wait out the fog. The turbines wind down and the rotor blades slow while the flight crews and grunts depart the aircraft to stretch their legs. Even though we've only been in the air twenty minutes, it will likely be a very long, unnerving day.

We're all grateful for the fog. Having to scrub the mission for thirty minutes or possibly an hour gives us the opportunity to walk around and shrug off some of our uneasiness. Talking with the grunts, it becomes obvious that their fear of today's mission is as great or greater than that of the flight crews. Cigarettes are lit and last minute adjustments are made to equipment while we all wait on Mother Nature.

After twenty minutes on the ground, a look to the west reveals that the fog is beginning to lift. The decision is made by Yellow One to give the weather a few more minutes to be sure the flight path is clear... just as mortars begin dropping in! We have obviously landed near the enemy and he's targeting our LZ! The first rounds land a safe distance from the ships, but as more rounds are fired, they "walk" closer. As soon as the first round is heard coming through the air, all crews and their passengers run for the aircraft, crank, and take off to the east. The enemy fire continues as the last ship departs. Gunships rain fire on the adjacent tree line where the enemy mortar tubes are suspected. Miraculously, none of the aircraft or personnel are hit. It's sweet revenge when the enemy expends so many of their valuable rounds carried all the way from North Vietnam, and is only able to bag piles of mud!

By now, the sun has burned the fog off the tops of the mountains allowing us to continue the task at hand. Heading back to the west, we're only seven or eight minutes out from the three mountaintops that will serve as our LZs. Continuing to our destination at tree top level, we're avoiding the artillery prep that is being directed toward our targets. The rounds are being fired from a couple of fire bases and are whistling through the air above our flight. The grunts fidget with their gear. Nerves are taut while we anticipate the fate that lies ahead.

Yellow One converses with the FAC circling outside the line of the artillery fire. Between transmissions, he's talking with Six, circling high over the valley in his Charlie-Charlie ship awaiting our arrival. The task for Six will be to direct the concert below. The "music" will likely be very loud!

Approaching the base of the mountains, we see the smoke from the artillery barrage. Simultaneously, the birds in the front of the formation begin to take small arms and automatic weapons fire while the accompanying gunships spray the area with minigun fire. The confusion of so many pilots calling in enemy locations, the voice of FAC, the artillery prep commander and Six, plus the loud voices of the grunts getting themselves psyched up, revs my adrenaline flow to the max. When I first started flying missions, it was all but impossible to separate all the different voices and what was being said over more than one frequency; though I am now able to understand the majority of the radio transmissions. During such an involved flight over the battlefield, flight plans must be changed with split-second decisions.

Flying closer to our assigned LZs, the crescendo of fire increases to a volume like none other. Willy Pete has hit the ground at each LZ signaling that the last artillery rounds have left the tubes and we're at least safe from that hazard. But another danger takes its place…we're taking on .50 cal. fire…and now, 37mm ack-ack is leaving its black puffs of smoke amidst our flight. We can live with the smoke, but if we get too close to it, the shrapnel within will eat our Hueys alive.

My heart feels like it's about to explode inside my chest! What have I gotten myself into? Will my premonition come true?

The gunships are doing a superb job of dusting off the anti-aircraft and .50 cal. sites with their tubes of rockets. At the same time, they're giving the lush jungle a good hosing with their miniguns and 20mm cannons. Without them, we'd all be history. The LZ we're approaching looks extremely hazardous. The breathtaking emerald green triple canopy jungle at the top of this mountain has a gaping hole carved in it from B52 strikes that took place early this morning and from the artillery prep that ended just moments prior to our arrival. The shattered trees and grotesque looking stumps scattered about are surrounded by dense jungle on all sides. The ridge line is very narrow, dropping off steeply for about two hundred feet on either side. It's a very eerie looking site...soon to be a fiery grave.

The approach and landing are a nightmare that I don't care to relive. But a Hand much more powerful than ours guides us to safely deposit our precious load of valiant infantrymen.

Except for a few bullet and shrapnel holes, all forty ships escape unscathed to pick up a load of fuel and another load of men to reinforce those already engaged with the enemy at the LZs overlooking the Ashau Valley.

On the second insertion, our luck runs out. Even though we receive the usual small arms and automatic weapons fire and have an occasional .50 cal. round slung at us, the AAA appears to be quiet. Making our approach to the same LZ where we did the first landing, the "pucker factor is still in the brown arc." The grunts on the ground are giving us cover fire to keep the Gook's heads down as my gunner and I are hosing the area outside the perimeter with our 60s, leaning out the doors and watching for tree stumps that could abruptly end our flight. Our ship comes to a two-foot hover enabling the grunts to bail out.

Adding power, the pilot begins the takeoff while we're on the guns and watching for stumps, when suddenly…we find one… with the main rotor blades! The sound is horrendous while our expensive weed-whacker chews up the top of a tall stump. Mr. Jewitt hesitates slightly while grappling with the decision to either crash land in the LZ, outside of the LZ…into the hands of the enemy…or risk flying to a safer area. Crashing in the LZ will risk the lives of not only the crew, but also the lives of the grunts on the ground. If we crash here, we'll likely slide over the edge of either cliff. There will be no survivors. A departure with our severely damaged blades will probably not be a good choice. Adding the necessary pitch (and therefore, stress) to the rotor system for flight will undoubtedly cause further damage, and induce a fiery crash. It's a long shot, but Mr. Jewitt departs the LZ. We feel like we're inside a paint shaker, the vibrations are frightening. Split second decisions are an important makeup of an excellent pilot. The decision is made to try to clear the treetops and 092 did, thanks to the finesse of the man at the controls and the good Lord above. The aircraft is vibrating so badly I think she's going to shake herself to death.

Mr. Jewitt's voice is very shaky over the intercom due to the extreme vibrations of the chopper… Undoubtedly, a lot of the reason for the shaky voice is also due to his strong commitment to

215

keep us all alive. That responsibility now lies with the skill of the aircraft commander...not to mention God's powerful hand over us. Actually, let's put God first here...we need all the help we can get!

The A.C. now asks, "Pete, do you think the old girl will make it back to Evans or shall we try to land it in the treetops? I think we can walk away."

"Why are you asking me, sir? I'm only the crew chief! But, it doesn't feel or sound very good! You'll have to caress her all the way home."

That's an understatement! This thing sounds and feels like it is going to scatter itself all over the mountain!

"Ok, guys...we're going to attempt to limp back to Evans."

"Mayday, Mayday, Mayday! Yellow Five needs an escort. We've hit a tree and have severe damage to our main rotor blades. We're going to try to make it back to Evans."

"Rog, Yellow Five. Yellow One will keep you company. We're on your tail."

"Thanks for the cover, Yellow One...We owe you one."

"We hope you'll never have to return the favor! Yellow One, out."

It's impossible to tell exactly where the blade damage has occurred. Mr. Jewitt is careful not to pull any excess power. The last thing we want to do is shed an entire blade, or even a large portion of one. We're already in deep doo-doo. Calling ahead, the pilot asks for the crash crew to foam the runway at Evans for a running landing that allows for a shallow approach to be made without pulling very much pitch in the blades and adding additional stress to our barely flying machine. The foam allows for a safer landing with less friction, reducing the risk of fire.

After what seems like an hour, our twelve minute flight puts us on final for as shallow an approach as possible, and being cleared to land, we see the fire trucks standing by. Jewitt finesses 092 into the long ribbon of foam that appears to be about three feet deep. The aircraft skids to a halt after sliding down the runway for about one hundred yards. Now covered with foam, the aircraft is shut down and the damage surveyed. The last two feet of both blades look like they've been run through a stump grinder! It's a miracle that we didn't crash in the LZ. A helicopter shouldn't fly at all with this kind of damage to its main rotor blades! Now that the flight is finished, we're all badly shaken…almost to the point of having to change our shorts! Typically, during an emergency, even though the tension is extreme, it seems that the full impact doesn't register until it's all over. The Almighty has protected us once again!

Walking weak-kneed to the waiting jeep for a ride back to the company area for a well-deserved break, we're all nervous wrecks. We've beaten the Grim Reaper again!

After our break, we head back to the airstrip to check our ship for further damage. Besides desperately needing a new set of main rotor blades, there are several bullet holes from AK47 and small arms fire. Fortunately, none of the rounds hit anything really important, so we go to work to replace the blades. After a couple hours, with the help of the maintenance crew, 092 has a new set of rotor blades that we've tracked and balanced, making the ship ready for service once again.

The tally is released at the post-flight briefing at the end of the day. This has been an expensive day for the taxpayers and a frightening and deadly day for a lot of us. The toll is: two engine failures with causes unknown, leading to crashes. Four slicks and one gunship have been shot down. In addition, two Chinooks and one Flying Crane crashed while bringing in artillery pieces, ammo, food and water. We had a total of nineteen of our comrades killed in action from crashes. Of these nineteen, twelve were crew members from several participating companies and the other seven were grunts. A memorial service will follow the briefing. Why do so many young, dedicated men have to die not only prematurely, but also in such horrific ways? We're all humbled when we realize how fortunate we are to have survived such terrible odds. Our hearts go out to those loved ones back home, who will soon receive the sad news that their son, husband, father, or friend has died in this very unpopular war.

According to intelligence, there are expected to be at least two NVA divisions in the Ashau Valley. There is not only a good and well-used road down the middle of the valley, but three airstrips that are being utilized by Charlie, and several LZs where they're landing helicopters. Many of the convoy drivers hauling in supplies for the enemy are thought to be Chinese. The enemy's arsenal includes not just the usual automatic weapons and small arms, but they're loaded to the gills with .50 caliber singles and quads, .51

caliber, recoilless rifles, and they have a good accompaniment of 37mm anti-aircraft. They're ready for a long engagement. This valley is not accessible from the east by helicopter much of the year due to weather. But we have a weather window now. We're ready to kick butt, but know there will be many more sad days.

One hundred and twelve days to go!

CHAPTER 53

NIGHTMARE

23 April, 1968
Camp Evans

After a fitful night with very little rest, I feel very uneasy about continuing on flight status. My nerves have been stretched to the limit. I've made up my mind, after much soul searching, to file a 1049 today and request that I be removed as a flight crew member. Up until now I've enjoyed the adrenaline rush that comes with being a Huey crew chief/gunner. Upon opening my eyes this morning, I made my decision. I've talked to my buddies about changing jobs for some time and it has now come to a head.

All through the night, I had a bad feeling about today's flight for some odd reason. If it's just paranoia, it feels very real. I woke up several times with a start, dreaming that my ship crashed and burned in the LZ. The next crew chief in line to get a ship is waiting for another crew chief to rotate back to the states after completion of his twelve-month tour, or due to severe wounds, being killed, or... just deciding he is too close to the end of his tour for this line of work.

Slipping on my fatigue pants and boots, I still have mixed emotions while walking to Allan Ney's tent to wake him with the "good news" that he can begin crewing my ship today. Will he and the rest of the company look down on me for shirking my duties? Allan is a good friend...certainly he'll understand.

With the nightmares I've just had about this flight, should I be asking a buddy to take my place?

Waking Allan, I tell him both sides of the story including the horrendous nightmare. During our conversation, I make it very plain that if he would rather not fly the mission that I would go.

"Are you kidding? Do you know how long I've been waiting for a ship?"

"Will Eddie stay with the ship as gunner?"

I assure him that Eddie had said he would stay. His gear is on the ship, and he likes the way 092 flies.

"I can be on the flight line in twenty minutes. Thanks Pete. Enjoy your day off."

This is too easy! Am I making a mistake? Maybe I should change my mind and take the flight myself. How will I feel if my premonitions come true and my buddies crash?

Deciding to sit in on the preflight briefing, my suspicions are confirmed. It's expected to be a day much like yesterday with lots of AAA, .50 and .51 caliber fire, and the usual popping of small arms and automatic weapons fire.

Shaking hands with Allan and Eddie after the briefing, I voice my concerns and wish them the best. My stomach is tied in tight knots. I'm so concerned for their safety, that I find myself accompanying them to the flight line for the preflight. I just want to be assured everything is just right…at least up to the point of departure.

When Yellow One calls the flight to crank, I step back to the edge of the flight line and watch the gaggle of choppers depart to the west, away from the rising sun. I say a short but audible prayer for the safe return of all aboard. My gut churns when the choppers are almost out of sight

Walking down to Flight Operations where I will spend the rest of my tour, I can hear the radio chatter from the flight.

While enroute, the flight is informed that once again the valley is shrouded in fog with a low overcast over the mountains, so a hold is again necessary to wait out the weather.

At 0900 hours the weather clears sufficiently to begin the assaults on the well-fortified, formidable valley and surrounding mountain ridges. The CO, Major Burkhalter, will be the flight leader. He has chosen my ship (now crewed by Allan) for Yellow One. LZ Pepper is the target for the insertion, on a high pinnacle along a ridge line, four kilometers southwest of LZ Tiger, where our ship hit the tree on the previous day. Charlie Company made up the Yellow Flight with Alpha Company following as the White Flight. They're setting up for their approach from the north.

Approaching the ridge line, the fireworks begin with a warm welcome by the .37mm batteries, followed by .50 and .51 caliber gunfire. Vollies of automatic weapons fire join the crescendo as the choppers close in on the LZ. The black puffs of smoke from the AAA and green tracers fill the sky. The radios are crackling with enemy gun position sightings and reports of hits while the flight continues its mission to insert the grunts into the stump-studded mountaintop.

On short final, the tracers are coming from all quadrants while the door gunners join in with the gunship escort hosing down the area, when suddenly a Gook manning a .50 cal hits the jackpot... Yellow One's tail rotor. With the loss of tail rotor effectiveness, 092 begins to spin out of control while it continues toward Pepper. Just below tree top level, the main rotor blades strike a tall, bomb-splintered tree. Allan is not wearing his seat belt and is thrown out the left door and into the muck below. A lieutenant, sitting on the edge of his seat next to Eddie, disappears out the open door, while 092 continues its uncontrolled descent before crashing and rolling over on its side. Helicopter parts scatter throughout the LZ. Fortunately, the Lieutenant has landed in a bomb crater clear of the aircraft.

Finding himself with his back jammed against the transmission wall while tracers are raking the LZ, Eddie scrambles to his feet and while standing on the transmission wall unhooks his M60. He tosses the 60 to the ground along with a box of ammo and his M16.

With his firepower on the ground, and adrenaline pumping, Eddie climbs out the door and jumps to the ground. His first thought is to get the rest of the crew out while the grunts are scrambling for cover. Looking through the windshield it appears that Major Burkhalter is in shock and frozen on the controls. With the help of the co-pilot, they bust out the windshield, release the aircraft commander's seat harness, and drag him to safety. Although the aircraft is on fire, it is not yet totally consumed and someone is screaming that he's pinned. Running to the left side of the ship, Allan is found pinned to the ground with the top edge of the aircraft door frame across his legs. With the earlier artillery and air strikes having done a thorough job, the ground is pulverized. Eddie scrambles to dig the crew chief out. With the weight of the aircraft against his legs, it appears that Allan can't be moved. However, the earth has been churned up sufficiently by the impact of the artillery rounds, softening it enough to slide the crew chief out. Eddie drags him to safety atop a knoll to the front of the crash site just as the ship blows up. Although Allan has back and neck injuries, his life has been saved by his courageous gunner.

Being a single ship LZ, with a burning aircraft in the center of it, an additional Huey hovers alongside Pepper while the 2/9th repels with chain saws to enlarge the LZ. Fortunately, this ship and the crew aboard were part of the mix. When the mission was planned, the wisdom to add the chain saw gang was great foresight.

Several trees are cut in record time before a third aircraft loaded with grunts drops its load and begins its departure. Another broken tree trunk catches the rotor blades pulling it back to earth. It makes a very hard landing on its skids.

The crew and grunts are frantically trying to escape. The turbines are screaming at full takeoff power and fuel is pouring onto the ground. Several men scramble down the hill to the aid of the crew. Eddie opens the nose cone of the chopper and disconnects the battery cable to effectively shut off all electrical power to the ship. Looking around to see if all the men have gotten free of the bird, he can see Ted Lamb, the crew chief, still sitting in his seat, holding onto the support post with his right hand. Ted's thumb is caught in a hole in the door frame post, where it had collapsed due to the hard impact. He had been holding onto the post prior to impact. Being a butcher by trade, Ted always carries a sharp knife and is reaching for it to cut his thumb off in order to free himself from the wrecked bird in an attempt to beat the real possibility of the aircraft burning. As soon as the dust settles, Eddie scrambles to the ship and convinces Ted to sit tight while he and several other men grab a shattered tree trunk that they use as a lever to rock the ship sufficiently to get Ted freed. It worked!

Because of the two crashes, only one infantry company was airlifted to the mountaintop before the weather set in, curtailing any further assaults into the valley for the next two days. Our heroic crews spent the next two nights on LZ Pepper.

For his heroic actions under fire in an extremely tense situation, Eddie Hoklotubbe was awarded a Soldier's Medal. He has always been a hero to me...always there in life and death situations to do whatever he can to help his comrades while selflessly putting his own life on the line. Despite extreme conditions, God miraculously spared the lives of all the men involved in both crashes.

During the course of this entire mission, I am glued to the radios listening to all the commotion. When the first ship crashes, my premonition has come to pass and I feel helpless. Not knowing whether or not my buddies are alive or dead, I am beating myself up for not going on the mission myself. I was very thankful when I found out the crews survived. However, a black cloud of guilt hung over me for years. I have still not shed that guilt.

Within a few days of this crash, I received a very concerned letter from Dad. He was watching the nightly news with the family, to catch up on the war. One of the camera crews had been filming on LZ Pepper when my ship crashed. They recognized the tail number as being that of my ship, and assumed I was involved in the crash. The report stated that there was no word of survivors. Typical news crew, they did not get all the facts prior to sending out the report!

CHAPTER 54

POLICE ACTION

23 April, 1968
Camp Evans

Dear Dad,

My 1049 form was accepted immediately. I'm looking forward to my new assignment to flight operations with mixed emotions. I'll be staying in the same tent with my platoon, and that's great. I'll know where the crews are at all times and be in contact with them by radio. I'm sure I'll miss the excitement, but feel I'm ready to let my heart rate slow down a bit.

During a lag in radio traffic this morning, I decided to do a little surgery and dug several more pieces of shrapnel out of my arm and shoulder. Before beginning, I could count thirty nine pieces that were near the surface. A film canister will easily hold today's collections for posterity.

I was actually able to go to the mess tent for lunch today. I haven't done that for months because of my flight schedule. Leaving Flight Ops, I walked only a short distance before I heard someone call my name. Looking toward the person who called, I saw my buddy from home, Ernie Haight! It was so neat to see someone from my hometown! I knew he was in Vietnam, but had no idea where he was stationed. He's with 2/7th infantry whom we support. Things happen so fast around here, he has likely been aboard my ship for some assaults. He's usually a point man, and understandably so. As you'll recall, Dad, Ernie and I spent a lot of time hunting and trapping together. He's like a fox in the woods! He'd make a fantastic point man! We talked for two and a half hours before he had to get back to his unit. He's currently bivouacked on Evans, but expects to be inserted into the Ashau Valley within a couple days. I'm worried about him. He'll have one of the toughest jobs in the valley! I hope he makes it home in one piece!

    Love,

    Bill

Following is a letter that I wrote to my cousin and very good friend.

26 April, 1968
Camp Evans

Dear Gerry,

    For the rest of my career in Vietnam, I've elected to work in Flight Operations.

    During the initial assault into the Ashau Valley a few days ago, we received extremely heavy enemy fire. The resistance was unbelievable! While on short final, our ship hit a tree as it was fired on. Even though we had a horrendous vibration, the pilot elected to limp the aircraft back to base rather than setting it down in such rough terrain, an enemy beehive.

    After seeing and/or hearing of ten of our choppers being shot down, having more lead thrown at my ship than on any other mission, and the loss of several buddies, my nerves are really shot. I've decided to resign from flight status. The Doc here has been pretty insistent. I'm afraid if I continue flying, I'll be a hazard to the rest of my crew and may make a deadly mistake and either cause someone else to die, or be killed myself.

    Flight Ops is a very interesting job because I'm on the radio a lot. The only problem is, when our ships get in trouble, I feel totally helpless. I'd like to be on each mission so I could help my buddies. Sarge has assured me that if I get the urge, I can fly as gunner for any of the crew chiefs whenever I wish.

    Though I often feel guilty for this decision, I think it was wise.

Maybe now we'll get to take some of those canoe trips together.

One hundred days to go,
Bill

29 April, 1968
Camp Evans

Flight Ops isn't what it's cracked up to be. Yesterday I had to find replacements for seven sick crew members and five more so far today. It's only 1230 hours. It appears that a major part of our Division is down with a severe case of dysentery. I've had more calls asking for replacements in the last two days than calls reporting enemy positions. If this keeps up, Charlie may as well go on vacation!

A call just came in on the radio reporting a .50 cal. position just east of LZ Stallion in the Ashau. There's a low-level supply airdrop operation going on in the valley right now with C130s. They're a huge target and not real maneuverable, but seem to be able to take a lot of lead.

When I was shot down in January, I had filed a damage claim for a camera lost in the crash. I just filed another, since Uncle Sam has now lost the previous four that I had filed! Not only that, but now they tell me that a receipt has to be filed with each claim. I can barely keep track of my own boots, let alone receipts! No wonder this war is taking so long when it takes the Army over one hundred forty days to process a simple piece of paperwork!

I've not had an opportunity to read much news since I've been here, but I did find an article today that certainly expresses my feelings about this "Police Action." Senator John G. Tower from Texas stated, "The Administration is doing what a number of us have been saying for two and a half years...that you cannot win a war by a gradual response of gradualism; that the only way to achieve military victory is through military power...to achieve the objective at the earliest possible time, with the maximum of impact."

Amen! We certainly have the firepower to deliver a death-blow to the enemy. A lot of people would die...those we are fighting, and yes, some of our own men, but over the long haul, we would lose far fewer American soldiers and we could all go home in a relatively short time

A transmission froze up on one of our gunships yesterday in the Ashau killing all four crew members. A Chinook went in and lowered our Medic, Tiny, and our Flight Surgeon down on a rope with the intent to haul the bodies up. As soon as the rescue party reached the ground, the Chinook was shot down killing three of the crewmen. Tiny and Doc got in a firefight and held the Gooks off with a 12 ga. and grenades until another ship was able to pick them up. Tiny had his leg broken by an AK round. He only had thirty seven days left in country but will be evacuated to the States tomorrow.

CHAPTER 55

AGENT ORANGE

2 May, 1968
Camp Evans

Dear Dad,

The Battalion Commander came down with a real important mandate today. "All mustaches shall be free of long handles." Now isn't that intelligent? Nothing like brass who have nothing but time on their hands and could care less about the job at hand. For those of us who are able, mustaches are a symbol. A symbol of what, I don't know, but most of our flight crews have them. Some are rather scraggly, but there are several long handled mustaches that look super.

The skin on my hands is getting much worse. I guess I've made too many flights into the jungles, either during Agent Orange spray operations or right after. We occasionally fly right behind the aircraft that are doing the spraying and drop the troops off in the same area. The chemical gets all over us when the rotor blades stir it up. It's pretty powerful smelling stuff. When it's sprayed on triple canopy jungle the trees are completely defoliated in a matter of hours! Pretty good weed killer! But I must say, it makes our job easier when we can actually see to the ground. It's amazing how many bunker complexes, roads and trails are revealed after a spraying operation. As strong as that chemical is, I wonder how the grunts are fairing on the ground…living in that chemical contaminated jungle and drinking the water.

The Ashau Valley is pretty well enemy free now, or at least a lot better. Now that the Cav is there in full force, the areas around Hue, Khe Sahn and Quang Tri are heating up again.

Evans was hit on April 27, 28 and 29 in the middle of the afternoon with 122 mm rockets. A pair of Cobras found the launching sights and turned them into mincemeat.

5 May, 1968
Camp Evans

Dear Dad,

The thermometer is pegged out today and the heat is unbearable!

Our Division is experiencing an outbreak of hepatitis so we'll all have to get jabbed in the rear end with five ccs of some concoction that's more painful than getting rear ended by an AK47!

I had the evening shift in Flight Ops yesterday, so got to sleep in this morning. At 0955 hours when I was about to roll out of bed, Charlie spurred me on by dropping in 122mm rockets for the next thirty minutes.

The word is that General Tolson is coming soon for an awards ceremony. The skinny is that all Ashau crews will get DFCs. My bet is that only the Officers will get the DFCs and the rest of us will only get Air medals with V devices.

As I recall, several months ago when we answered the call to pick up three Marines who hit a land mine with their jeep, the pilots got DFCs and my gunner and I came out with nothing. Personally, I don't think anyone should have been decorated, as it was just an everyday mission. Sure we were drawing a lot of fire from the tree lines, but that's an everyday occurrence.

When I think back, it's been a long, hot, discouraging, bloody, dangerous, and challenging nine months, but I wouldn't trade it for anything. I've certainly learned a lot about getting along with a lot of different types of people in an extremely tense situation. I've made a lot of friends who I feel will be friends for life. In addition, I've learned more everyday of God's love and mercy and His protective hand over my life. This has been a heck of

229

a way to grow up quickly and I feel I've changed a lot. Hopefully, that's a good thing.

Waiting to go to work this morning is really getting old. Not only am I bored, but the sun is absolutely baking this tent. Even though the flaps are open, there is not a whisper of a breeze and the temp is hovering right around 120F at noon! The mosquitoes are having a feast on my sweat-soaked body. Actually, I think they're just here to drink my sweat! I'm already missing the flying. A few days ago, I didn't think that would happen. But I miss being with my flight crew buddies and helping out the grunts. Yes, I even miss the adrenaline rush!

I know it's been a rough year for you and the rest of the family not knowing from day to day what is really happening here. Though I miss flying, I feel good about my decision to go into Flight Ops. This is obviously a much safer job. Hopefully, that will make you feel a lot better, and now that my DEROS (date of expected rotation out of service) is drawing closer, I'm starting to feel more positive about coming home in one piece. I'm sorry for all the stress I've caused all of you. I hope you can breathe easier now.

I love you,
Bill

CHAPTER 56

BUNNY IN THE BUNKER

9 May, 1968
Camp Evans

Sleep generally comes quickly in this place. I think the reason is that we never know when the next attack will take place. When I went to sleep last night, my intention was to sleep until 0800 hours since I wasn't scheduled to show up in Flight Ops until 1000 hours. But once again, Charlie changed my mind when he started firing rockets at us at 0720 hours this morning. Several rounds landed right next to our company area and, with about ¾ of the second platoon with less than one hundred days left in country, our nerves are a bit stretched.

Although Sergeant Tucker promised I would have the night off after having worked the early shift, I was called in at 1930 hours to help out in Ops. A call came in from a seven-man LRRP team that was in heavy contact seven and a half clicks to the northwest of Evans.

An infantry platoon was choppered in nearby, with the intention of moving in from the south, but they too ran into trouble and got into a heavy firefight. We then sent two flare ships and four RF ships to pull the LRRPs out. By 2130 hours, between the reinforcements and the LRRPs, the toll was heavy. There were two men killed and fourteen WIA. It looks as though the Gooks are trying real hard to get our attention away from the Ashau Valley.

The absence of flying in my daily routine is beginning to bother me. As the days drag on, I realize how rapidly time passed while I was a crew member. When I talk to the crews on the radio and hear the stories upon their return from missions, I must admit that I yearn to get back out there. When I mentioned this to the first sergeant, he said I could volunteer to be a gunner at any time. That sounds good to me…at least today. With the temperature climbing every day, flying around with the doors off would feel a lot better than spending my time either out in the hot sun or in a hot tent. But then, I'm not drawing lead every few minutes either. I still feel like I made the right decision about getting off flight status before winding up in a body bag. Of course, that could still happen, but I think my odds are better on the ground.

11 May, 1968
Camp Evans

The heat must be frying my brain. Chris Noel was here yesterday as part of a USO tour and I barely remember it. She was only here for a few minutes while she talked to the troops and handed out 8x10s. It was great to see a round-eyed woman again… it's been months, but the heat was wearing even on her. She was wearing a great mini-skirt, but still sweating like the rest of us.

I'm amazed at how many celebrities are willing to risk their lives to come into a combat zone to visit us. It's really a morale booster, even if only for a few short minutes. And even though it makes us more homesick, it's nice to see someone willing to give his or her time to entertain us.

Our Ops NCO is Sergeant Tucker who used to be a recruiting NCO. He hasn't forgotten his techniques. Whenever I run into him, he likes to give me his pitch on why I should re-enlist. I must say, even though he comes up with a different tactic every day, he'll never convince me that I should make the Army my career. Not a chance!

15 May, 1968
Camp Evans

Dear Dad,
    During my shift on guard duty three nights ago, the sky was as black as tar. At about 2030 hours, a trip flare went off in the wire. Whenever that happens, it's usually Charlie trying to crawl through the concertina. I woke up my other two buddies and we threw several grenades in an attempt to ruin the evening for Mr. Charles. The trip flares only light up the area momentarily, so it soon appeared darker than before since our night vision was ruined temporarily by the sudden brightness of the flare.
    The field phone rang with the duty officer wanting a SITREP. When we told him what we had observed, he put everyone on full alert. We were all wired pretty tight not knowing whether or not we killed the Vietnamese. Trying to pierce the darkness, we searched the perimeter for any sign of movement, with our cars tuned for any slight sound other than the chorus of crickets and frogs. It was really creepy.
    About fifteen minutes after the flare went off, something came through the ground level window of the bunker, hit the floor with a thud and bounced a couple of times. Not one of us decided to be a hero and have the Medal of Honor awarded posthumously, so we all simultaneously hit the dirt and covered our heads while we waited for the satchel charge or grenade to blow us to pieces. Several seconds passed as we each watched our lives pass before us at lightning speed. When we decided it was a dud, there were a couple more thuds that seemed softer and we again tensed up waiting to be zipped into a body bag. After a few more seconds, I chanced a look in the vicinity of the last sound in the far corner and was able to make out a slight movement. The deadly charge turned out to be…a rabbit! Our fright quickly turned to laughter. That's the best laugh any of us have had since arriving in country! In just a few seconds the field phone rang. The duty officer wanted to know what was so funny when everyone else was so intent on peering into the darkness for the enemy. We just told him it was a private joke. We decided to keep the bunny in the bunker for the rest of the night so he wouldn't give us any more thrills.

While trying to get our nerves under control again and quietly chuckling about Peter Rabbit, we watched as three rockets came streaking in at 2355 hours. They hit our flight line. After a slight lull, seventeen more followed. The fifth round hit the POL dump. Very lucky shot! What a sight when all that fuel ignited!

At daybreak, we decided to let Peter go rather than put him in the stew pot. He seemed happy to have his freedom again and hopped down the hill.

At 0800 hours we were relieved from guard duty and went directly to the flight line to see what damage had been done. We lost one ship. The POL dump was still burning.

Hopefully, you and the rest of the family are less worried now that I'm off flight duty. Even though we still get rocketed and mortared, and an occasional ground attack, I feel much safer than when I was flying.

I'll be home soon.

I love you all,

Bill

CHAPTER 57

MAIL CALL

17 May, 1968
Camp Evans

Dear Dad,

This morning while on a resupply run, two of our Huey's landed in a two ship LZ to drop off their loads of ammo when mortars started dropping into the small clearing. It was to be a quick drop; just land where the grunts are waiting alongside the LZ, spend a minute or so on the ground while the goodies are unloaded, and takeoff ASAP. The enemy gunners had the LZ pegged, and both ships were pretty well peppered with shrapnel holes. The two aircraft made it back to Evans, but the crews were well shaken. As a result, one of the crew chiefs requested ground duty. I understand exactly where he's coming from.

Today's mail call brought a most welcome package from home. After hungrily ripping the box open, I was treated to several large candy bars that were very well wrapped and so were still intact, rather than oozing out the corners of the box. There was also a fairly large folded piece of cardboard that turned out to be, of all things, a Kodak advertising poster with the Kodak model nicely adorned in a swimsuit...almost life-size. I know I'll have some fun with this! Included in this package was part of another shapely girl. After unrolling a strange looking tan colored piece of plastic and inflating it, it took on the shape of a lady's leg! When the crews get in tonight, this ought to be the talk of the camp. Now I'll have to find a place to hide these items so they aren't swiped by some other crew member!

That package made my day! It's so good to recall that there is an outside world where I have a family that cares for me. Even though you're going through a lot of stress by not knowing from day to day whether I'm having a good, bad, or indifferent day, or whether I have gotten sick, wounded or killed, you still have a sense of humor.

Thanks for your support. I love you all.
Bill

CHAPTER 58

WIDE-EYED COMRADES

> "I have seen Christ doing Christly deeds;
> I have seen the Devil at play;
> I have gripped to the sod in the hand of God,
> I have seen the godless pray."
>
> John Oxenham

20 May, 1968
Camp Evans

Dear Dad,

After a busy day of missions for our company, all aircraft were on the ground tonight with no scheduled night flights. With all birds on their roost, it was a great time for Charlie to hit us with the possible reward of hitting several or all of our sitting birds. But it was a very peaceful evening with the frogs chirping their melodic tunes down in the rice paddies - a great night to spend catching up on correspondence and generally kick back and relax.

Having spent a long day in Flight Ops, typing up aircraft hit reports and plotting enemy gun positions on the area chart, I was able to sit down in the mess tent and eat a leisurely meal for the first time since I've been here. Supper was nothing special, in fact, it was barely edible. SOS is by far my least favorite delicacy. But, I actually had time to sit around and talk to some buddies while we ate. Spare time has been a rare commodity over here.

After supper and a shower, at exactly 1900 hours, I was sitting in the tent writing a letter home, and talking to several friends, when we heard the all too familiar sound of incoming rockets. Ssssshhhhhh…a slight hesitation, and…boooooom! This happened two or three more times in rapid succession before we all dove through the side of our tent where we have the flap rolled up, just for quick exits, into the sandbagged trench and crawled as fast as we could to the relative security of our bunker. Mortar fire joined the rocket fire and the noise and dust increased with the attack continuing all across the compound.

There was too much enemy ammo being expended to chance not being under cover, so we took turns standing watch just inside the entrance to our bunker with a .12 gauge pump loaded with buckshot, just in case any enemy soldiers darted past in their haste to escape being hit by their own incoming. There were so many rounds falling that we fully expected the enemy to be running all over the camp in a full-fledged ground attack.

Suddenly, the excitement built as the night sky exploded into daylight. The explosions were so fierce our bodies were flung around inside the bunker. The Gooks hit two bull's eyes…the ammo dump and POL dump. Soon the incoming were joined by our own rounds exploding in the ammo dump and by our Jet A, Av gas, and diesel fuel burning profusely.

It wasn't long before the shrapnel from the enemy rounds was joined by secondary rounds from the ammo dump, exploding not only within the confines of the dump, but propelled throughout the camp. The shells from the ammo dump consist of rockets, mortars, grenades, .223, 7.62, .12 gauge rounds, M79 and a large array of artillery rounds. Many exploded where they fell. The artillery shells weren't armed, so they just flew through the air and landed with a deep thud. Flames shot hundreds of feet into the air and turned the black night into an eerie yellowish nightmare.

The Gooks must have had a wild party while they watched the First Cav operation go up in smoke. They hit the jackpot!

The fireworks worsened as rounds were dropping throughout the base and beyond, hitting jeeps, trucks, aircraft, buildings and tents at random. Every time an aircraft was hit and ignited on the flight line, the magnesium burned out of control. Aircraft fuel cells ignited with a tremendous explosion. Soon, our tent was hit and began to burn to the ground, igniting ammo and grenades stored under our cots, and destroying our meager personal property.

Despite the fact that we were holed up in a well-constructed bunker, we were often lifted off the ground and thrown about, when several huge explosions rocked the earth.

While the ear-splitting noise continued, we were all living with the agonizing fear of meeting our Maker before daybreak. Sometimes, folks say they have their lives in order and are ready to die. At an average age of nineteen, I don't believe there were many young men in our bunker that felt that way. We have a lot of living left to do and prayed that God would spare us.

Conditions that were bad when this first started last evening worsen as the bombardment and fires increased after midnight. Many of the tents in the company area have burned. The frag grenades, ammo, and smoke grenades that were left behind cooked off in a rapid-fire mode.

A massive explosion right next to our bunker sent all of us airborne again in our sandbagged hole that now seemed inadequate to save our lives. It may have been an enemy rocket, or one of our own artillery rounds that sailed through the air from the ammo dump. It doesn't matter whether it's enemy or friendly fire. It's all deadly. The shrapnel could be heard ripping through the sandbags and tents. The round ignited the side of our tent adjacent to our hole in the ground. A belt of 7.62 machine gun ammo and several grenades exploded from inside the tent and sprayed shrapnel into the tunnel leading into our hiding place. We all huddled in the far corners of the bunker to avoid friendly fire. The sandbags surrounding our shelter ignited, and while they smoldered, the sand began sifting into our bunker.

We decided that staying where we were was unwise and elected to make a dash for the Flight Ops bunker. The Ops bunker was a little further up the hill, closer to the flight line. The ultra-bright light of the magnesium fires consuming the choppers lit our way.

One by one we made a beeline for the other shelter in hopes that we'd be better protected from the onslaught. When it was my turn, I low-crawled faster than a lizard on steroids, hugging the ground as tightly as possible. There was an explosion several yards to my left and I felt a burning sensation on my left hand. Determined to get to the safety of the Ops bunker, I reached the trench leading into it and dove in head first to cheers from the guys huddled inside. Another comrade made it to safety. Borrowing a cigarette lighter when my shakes subsided, I investigated why my hand felt like something warm was running down the backside. I had been hit in three fingers by shrapnel, but luckily, the wound wasn't serious.

It was difficult to tell when daylight arrived by looking outside as the fires continued to consume what little is left of Evans. By 0600 hours the majority of the rounds had expended themselves, so we crawled out of our holes and began to search for comrades who may have been wounded...or worse.

We've been in a state of shock all night, but nothing had prepared us for what we saw when emerging from underground. We had twenty-three tents in our company area. Nine are still standing, riddled with holes from shrapnel or fire, some barely hanging from their ridgepoles and side poles. All are still smoldering along with our personal belongings.

When each of us left for Vietnam, we were given a list of what to take along and were told to keep our personal belongings to a bare minimum. Looking at our individual platoon tents and seeing the destruction of our minimal treasures, tears come easily. Most of the company tents are either riddled with holes or burned to the ground. Out of Charlie company tents, ten were completely consumed by fire. Many have partially burned and some are still smoldering. The small refrigerator that kept our drinks cold is destroyed. Many of us have lost everything: clothes, boots, sandals, bed, sleeping bag, mosquito netting, poncho liner, web gear, weapons in some cases, and toiletries. More importantly, letters saved from sweethearts, wives, children, parents and friends are gone. Trinkets sent from home, though maybe small and unimportant in another situation, are now real treasures...lost forever. For those fortunate enough not to have lost everything, things are not quite as bleak, but there wasn't a dry eye in the place.

While sifting through the ashes, a light rain began to extinguish the fires and turn everything into a muddy mess again. Encircled by several rows of burned out sandbags, in the corner of where our tent had been erected, I saw another crew chief, Twiggy, sitting on an ammo can. His shirt was off and his tanned back was rain-soaked while he hunched over a small pile of smoldering letters

240

from his girlfriend. Reading what was left, his tears flowed into the rain already running down his face.

There are live artillery, rocket and mortar rounds, live ammo, grenades and mines of all types scattered throughout the company area and flight line. Top had warned us all to walk gingerly due to all the hazards lying around. Some are just lying on top of the ground, while others are embedded in the earth.

Several of us walked out to the flight line to see if there was anything left. Most of the ships that were waiting for today's missions are totally destroyed, either by fire or shrapnel. All are damaged sufficiently to be grounded until repaired. Some are still burning.

By mid-night, the word came down that miraculously, no one on the base was killed though there were several WIAs. The final count is not in yet and hopefully the number of KIAs will not change. Over one hundred aircraft on the LZ were destroyed including helicopters and airplanes. All others received substantial damage.

Two good things happened through all of this…one for Charlie and one for the Americans. It was the very good fortune of the enemy to have scored such direct hits on our base, virtually destroying almost everything that was above ground. Our good fortune is to not be shipping any of our men home in body bags.

No sooner had we been warned about live rounds throughout the area, than we heard an explosion nearby. While walking to the flight line to check on the aircraft, one of the warrant officers, Mr. Hammond, stepped on a stray mine that had come from the ammo dump explosion. His left foot was savagely ripped open. Instantly he had a large hole where his anklebones were shredded. A ticket home. Unfortunately, his flying days are finished.

Demolition teams are at work throughout the camp searching for and dispensing live rounds. They certainly have their work cut out for them.

Word is being passed around that replacement tents and equipment will be ordered today. Until the needed items arrive, we all have a lot of cleaning up to do. Again, working as a team, we'll have the place back in shape within a few days. Until then, we'll make do with what we have available.

Dad, I know this sounds horrible, but you wanted to know everything that happens in our unit. I am reminded of the verse you recited for me just before leaving for war: Psalm 91:7, "A thousand may fall at your side, ten thousand at your right hand, but it will not come near you." Once again, God spared me. I have a great deal of faith and believe I'll be going home as planned.

I love you,
Bill

Note: My father read everything and watched all the news stories he could about Vietnam while I was stationed there. The news reports barely made mention of our ammo dump explosion and devastation, not to mention all the aircraft that were destroyed. This proves the fact that although our military reporters did a great job of reporting the facts, it was all highly censored prior to reaching the U.S. In contrast, it was the front page story in Tokyo, Japan. Had our government told the truth about all our losses in Vietnam, rather than only our victories, Americans would have had a very different attitude about our "Police Action". This is a very large burr under my saddle!

CHAPTER 59

WHERE ARE YOU GOD?

> "I have sped through the hells of fiery hail,
> With full red-fury shod;
> I have heard the whisper of a voice,
> I have looked in the face of God."
>
> John Oxenham

"Foxhole religion" is not fictitious. I witnessed it firsthand on many occasions. When a soldier is being shelled, whether he's in a foxhole, above ground returning fire, or in a helicopter, it doesn't matter. He's scared. A lot goes through your mind when you're faced with possible, or even worse, probable death. In many cases, God is in the forefront. You think you're about to meet your Maker and want desperately to clear things up with Him. Often, when the action subsides and you find yourself in one piece, you forget about the promises you made to God just moments before. However many hold those promises dear, and are thankful to Him for protecting them through a life or death situation.

During an ammo dump explosion later during my tour the following example of foxhole religion took place.

While the horrific nightmare unfolded throughout the night, we all prayed to our god of choice, with some of us recommitting our lives to Christ, or even accepting Him as our personal Savior. At the time it seemed to many of us that God is the only answer to save us from certain death. There is a wide spectrum of religions amongst the troops. Some of the men prayed aloud with their voices barely audible amidst the shelling, while others admitted later that they

243

were praying silently or thinking of home and family. Many thoughts went through my mind, including praying that since God has protected me through so much already during my tour, perhaps He has a plan to see me through this carnage as well. A huge amount of faith is required, as the explosions continued to jar us, even underground. One of the men mentioned that he had already done enough praying to be a full-time preacher! At this point, I think even the atheists are having second thoughts.

When I left for war, I already had a personal relationship with God. To this day, I know without a doubt that He protected me through many close encounters with death. For that I will be eternally grateful.

The following letter was written by my father while I was in Vietnam.

21 May, 1968
First Air Cavalry Division Association
Albuquerque, New Mexico

Gentlemen:

Our son, Bill, a crew chief with the 227th AHB, lst Air Cav has often written home about White Robe Six, the First Team's name for God. We thought the inspirational traditions of White Robe Six should be perpetuated and included in the legend and lore of the famous Air Cavalry. And so, "White Robe 6 calling Yellow One" came into being.

My brother, a Baptist minister and Chaplain in the Naval Reserve, wrote the text. Bill's brother-in-law, Jim Worden, did the artwork. As a proud father, I was privileged to pay the bill.

Twenty thousand copies of this little tract have been shipped to the various chaplains of the Cav, under the direction of the Division chaplain. We trust that these will help the gallant troopers to become better acquainted with White Robe Six and that the tracts will be a source of inspiration to them. Hopefully they might also make the work of the chaplains a little easier. So far the response we've had has been most gratifying. To be able to make this small contribution to the First Air Cav legend has been a labor of respect and admiration.

Respectfully yours,
Gene and Eileen Peterson

CHAPTER 60

TYPHOON

27 May, 1968
DaNang

After being in Danang on R&R for two and a half days, I'm ready to go back to the war. I spent most of the time on the beach getting burned and learning how to surf. There was a floor show and movie every night, giving me a chance to really kick back and try to forget about being shot at every day. There were great restaurants where I was able to eat all the burgers, fries and steaks that I wanted, and I wanted a lot! But I stay very antsy wondering how my buddies are doing. You would think that a couple days away from the rigors of war would be enjoyable...and it has been. The closeness I feel to all the crews in my company can't be described. I feel almost as close to them as I feel to my own family. Both are always in my thoughts. I miss them.

On the way back to Evans, we landed in Phu Bai with maintenance problems so we spent the night there. I met a guy who has been in country eleven days and wants to be a door gunner. After talking with him for a couple hours, I think I have him convinced that he should look into something where he might have a little longer life expectancy.

28 May, 1968
Camp Evans

Last night while I was listening to a tape from home, sniper rounds came zipping past my tent. I went to the perimeter to join the guys who were returning fire. The sniper fire continued sporadically throughout the night, but no one was hit. It was just another of Charlie's ploys to keep us on edge.

This afternoon we had a flash flood. The storm only lasted a half hour or so, but it rained buckets rather than drops. The rain was so fierce, that the bunkers were filled to the roofs. Several of us took advantage of the fresh water supply and grabbed our bars of soap for a refreshing scrub-down. Just as we got lathered up, a fierce wind forced us inside the tent. We had to grab the center pole to try to keep from losing the tent. We were too late…The wind leveled the tent while we watched the few possessions we had left float down the torrential river passing through the center of where our tent had stood. The integrity of the tent wasn't great prior to the wind, as one side was burned out from the ammo dump fire eight days before.

This is certainly "the land of plenty". plenty of bugs, plenty of rain, plenty of heat, plenty of mud, plenty of rockets, mortar, and sniper fire, plenty of dust, plenty of wind, plenty of snakes, plenty of disease, and certainly plenty of enemy.

CHAPTER 61

FLIGHT OPERATIONS SPECIALIST

2 June, 1968
Camp Evans

Dear Dad,

Sixty-eight days to go!

We seldom have formations over here; they're held whenever the Brass feels a need, which fortunately isn't very often. But tonight's the night for another. A new battalion C.O. has arrived, so we have to show up for another "Do's and Don'ts" lecture. This guy is a Full Bird, so I suppose his expectations will be higher than our last C.O. who was pretty laid back.

The G.I. trots have hit me again, but at least this time I don't think it's a virus. The officers had a party last night for the outgoing C.O. Since I happened to be on KP, I managed to put away some great chow...like three steaks, four plates of fries and mounds of ice cream with pineapple. Actually, the runs started about two hours later and haven't let up. It's miserable, but well worth the great food. The new C.O. promised a similar party to the enlisted men in a couple of weeks. I'll believe it when I see it.

Our afternoon rains are more fierce each day. After having two flash floods in our tent in the last couple of days, the communications chief and I took a ¾ ton over to the Seabee camp and scrounged up some wood. We built a floor in our tent. It'll probably float next time we get a hard rain, but at least for now, our gear is high
and dry.

A week ago, a can of nuts and chocolate arrived from home. We had to inhale the chocolate quickly before it melted any further. The heat is getting unbearable and suited only for tropical candy bars. The only problem is, all they're good for is dropping out of helicopters to the kids below. Even they don't seem to like them. The next time we fly over, we often get shot at!

The food is worse than ever. I came across the pond as a healthy one hundred and sixty pounder and am down to about one hundred and thirty now. I've always been a picky eater...pretty much a meat and potatoes kind of guy, with nothing on it...no gravy, ketchup, mustard, bar-b-q sauce, etc. When I went to chow tonight, they served bar-b-que spare ribs. The meat was "spare!" I was so hungry that I ate the stuff. There really wasn't but a hint of meat, so I just licked the sauce off the bones. If the Army moves on it's stomach, it's about to come to an abrupt halt here!

Our cook, Pierre, is a great guy. He's a French Canadian from Quebec who talks incessantly! He's pretty antsy here and I think talking non-stop is his way of releasing tension and not having to contemplate the danger he faces every day with the rest of us. He's a pretty good cook, but he can't perform miracles.

Charlie, one of our gunners, got a care package from his girlfriend today. She sent a can of Ice Blue Secret that he just sprayed in our tent. Talk about a tent full of turned on G.I.s! It doesn't take much to arouse a bunch of war-weary guys!

6 June, 1968
Camp Evans

Today I received orders for a new MOS, Flight Operations Specialist, 71P20. That's what my everyday duties are now, but for some reason, I didn't expect to be assigned another MOS. My real concern is that both of my current MOS's are critically needed in this theater of operations. Since I will still have eighteen months of active duty left when I DEROS from here, there is a very good chance that I'll be welcomed back to this God-forsaken place before my enlistment is up.

When I enlisted, the recruiter told me that once I got in the Army, I would have the opportunity to get to go to several different schools that interested me. I have requested to go to the USA Northern Warfare Training Center at Ft. Greeley as my next assignment. I'd like to go through the training there and then become an instructor. We'll see. Recruiters are like used car salesmen, promising you the world and giving you the shaft.

7 June, 1968
Camp Evans

Rob is one of the few crew chiefs left in our company that I feel very close to. The others have either been killed or made it back to the States. I had planned on flying with him today as his gunner, but then checked the board to see the roster of pilots for each ship. The Old Man is the AC. He doesn't get a very high grade in my book for pilot skills. Besides, with only sixty three days left, I'm pretty choosy about my flying partners. I guess I'll stay in Flight Ops today.

We're sending a recovery crew into Laos to pick up a Huey shot down there two days ago while doing a Green Beanie insertion. The entire crew is MIA. The crash sight was too hot when the aircraft was shot down to insert grunts to secure the area and search for survivors. The cobra pilots stayed on station as long as they could, but couldn't see any sign of life. Though the helicopter didn't burn, it went into the trees pretty hard and was damaged badly. Another sad day.

Two of our gunships were shot down two days ago. The crew chief on one was killed in the burning wreckage and his AC was listed as MIA. He was a pilot for Charlie Company before being transferred to fly gunships for Delta Company, so those of us who knew him were pretty disheartened. But it turned out that he had escaped the crash site and crawled into the elephant grass to hide. As he continued his escape, he thankfully found a road where he waited until an American jeep came by and hitched a ride back to Evans. His head and face are pretty beat up, but he is no longer MIA…or worse.

I've had numerous comments on the tract, White Robe Six. The men seem to really like it and a lot of copies have been sent home to family members.

We've been here at Evans so long that we actually built a new shower. We even poured a cement floor below the four sprinkler heads and have hot and cold water. That just means that we'll be moving to another base soon. It seems that every time we make any kind of improvement…new outhouse, mess hall tables, or a shower with a real floor...we pack up and move. The worst thing is that, since we are an airmobile unit, all the good stuff gets burned and left behind, while we pack up what we can get in the helicopters and go off on another adventure.

When the ammo dump exploded in May, all our medical and dental records were destroyed in the attack. With each of our histories in ashes, we're in the process of having new records made. It'll be interesting, but discouraging I'm sure, to see what ramifications this will have for each of us in the future when we need to reference our old files for whatever reason.

Though the days are passing at what seems like a very slow rate, I can see the end to my tour not far off. Looking forward to that great day!

I love you,
Bill

CHAPTER 62

PONY SOLDIER SIX

11 June, 1968
Camp Evans

Dear Dad,

     Today Bennie and I had to run a few errands and scrounge up some more wood to build some shelves. While driving across the base, we noticed a First Cav Museum. Since we had an hour or so to kill, we stopped to see what it was all about. It was a large, cheaply assembled frame building with plywood sides and a metal roof. That's as good as the buildings get here. The contents consisted of equipment that the Cav has captured from the NVA. It was interesting to see some of the stuff up close that has blown so many of our helicopters out of the sky. They had everything from AK-47s, to .51 cals, .37mm anti-aircraft guns and ammo, to Chi-Com satchel charges. It was nice to see so much equipment that has been taken out of action. Of course, this museum is just a sampling of captured munitions and supplies. We've hauled literally tons of stuff out of the bush, but the fight continues and likely will for years to come since the Gooks are also hauling tons of supplies down the Ho Chi Minh trail and into Vietnam to continue their dedication.

12 June, 1968
Camp Evans

Dear Dad,

Mail from home is the greatest thing! Today brought three letters from you and Mom, and one from Cindi. Not only that, but Bennie, Lizard and I each got care packages. Yeah, Lizard is really the label put on this guy. I'm not sure why, but it seems to fit him well.

Yesterday Captain Brownlee approached me excitedly with the message:

"Pete, shine your boots, press and starch your fatigues (with what?), get a haircut, shave, brush your teeth, comb your hair, get a new helmet cover, clean your weapon, and have clean socks and underwear standing by for 0830 hours tomorrow. You're going to be interviewed by General Tolson. What did you do anyway?" Naturally, I had no idea. Just like the military...keep you in the dark until the excitement is over.

So, I spent an hour or so haphazardly polishing my boots that hadn't been shined since they were issued to me ten months ago. Even though I had no idea what was going on, I just couldn't get my heart into whatever was scheduled to happen the next morning. Having spent the better part of a year in a war zone, I've gotten accustomed to treating most of the brass as just members of the team. Not saluting has become a custom, not out of disrespect, but out of the will for survival. Officers don't like snipers any better than the rest of us, and would rather Charlie not be tipped off as to just who is who as we move around the compound.

Well, apparently this is some big deal. My special day is here, and I'm getting a little nervous. Numerous people who seem to want me to make a good impression on the Old Man, have come by my tent to inspect me.

At 0815 hours, I hike out to the flight line in an attempt to be early for the big ceremony. Thinking that I'm just going to meet the General on the flight line, I'm surprised to hear music. As I crest the hill overlooking the revetments with a few choppers that hadn't yet departed for their scheduled missions, I'm shocked to see a band playing and a flight line half covered with men milling around as they're being instructed to get into formation! It turns out that the band is only practicing since the General's chopper hasn't arrived yet. I can't believe the crowd!

Even this early in the day, the sun is beating down mercilessly and the sweat is soaking through my clean fatigues. At 0825 hours the General's chopper circles Camp Evans and lands in a cloud of dust in the middle of the flight line at precisely 0830 hours. The old codger steps out of the bird with his entourage. The band exuberantly breaks out in a loud fanfare. I have no idea what they're playing…my mind is confused. Watching the men exiting the aircraft, it's obvious who the General is. His slightly worn jungle fatigues are smartly pressed with the sleeves rolled up precisely to regulation height, with the legs bloused perfectly over his highly shined jungle boots. His fresh helmet liner adorned with his stars, sits smartly atop his head of white hair. Slung around his hips is a wide black pistol belt adorned with his holstered pearl-handled colt forty five. My skin starts to grow goose bumps! What have I done to deserve this kind of stress? My mind races. I can't figure out why a hick from the Upper Peninsula of Michigan is about to meet face to face with our Division Commander.

When the music stops, a change of command ceremony for our new Battalion Commander commences. I have no idea what is being said. My mind is still spinning. As long as the army has gone to all the effort of gathering all of us in one place, General Tolson feels obligated to do a cursory inspection of the troops. Walking down the formation lines, he stops occasionally to ask a soldier how their year is going, where he's from, and generally thanking him for the fine job he's doing for our country. All this time, Peterson is standing where I've been instructed to stand, in front of a freshly polished Huey. I'm shaking in my boots. I'd rather be in my ship under heavy enemy fire than standing here and not knowing what is going on.

Finally, after what seemed like hours, but has probably been thirty minutes, the General, accompanied by his original crew, do an about face and march toward me. I gulp trying to swallow my uneasiness, but it doesn't work. Though my heart isn't in it, I whip a salute on the old war-horse and nervously address him.

"Good morning, Sir."

"Specialist Peterson, I received a letter, placard and tract from your father."

Now that I know what we're standing here for…I'm still shaking the polish off my boots.

"Specialist, I never get enough mail. I really appreciated the fact that your father took the time to send me a letter along with the enclosures."

Gee, the guy seems almost human.

I begin to relax.

"Peterson, I really like the White Robe Six tract, and think it'll be a real asset to the First Team. Tell your Dad that we could use an old decrepit B-17 pilot to help us out over here. You have a great military record, Specialist, and I think you ought to re-up and go to flight school. You'd be a great candidate. You could sign up today and get a guaranteed assignment, if you'd only be willing to give the military a little more of your time."

"Sir, I'm very proud to be a member of the First Team, and I appreciate your offer. But after my current three-year obligation, I have other plans."

The photographers are standing by from the Stars and Stripes and after shooting several photos, the General and I chat for a few more minutes before he wishes me the best of luck and we exchange salutes.

The Editor of Stars and Stripes, along with one of his cronies, bombards me with questions. General Tolson had told them he wanted a very thorough report on me.

It was a real honor to meet the General. Even more humbling though is that the White Robe Six tract is now in circulation, not just in Vietnam, but also in many branches of the service across the globe. My hope and prayer is that it will meet the G.I.s right where they are and help them realize that God is real and can see them through every situation in their lives if they only put their trust in Him.

Thanks Dad, for all the work you, Uncle Oliver, and Jim put into White Robe Six. It's getting great reviews.

Love,
Bill

CHAPTER 63

ANTSY

18 June, 1968
Camp Evans

 Just when I thought the mercury couldn't go any higher, it fooled me. Every breath is an effort. I feel like I need oxygen. The heat is tough enough, but the humidity is unbearable. I guess I shouldn't complain. I can't imagine what the grunts must feel like on a day like this while humping through the jungles and struggling up and down the mountains.

 Communist helicopters have been spotted the past three nights just thirty miles northeast of here. There was also a report of one being seen three miles west of Evans, but most of them were near Dong Ha. Ten or eleven of them are still there...destroyed. The enemy ships shot up one of our friendly positions. Gunships, artillery and Air Force F4s were called in and were credited with the destruction of the choppers, some of which were caught on the ground dropping off troops. There have been a lot more fighters flying in the area since the sightings, both day and night. We're also putting up twice as many choppers every night.

 The NVA is moving an enormous amount of supplies by sampan right now. They usually don't risk this during the day, but as soon as darkness closes in, they throw off the camouflage and begin their deliveries. Our birds sank six just two nights ago and ten last night. The chopper crews are having a ball! I wish I were with them! I not only miss the adrenaline rush, but the danger as well. I'm torn between volunteering for the missions as a gunner or staying on the ground in relative safety since I'm so short.

This morning at 0620 hours we received several rockets and mortars. This is the first time we've been hit since May 20th. We've had a few small fire-fights, but they haven't amounted to much. We just level the big tubes on them and blow them away.

24 June, 1968
Camp Evans

A few days ago, I contracted some weird virus that has gotten worse, so I've been on quarters for the past couple days. I'm getting tired of lying around so plan to go back to work tomorrow.

As promised by the new C.O., we had a company party last night. What a surprise, and what a night to be sick! I really wasn't hungry so was only able to put away two steaks and five cokes.

After the party, Bennie and I were eating some very stale Spanish peanuts. They were so bad that we couldn't eat anymore, so decided to use them for marbles. Lying on the floor of our tent, we were shooting them into a hole in the floor when Top walked in. He wanted to know what we were doing on the floor, especially since I was sick. We tried to explain that we were exercising, but he didn't buy it. He also wondered what all the peanuts were doing on the floor. When we told him, he just walked away, shaking his head. There isn't a whole lot of opportunity for recreation.

1 July, 1968
Camp Evans

The Old Man is getting to be a real pain. He's now scheduling training classes, unnecessary formations and even inspections. This is far from the good ole' USA, but he is treating us like we're back in the States. It's getting old fast. Guys who have been here a lot longer than he has don't stomach that kind of nonsense for long. It makes me realize why guys extend for another tour in Vietnam. None of us want to go back to the unnecessary duties that take place in the States. That's one thing that's been great while here. We do our job and work together as a well-oiled machine. The work gets done efficiently and we haven't had to put up with ridiculous rules…until now.

I finally got my orders for SP5 today…only four months after the fact. The biggest plus is that I'll no longer have to be on KP rotation.

I've been real antsy staying on the ground. I've volunteered to gun for several crew chiefs, but every time we plan it, something comes up in Flight Ops and the XO won't let me go. Several of the guys won't take me with them since they think I'm too short to take those chances. I suppose they're right, but I sure miss the action.

CHAPTER 64

SLEEPLESS NIGHTS

10 July, 1968
Camp Evans

One month to go!

Today my claim finally came through for the camera that was ruined when I dove into the rice paddy in the first crash in January. I had claimed $221.00, but the government only approved $132.20. I guess they figure they're already over-paying me for my services in the Army. Of course I'm disgusted with the whole deal, but have decided to settle with them since I'm tired of fighting the system.

This Saturday, Bennie and I are planning to make the laundry run to Dong-Ha. It'll be a welcome break from the daily routine and it's only a thirty-mile drive. The C.O. had announced a full inspection of the tents, men and equipment that morning, so it wasn't out of our generosity that we volunteered for the laundry run. This colonel is really hung up on himself and seems to be trying to make an impression on us. He is doing just that, but it isn't a favorable one. We all tend to be a bunch of slobs at times (whenever we can get away with it), but with the kind of schedule we keep, there isn't much time to keep everything as neat and tidy as the Old Man would like.

A care package arrived yesterday from home with six pizza mixes. Pierre promised he'd do the baking for tonight's party… assuming a hot mission doesn't come up.

My new assignment came in today. Rather than Alaska, as hoped, I've been assigned to Ft. Sill, Oklahoma. Since orders haven't arrived yet, I don't have a clue what I'll be doing there. I don't even care. I just want out of this place!

Yesterday one of the new pilots was in the officer's outhouse...yes, even there we are segregated...and while sitting there in deep thought, three sniper rounds came zinging by. He hastily pulled up his britches and beat feet to Flight Ops to report the incident. When he came in, we knew he'd been shot at for the first time. He looked very pale with wildly dilated eyes. Secretly, we call him Snow White. In his defense, I recall the first time I was shot at. I'm sure the color went out of my face too.

23 July, 1968
Camp Evans

My orders came today. I'll be leaving here between August 9-11 and after four to five days leave, I'll be assigned to Ft. Sill as I was told. I'll be a Flight Operations Specialist for the Artillery Aviation Command. I'll definitely request additional leave, since the time they've allowed won't come anywhere near taking the edge off my nerves.

Last night, while on Guard Duty near the ammo dump, we had a little excitement. I was on bunker number three and had a report that the enemy had infiltrated through the perimeter wire and were suspected to be between bunkers number three, four, and five. It was blacker than Gook's teeth all night. Our bunker was the only one with a starlight scope, and though using it all night, we had detected no movement. My two partners and I decided that bunkers number four and five were "blowing pot" since they were reporting some very strange sightings and noises. At 2330 hours, machine guns opened up at a Gook that was supposedly crawling toward the ammo dump. The rounds went right over and in front of our bunker, so we, of course, kissed the dirt. I crawled behind my M60 and sent a stream of lead where the "ghost" was and then at the wire and tree line where three more infiltrators had been spotted.

At 0130 hours bunker number four called the CP claiming they had AK-47 fire coming from the ammo dump. Deciding to investigate, I told them to hold their fire so I could sneak up the hill and peak into the ammo dump to see if I could spot anyone. I spent an hour searching with the starlight scope and listening, but saw and heard nothing except the whispers from Bunker Four and Five. When I called in my report, the CP called out the "Big Eye" to check out the area. They couldn't find anything either. The sergeant in charge of the CP was obviously scared to death. Every time he spoke on the radio, you could detect the fear in his higher than normal voice. He had us hammer the perimeter every few minutes throughout the night with M79, M16, M60 and grenades.

Searching the perimeter the next morning, we couldn't find any bodies or blood.

27 July, 1968
Camp Evans

Unfortunately, Delta Company is just to our west and they obviously have a detail out doing a bar-b-q this morning. The only problem is, they aren't grilling steaks; they're emptying the outhouses and torching the excrement! Oh, to get back to the "world" and septic systems!

I've wanted to go on at least one more mission before leaving for home. But since I had two more buddies killed in a crash a few days ago, I'm having second thoughts.

One of the new warrant officers was out with another pilot in a deuce and a half this morning. When they came back through the gate, after having driven into the local village, they were trailing about fifty meters of concertina wire behind them. They apparently got too close to the wire someplace with the rear bumper and didn't realize it. It sure stirred up a lot of dust, not to mention roars of laughter. They should stick to flying helicopters...or...maybe not!

There have been a lot of sleepless nights lately. The enemy has stepped up their attacks. They not only hit us at night, but usually lob a few rounds in during the day, too. Coupled with that is my anxiety over going back home. The past several nights I have felt like I used to feel the night before deer season...too keyed up to sleep! Though I certainly look forward to getting home, I wonder if there will be any difficulty in adjusting to a quieter lifestyle without the constant threat of death hanging over my head. I still spend hours thinking about whether or not the adjustment will be difficult. I'm anxious to find out!

CHAPTER 65

MIXED EMOTIONS

9 August, 1968
Camp Evans

    Tonight Top walked into my tent and told me to say my goodbyes. There will be a chopper leaving for supplies at 0830 in the morning and I'm supposed to be on it. Finally, the first leg of my trip back to the world.

    Though I knew this day was coming, and looked forward to it with great expectations for the past three hundred and sixty three days, doubts and fears fill my mind. How can I say farewell to all these guys who I've grown so close to? I just can't do it tonight. I'll wait until morning and catch them on their way to their missions. Maybe that will be easier.

    Making small talk the rest of the evening to those who aren't out on night missions, the time passes quickly. I find myself refusing to get into any intimate conversations. An imaginary wall has been erected between me and those I've served with for so many months. I don't want to get close. Saying goodbye will be hard enough without getting any closer.

    At 2200 hours, the balance of those not already asleep hit the rack. Sleep comes easily for most, exhausted from today's missions. With the passing of each hour, I lie awake with my eyes closed hoping for sleep to interrupt the movie running rapidly through my mind. The entire past year is replayed in nightmarish scenes. I can't get rid of the vivid images of the missions. I see all the fearful faces, and those of the wounded and the dying. I see the ashen faces of all those KIAs who I accompanied on their last helicopter ride. I can hear the excited sounds and see the fearful looks on the faces of the grunts about to land in a hot LZ. Heard also are the haunting moans and screams of the wounded and the dying. I can see my gunner buddy trapped between the mast and his machine gun. I still see him vividly looking at Eddie and me while the flames engulf his body. I smell the burning flesh of my buddies...and of many men I do not know.

I can see the young boys in the bunker, praying for safety from the enemy shelling. The rapid transformation of these boys into mature men is incredible.

After listening to sporadic fire coming from the perimeter, sleep finally interrupts my daydreams that now transform into nightmares.

When the CQ arrives at 0500 hours, I hear him awakening the crews for the early morning mission. It's time for me to crawl out from under my poncho liner too. I need to talk to these buddies once more. After our daily routines of emptying the critters out of our boots and getting dressed, we head for the immersion tank to fill our steel pots with hot water for our G.I. shower and shave.

After a quick breakfast of toast, reconstituted eggs and sausage, Tang and coffee, the crews are ready for the morning briefing. I decide to tag along.

The first mission this morning will be fairly normal. A battalion will be inserted into a hot LZ for a search and destroy mission. The known enemy gun positions are pointed out on the area map, and call signs and freqs are given out. Just another day in the life of Charlie Company.

Following the briefing, the crews head for their tents to collect their gear for the flight. Feeling like a lost puppy, I decide to accompany my comrades to the flight line. As a group, we arrive at the first revetment where, typically, the crews separate and walk to their assigned ships. My voice breaks the relative silence as I make the announcement that I wish I could go along just once more, but I have a chopper to catch. They all knew I was leaving, but no one has mentioned it. They probably all had the same reasons for silence that I did. Gathering around in a tight group, we embrace each other and say our farewells. They talk about envying me. Oddly, I say the same thing. As frightening as it is, something inside me says I really want to stay. In the early morning light, tears can be seen running down the cheeks of many. It's obvious I'm crying, in fact, sobbing at this point.

How can I leave all these combat brothers?

One by one my heroes leave to prep their ships for takeoff. I stand and peer through the light early morning fog, watching them mounting the machine guns, loading the ammo and grenades and preflighting their aircraft. Soon, the pilots begin to filter up the hill from the company area. Greeting each one, we go through the same grueling ritual before they each head for their assigned ships.

Five minutes prior to the prescribed departure time of 0600 hours, Yellow One's beacon flashes its signal to the rest of the flight that the time has come to crank the turbines. With the starters engaged and the jet fuel introduced, the turbines light off, and the blades stir the fog. As the blades come up to full RPM, the eerie red glow of the instrument panels is reflected on the pilot's helmets and faces. I can tell which aircraft need to have their main rotor blades tracked and balanced by the gyrations of the pilots belted into their seats. They all vibrate, the nature of the beast, but some are worse than others.

In sequence, each aircraft comes to a hover, to do a final instrument check prior to takeoff. With beacons flashing, they back out of their respective revetments, and in a cloud of dust, depart to the northwest to pick up their payload of grunts at LZ Stallion.

The tears are flowing as I say an audible prayer, asking God to protect my buddies, not just today, but throughout the rest of their tours so they too can go home on schedule.

As planned, I have my gear ready and waiting at the maintenance chopper before the 0830 hours departure. Today, I am the only one leaving for home. I almost feel like a VIP with an entire helicopter to myself. The crew are guys I've flown with, but they're all fairly new and haven't been in Vietnam for very long. The flight to An Khe is at low level and uneventful, a time to reflect more on my tour, and what it will be like to finally go home. As the rice paddies, villages and jungle race by in a blur, I can't help but be concerned for all the guys I've left behind. I really want to go home, but a large part of me wants to stay to try to help protect those men I so respect. Besides, I don't want to miss out on anything. A very odd feeling.

I don't expect to ever again be associated with such a noble, unselfish, gallant, loyal, courageous, devoted, and brave team of men such as these…my comrades for the past year. What a privilege and honor has been mine. I love these guys! I'll never forget them. Our blood has been thoroughly bonded with those who have lived and those who have died. There have been no racial barriers. Black, red, yellow and white have melted all biases. We're all equal under God. Through adversity, we've become brothers in the grandest sense.

While out-processing at the Cav's headquarters, I'm introduced to a guy in new jungle fatigues, with newly issued boots. I'm told he's my replacement, and will be leaving for Camp Evans on the same ship I arrived on. He bombards me with questions. Though I tell him about some of the hazards he's about to face, I also tell him that he'll be working with some of the finest men in the country. Under his steel pot with its brand new helmet cover, I see an innocent boy…clean-shaven, with pale skin and soft eyes. That look will quickly change. In a few short months, his innocence will disappear and be exchanged for a serious, hardened look, one that shows he has looked into the face of death and has experienced uncomprehending fear. On those days when he has time to shave and looks into his mirror in the dim morning light, he'll see that metamorphosis. At first it will alarm him…after a few months, he'll be proud of the look of a rugged combat veteran. I wish him the best of luck in his new adventure. I pray he'll make it home alive and in one piece.

After turning in my weapon and field gear, the orderly tells me to throw my duffel bag in the jeep waiting outside the tent. A five minute ride along a bumpy, rutted road and I'm dropped off at a waiting C130. Joining another group of combat vets, we're ordered to board the aircraft for our flight to Cam Rahn Bay. When we're all strapped in our seats, the crew chief closes the clam shell rear door just before the aircraft taxis out to the runway. Holding the brakes, the engines reach full RPM while the pilots make the necessary pre-takeoff checks. Rolling down the runway, the takeoff distance is amazingly short, followed by a steep climb to five thousand feet. Charlie won't be able to reach us here…at least not with small automatic weapons.

The noise in the cabin makes conversation impossible. We're all silent with guarded excitement. Gazing at each other, we all look fairly grizzled, some more than others. As our eyes meet with those of other comrades that we don't know, we can usually manage a weak smile. This is unlike the trip to the field from Cam Rahn Bay a year ago. None of us were smiling. Our smiles are guarded...not yet ear-to-ear. None of us can believe we're actually going home, after the past year of horror. Many of us may be experiencing a case of reality shock.

In Cam Rahn Bay, we're greeted by an E-5 who explains that if we cooperate and have the patience we need to out-process, the freedom bird will leave this hellish place in a few hours.

The myriads of forms we have to fill out to get out of this war are wearily, but joyfully completed. We're all eager to see our loved ones at this point. The reality of going back to the "world" is glimmering on the horizon.

As promised, by mid-afternoon, we're bussed to the flight line and climb aboard a 707 for our trip back to the country for whom we fought. Surprisingly, there is very little talking while the cabin is readied for takeoff. All talking ceases when the jet engines begin to whine and it's very quiet while we taxi out. When the brakes are released at the end of the long runway, apprehension hits us all.

The aircraft breaks ground, and a weak cheer is heard. We're still unsure that this isn't just a dream...it feels very odd. In the short time it takes to climb to ten thousand feet, we're all staring out the windows, amazed that we've survived. Taking our last look at the country we defended, my emotions begin to run away with me. I have a feeling of attachment, even love for the Vietnamese...the other side of me reminds me to hate them for what they have done to so many close friends and, yes, even me.

Will these feelings ever pass?

In a short time, the Captain warmly welcomes us aboard, thanks us for our honorable service and tells us the flight stewardesses are anxious to serve us. The planeload of war-weary veterans erupts in cheers, laughter and...tears.

The airlines have chosen terrific stewardesses who serve us like kings for the entire long flight home. Fortunately for them, after a short time, the majority of us fall asleep. After a short stop in

Guam to refuel, we fly the final leg to Seattle, where we board a bus to Ft. Lewis, Washington. Additional paperwork, a hot shower, fine steak dinner, and the issuance of new uniforms prepares us for our trip home. As soon as we complete the requirements at the out-processing center at Ft. Lewis, we're free to go.

Taxis are standing by on the street. When four men climb in with me for the short drive to the airport, we find that the fee will be $20.00…each. We all think $100.00 for a ten-minute taxi ride is a bit steep. But, at this point, we'd pay any price to go see our loved ones.

Thankful to get a seat on a flight headed to Chicago in just a couple of hours, I take some time to try to calm down and convince myself that I really am "home" and safe. Nervously, I call my folks to tell them that I'm safely back in the States. They're elated, and now…so am I!

After shaking off the nervousness of the phone call home, it's time to give Cindi a call. Though the call is relatively short, we're definitely ready to see each other. It's been too long to be away from the girl I've been dating for four years.

When Cindi and her folks pick me up, the reunion is super. We travel from Chicago to their home in Madison, Wisconsin. It doesn't seem like it's been twelve months since we've seen each other. After spending most of the night catching up on news and getting reacquainted, we leave the following day for Oshkosh, Wisconsin to pick up a new MGB that I've ordered. Saying goodbye this time isn't nearly as difficult, as I know I'll see Cindi again in a week or so.

Firing up my new sports car for the drive north, the movie of my year in Vietnam plays through my mind again. I forcefully push it out of the way, reminding myself that I'm back home and can forget about all that happened in the past year. It is now history. When I replace these thoughts with those of home and my family, I find myself being apprehensive. Though I am anxious to see my mom and dad, my brother, four sisters and all my friends, I suddenly feel like it will be awkward. We've always been close, but now I feel like there will be a big gap. I know I've changed a lot. That I can see. What can't I see that they will? That thought worries me.

After a three and a half hour drive to Upper Michigan, I slowly pull into my parent's driveway. Before I can turn off the ignition, the den door bursts open and the family piles out. Mom gets the first big hug and we all break into tears. Stepping over to my father, he reaches out his hand to shake mine, and pulls me into a hug. He later tells me that he didn't know whether to shake my hand or give me a hug. His young son has turned into a grown man. When the rest of the family is greeted and cried over, we go in the house to a pile of food. For a while, the questions they all ask are general and easy to answer. After a few days the answers become more difficult. I know they can sense when the questions are too straight-forward, and kindly back off. I'm just not ready to talk about my whole tour. It will take time. Little did I realize, it would take years.

It's great to be home! I only wish all my buddies could say the same thing. May God bless each of them.

CHAPTER 66

HEALING TEARS

Fall 1999
Washington, D.C.

Several years after returning from Vietnam, I attended flight school as a civilian. I received my Flight Instructor ratings in both fixed and rotary wing aircraft.

For the past fifteen years I've been a corporate pilot flying everything from helicopters to business jets. Being fortunate enough to have seen most of this great country from the air, I flew one very special trip that has helped me immensely in the healing process concerning my experiences while in Vietnam.

In 1999 my co-pilot, Steve Lay, and I were asked to depart Bristol, Tennessee, early in the morning to fly several company folks to the Dulles International Airport in Washington, D.C., for a business meeting. Our return to Bristol wasn't scheduled until late in the afternoon, so we had some time to kill. We decided to walk to the nearby Marriott Hotel for a leisurely breakfast.

After being seated by the hostess, we noticed that none of the waiters and waitresses were Americans, but were from various parts of the world with their nationalities printed on their name badges.

While reading the menu, a beautiful lady walked toward us. Her coal black hair hung most of the way down her back, and her silk slacks and beautiful white silk blouse flowed as she gracefully approached us. Drawing nearer, I could see that her features were very much Vietnamese. Her slight build and high cheekbones increased my suspicions. Approaching our table with a pleasant smile, she greeted us warmly and asked if we would like a cup of coffee. Her name tag caused my heart to skip several beats. Amy Trinh was from...Vietnam.

I was almost in a trance. While Ms. Trinh went to get the coffee, all I could do was stare as she walked away. Steve knows me like a brother and broke the silence when he asked if I was planning on talking with her. I shallowly answered that I felt I had to. I had no idea what I was going to say, but a strong urge came over me to find out all I could about this lady. The adrenaline was pumping through my body. I was scared. I felt in a very strange way that I was again facing the enemy, but in a totally different aspect. I wanted to run out the door, yet something inside held me back and I knew I needed to explore whatever lay ahead this morning.

When our smiling waitress returned with the coffee pot and memorized our order, I asked where she had lived in Vietnam and how long she had been in America. She told me in very broken English that her home was in Saigon and that she had been in the US for five years. It was almost like a canned answer. I'm sure many other customers had asked her the same thing. Awkwardly, I told her that I was interested, because I had spent a year in her country in 1967 and 1968 while serving with the Army. Asking if she would have any time during or after her shift to sit down and chat, she assured me that as soon as she finished with her present customers, she would be happy to join us.

Now, what would I say when she returned? Somehow I felt I owed this lady an apology. For what...doing my job while serving in the military?

I had seen so much turmoil in her country, with thousands of refugees having to flee their villages. I had personally transported hundreds of them on my aircraft to a safer haven. Safer yes, but it wasn't home to them. Their village would be destroyed...their meager belongings ravaged by the communists. This was not due to atrocities by the American soldiers, but due to the fact that more often than not, these villages were infested with V.C. They either lived there or would come often during the night hours to recruit, and I don't mean voluntarily, threaten the villagers with their lives if they didn't cooperate fully with the enemy, and often torture men and children, while raping and torturing many of the women who were living in the village. Their innocent lives had been savagely

271

disrupted and often snuffed out after they had already experienced a lifetime of war in their own back yards. Did these South Vietnamese people realize that we were there to help them…to defend them from Communism? Americans had often herded villagers from place to place at gunpoint. We shouldn't be blamed for that. It was most often impossible to really know who the enemy was. They usually dressed and looked alike. There were no front lines in this war. These unfortunate people were frightened beyond belief and had no idea what their future would hold. Their families had been torn apart with their sons and husbands, and often their daughters, off fighting the war somewhere…or had they been killed? They had every reason to hate the Americans who were part of the cause for their disrupted lives. Even though we were in their country for a just cause, did they understand that?

All of these flashbacks played through my mind like a violent movie while this seemingly innocent waitress was serving surrounding customers. Where would I begin…and where would it end? I was apprehensively ready to get on with it.

Ten minutes seemed like hours when Ms. Trinh returned with, not only our breakfast, but two heaping plates of fruit and pastries…on the house. She was obviously ready to talk.

As Amy sat down beside me, with Steve looking on from across the table, I almost felt like I was in a dream. So many of my buddies had been killed or savagely wounded by the Vietnamese people. Admittedly, I often felt an extreme hatred for the Vietnamese. I had never imagined that I would someday sit down and carry on a conversation with a native Vietnamese!

Immediately I was asked where I had been stationed, if I had ever been to Saigon, and what my job had been while in South Vietnam. Most of these questions were easy, until I told her that I had been a crew chief…and door gunner on a helicopter. Surely she knew what the door gunner part meant. I had quite possibly killed many of her countrymen while not knowing whether or not they were enemy soldiers.

Feeling very uncomfortable talking about what I had done while stationed in her country, I asked about her life while growing up during the war. When I opened that door, she took Steve and me on a horrendous tour of memories.

Amy Trinh was born and raised in downtown Saigon. Her life, and that of her parents and older brother Robert, was torn apart by their country being at war for years. Her father fought for the South Vietnamese army for several years before being killed by the Communists when she was eleven years old.

Robert Trinh attended law school and became an attorney. During his stint with a law firm in his hometown, he had been involved in doing some work for the American government. At that time he thought the United States would conquer the communists in South Vietnam.

When the Trinh family was told that the Americans were preparing to depart Vietnam, they were doubly concerned for their future because they knew the Communists were not far away and would soon take total control of the city of Saigon.

Very soon after the American pullout, Saigon was overrun with Communist troops. Many documents left behind in the hasty American withdrawal contained sensitive material and named many of those involved as American sympathizers. One of those names was Robert Trinh.

One of the first tasks of the North Vietnamese troops was to round up all dissidents who were to be put on trial for war crimes. Not long after Saigon was taken, Robert Trinh was arrested for "war crimes" and removed from his home at gunpoint while his family protested loudly. He was taken to a makeshift prison. Amy and her mother were warned that they might very well be suspects too, and advised not to go anywhere.

Having lived for years under the threat of communism, Amy's mother told her that she was concerned for their safety and they couldn't take a chance on staying in their meager home. They must leave…that very night.

Gathering up what necessary survival supplies they knew they could easily carry, Amy and her mother sneaked out the door with their satchels well after darkness had fallen. They moved quickly through the back alleys on the edge of Saigon, hoping to avoid being seen by the NVA. When they reached the edge of the jungle, they went in a little ways to hide out and rest through the night.

At daybreak, Mrs. Trinh and her daughter fled deeper into the jungle with great fear in an attempt to evade their adversary.

Arriving at a small stream, they decided this would be where they would make their home as long as necessary. They busied themselves hacking away at the jungle foliage to build a makeshift shelter, gathered firewood and water, and settled in for many months. They lived totally off the land, eating mostly fruit, roots, fish and insects. During their stay in the jungle, Mrs. Trinh would sneak periodically into Saigon to talk with friends about the possibility of returning to their home.

The political situation was in turmoil for a long while. But after nearly two years of surviving in the jungle, Amy and her mother moved cautiously back to town. When they returned to their home, they found it had been burned to the ground. Seeking shelter, they were taken in by long-time friends.

They learned that Robert was still being held and would likely be executed by the Communists before long. It was at this time that Mrs. Trinh decided that she and her daughter needed to flee the country. Spending many days seeking a way to escape, she finally made connections with some friends who were planning to escape in their sampan, hoping they might be picked up by a friendly ship offshore.

As darkness fell on the following night, the four boarded the sampan and slowly paddled downstream on the Saigon River. Upon reaching the South China Sea, they quickened their pace. Fortunately, the seas were calm. Paddling all night, they were spotted by a freighter, and after being thoroughly searched, were reluctantly allowed to board.

They told the Captain their plight and he agreed to get them to America, the ship's ultimate destination.

Arriving in the US, Mrs. Trinh and her fourteen year-old daughter sought odd jobs and were soon taken in by an American lady. Eventually, they were granted citizenship and through many circumstances wound up in Washington, D.C. Mrs. Trinh got a job cleaning houses while Amy applied at the Marriott where she was hired. She is very proud of being granted citizenship in this great country of ours.

Amy told me of many more hardships that her family had to endure. Spending almost an hour talking with my buddy and I, it was time for her to go back to work.

All these years I had felt extreme guilt over having gone to war in Vietnam. I was proud of having served my country and knew I had done my job well, but I was carrying a heavy load of pain over the way the war was waged. The fact that so many South Vietnamese were not only displaced from their homes, but often killed and maimed by American soldiers stuck in my craw. Though a victim of circumstances beyond my control, I was ashamedly a part of that.

At the same time, ever since my first buddy had been killed with many to follow during my tour, I felt a deep hatred toward the Vietnamese people in general. I guess I lumped them all together, North and South alike. With the exception of the NVA who often wore uniforms, they all dressed and looked alike and it was impossible to tell them apart.

After hearing Amy tell of knowing nothing but war all her life, I saw that she had reason to dislike Americans too, for pulling out of her country and leaving the scraps to the Communist jackals, if nothing else.

Looking into Amy's eyes, I felt a surge of excitement. I was thankful that she had not only escaped Communism, but that she had shared her story with us.

After a brief moment of hesitation, a flood of emotion came over me, and I wept while I told her how sorry I was that we had created so many problems in her homeland. I explained that we Americans were there in an attempt to stop Communism in its tracks, but admittedly had created a real mess. My sorrow over her family's turmoil was overwhelming.

While emotions were difficult to suppress for both of us, we hugged...and cried healing tears together. I felt I had finally "come home" and had rid myself of a lot of bad blood. Better than that, I believe this innocent lady was finally "home" too.

CHAPTER 67

REUNION

May 2001
The Vietnam Veterans Memorial Wall
Washington, DC

On Memorial Day of 2001, the unit that I served with had a reunion. I was reluctant to attend after being away from those formerly close buddies for so many years...fearing the unknown. I was afraid of any more sadness relating to the war, yet felt compelled to go. Fellow warriors met at the Vietnam Wall in Washington, D.C., for a time of reflection. Emotions ran high while we hugged and cried as each man arrived. Watching "Rolling Thunder" and seeing all the support for the Vets was astounding, but when we walked with our arms over each others shoulders along the Wall, our hearts were burdened while we tearfully read the names of our many fallen brothers with whom we had fought all too many bloody battles. For those who had not been to the wall previously, it helped heal the wounds that have been festering all these years. I highly recommend this trip to any Vet or loved one...you will never be the same.

At the reunion, I was re-introduced to guys I hadn't seen or heard from in over thirty years. After only a few minutes, we felt the old closeness return. The bond of comrades had not weakened.

One of my buddies, Dale Erickson was there. I hadn't seen him since he was wounded during TET and evacuated to Japan. Spending many months in hospitals both there and in the States, he was told he would never walk again due to his severe leg and back injuries received when a mortar round landed next to him shortly after being shot down. The docs had made the decision to amputate one leg. That tough old Swede told them to leave the leg; "I'll need it to walk out of your hospital." After a great deal of therapy, Dale was walking at the reunion! Sadly, this warrior and very close friend was overtaken by cancer two years before this book was published. I owe him my life.

PTSD has been a major factor in the lives of most of us who have experienced combat. Its something we have to deal with every day. Some of the symptoms are more obvious than others. Talking with comrades helped many of us better understand through war stories that were retold. By confirming some of the things we remembered from so many years ago, it helped some of us realize that our imaginations had not run amuck. These horrid events or similar ones had actually taken place.

Though we were a young and naive bunch of kids when shipped off to war, that experience changed us all. As for me, I wouldn't take a million dollars for it. It has made me who I am.

For those Vets still fighting and beating yourselves up over what you did or did not do during that ugly war, I strongly recommend you seek help. For those of you who feel guilty over surviving when many of your best friends were killed, and those who may struggle daily with your thoughts and memories, start at one of the Vet Centers where free counseling is available. These counselors understand your problems and can help you as you cope with yourself and others.

Twelve years ago, after an appointment at the VA Center, I swore I would never go there again. However, the attitudes over Vets have changed dramatically and the care is great! Check it out, and get enrolled in a class for PTSD. You will be amongst friends...lots of them. With an open mind, you will begin to better understand yourself, and others.

EPILOGUE

Throughout my life, I've found it easy to make friends, but never like while I was in Vietnam. All the men I met there are very special to me and I feel a very close and special bond with them.

I didn't know the names of those who were passengers on my helicopter when I helped take them into battle, re-supplied, and picked them up again to take them to a safer area, on another assault, or to a field hospital. In all too many cases, our crew took them on their final helicopter flight out of the bush and on the first leg of their trip back to their mourning loved ones. Without knowing their names, I can still see the look on each of their faces, whether they were traveling to the rear, back into battle, to seek additional medical help, or headed to graves registration. Each man had a very distant look in his eyes.

Our missions of fire were underlined with an indescribable rush of adrenaline. Our alertness was always at its peak during those flights when we had to be performing at max capacity, keeping our wits about us while we flew into battle with our machine guns blazing. Our rounds joined those of the supporting gunships and often, jet or prop driven fighters and bombers. Because these flights were so brazenly accomplished, they are ingrained on my mind to the point that I think of many of those missions on a daily basis, as if they happened this morning.

Our missions of mercy, they too added excitement to our lives. The flights where we snatched men from the rice paddies and depths of the mountainous jungle, often surrounded and under enemy fire, are **unforgettable**! These missions were another shot at cheating death.

As flight crews, we never knew what we might see on the next lift. But we knew that these missions were critical to saving men's lives. Usually the medics and buddies in the field had patched these guys up and were able to stop the majority of the bleeding. We often retrieved wounded who had just been hit by enemy fire in the past couple of minutes. In many of these cases, they had not received medical attention as the rest of their unit was busy keeping the enemy at bay while our crews were busy loading the wounded on board. There are no words to describe the peak of adrenaline! It far exceeded "peak."

There were times when the wounds were still smoking from white phosphorous, or the steam might be rising from their still warm bodies. If there wasn't time to care for these soldiers on the ground, the task fell into the hands of the crew chief and gunner after the aircraft cleared the danger area. Too often the bleeding couldn't be stopped, with wounds too large for our limited supply of medical supplies. Though we were able to fly these soldiers to field hospitals for additional help, many died while aboard our ships. The field hospitals were very efficient and were able to send men back into battle, while more men went home for additional surgery. A lot of them left pieces of their bodies back in the jungle. They all left their blood.

The final missions of mercy were flown when the intensity of the battles became less intense or were complete. The unfortunate soldiers who were our passengers on these flights, were in no rush...their missions were complete. These brave, often young warriors gave everything in an attempt to save others' lives while trying to save their own. They returned home silently. Though I didn't know any of them, I felt there was a special relationship between us. That bond still tugs at my soul. We shared both life and death. The memories of them will be with us forever. Their names are written on the Wall.

Recalling our flights into various battlefields, I can still see the fear in the faces of the grunts, and the tears often being shed over the current battle, which might snuff their lives out in a split second. I can see, hear, and smell the gunpowder and JP4 from the blazing gunships, the fighter jets screaming by on their strafing, bombing, and napalm attacks, smoke-filled villages, fearful, tearful, and often screaming refugees, the bound P.O.W.s loaded on our chopper. I smell the overwhelming stench of enemy bodies laying on the battlefield, who have yet to be buried, due to the intensity of the battles.

I can easily remember how dry my throat was from fear every time I felt the icy touch of death. Although I didn't want to admit that fear at the time, I unashamedly admit it now, in all its vivid and unforgotten reality.

My survivor guilt, nightmares, and flashbacks have helped me to write more vividly. However, reliving my entire year in Vietnam over the past several years while writing this has been emotionally draining. Yet, I am grateful to God for the fact that He has also healed my emotions over my experience to a large degree.

After re-reading the letters I sent home and the copies that my parents saved of those sent to me by my family, I now better appreciate my insecurities and fears. I have also wept again over how difficult my tour was on my family, and on Cindi, who would soon be my wife.

My twelve month tour was both the longest and shortest year of my life. I spent every day and night wondering if I would survive.

Though I told my family a lot of what happened in Vietnam during my tour, it has taken me over forty years to tell it all in this book. Again, it is finally OK to let it all out. I held it in for years. Though I generally don't bring the subject up in normal conversation, I am willing to talk about it if questioned. I have found that after I discuss it with others who are interested, it is a great relief of pent-up emotions. Often those of us who have been in combat keep it all in. I don't believe that's healthy. For those of you who have been there, even if you don't feel able to discuss your experiences with your family or friends, try writing it down. You might find that is a good way to get it out of your system. You've been home a long time now and even though the horrors may still be forefront, look for a constructive way to get it out in the open. You will be glad you did.

Military discipline changes a person and, in my opinion, trained us to hate the enemy. This hate I believe saved many of our men's lives. I feel it saved mine on more than one occasion. Even while fighting against the enemy, in the midst of my hate, I was bewildered. The South Vietnamese looked so innocent and scared. I think they were more scared than I was. That's some kind of scared! I often had thoughts during my tour, and even more now that I'm back in civilian life, that the country we were attempting to save from Communism was in many ways destroyed by us. Granted, we were trying to root out the enemy, but look at what we did to that country. Vietnamese were torn from their roots. Many lost their homes and were transferred to refugee camps with thousands of others. Looking back, I have the utmost respect for the enemy. Whether they were VC, NVA, men, women or children, they were fantastic and determined warriors. Even though I called them Gooks, I had great compassion for them. Some of them had killed my buddies and tried to kill me, but they were human, just like me, with families.

They fought a guerrilla war that was very difficult for the Americans to fight. Sure, we killed a lot of them by using massive firepower, but the next day, those who had not been killed were back at it again. They were tenacious, dedicated, and proud. They were fighting for their lives just like we were, but under much harsher and more primitive conditions. Even though they fought on their turf, they didn't have the privilege of being re-supplied or evacuated by air. Everything they had at their disposal was brought in from North Vietnam. A large portion of their supplies were brought down the Ho Chi Minh Trail via trucks. But the dispersement of war supplies and food into South Vietnam was done on foot, by bicycle, sampan, water buffalo, elephant, or by whatever means they could devise.

Please understand, I am certainly not supporting Communism here. I am merely giving credit to the brave warriors with whom we clashed day and night.

I was angered by our government, and have been for years, over how they handled the war. Had the truth been told in America, I am confident that the war could have ended much more quickly with fewer lives lost. We cannot fight a war on a political front...it must be fought in the wretched mud of the rice paddies, the mountainous triple canopy jungles, and from the foggy skies in the country where the fight began. It must be meticulously planned and carried out by those with boots on the ground, rather than by those political fat cats sitting in their leather chairs, smoking those big cigars who don't know squat about what is really going on half a world away, and often don't seem to care! Were enemy body counts inflated to look as though we were winning what was a losing battle from the onset? This looked great to the American public back home. Those at home were fed untruths for years. Though they don't need to know classified information, taxpayers were kept in the dark like mushrooms and fed a lot of buffalo chips by our government.

Unfortunately, this is still true of our government! **When will we Americans wake up and demand accountability from those we elect, rather than let them run rampant like a bunch of spoiled teenagers? Remember: we pay their salaries!**

When we pulled out of Vietnam in 1975, I was furious! I still am. What did we accomplish? What about all that American and Allied blood we left over there, and the fifty eight thousand plus men and women who gave their lives? What about the thousands more who were wounded physically and mentally? I am extremely saddened for those who lost loved ones, and ask the same questions.

The US Military did not lose the war on the battlefield. We began losing the war in the press and on the nightly news. The press effectively convinced the American people that we lost the war. Excuse me...but they are dead wrong. We won almost every battle with very few exceptions. Our government and press would have you believe otherwise. Talk to any Vet who was in the thick of the battle. Very likely, he will tell you the same thing.

According to the Encyclopedia of the Vietnam War, edited by Spencer Tucker, the following are facts: The highest per capita ratio of casualties of any contingent of US. Combat troops in Vietnam were the army aircrews. American helicopters flew 36,000,000 hours. Lost to hostile action were 2,086, with 2,566 lost to non-hostile causes. Of the 8 generals killed in this conflict, 5 were killed while flying in helicopters. The attrition rate of aircrews was very high.

When I think of our heroic P.O.W.s, my hat is off to them! Once captured, they fought an entirely different battle, facing starvation, severe physical and mental torture, and the daily question as to whether or not they could hang on for another day, month, year or longer. There are still many warriors unaccounted for with families and loved ones still wondering what their status could possibly be. Some of course died in captivity, the others...?

AFTERWORD

Finally, to the families and loved ones of those killed in action...though I know it's not the same, my heart is as broken as yours. I watched many of these soldiers die, and I can tell you from first-hand experience that they died bravely. They are my heroes. You also are my heroes. I feel badly for all you had to endure while your loved one was off fighting a nasty war. Many of those men and women believed in what they were doing. Many did not. But they all fought valiantly for the freedoms that we enjoy daily.

To all the men and women whose names are on the wall, to those wounded physically and/or emotionally, to you wives, husbands, mothers, fathers, brothers, sisters, children, grandparents and friends...

I SALUTE YOU!

ABOUT THE AUTHOR

William "Bill" Peterson was raised in Michigan's Upper Peninsula where he learned how to hunt and was taught by his father to make every shot count. Little did he know at the time that this training would be extremely useful within just a few short years.

His father, Gene, was a B-17 pilot and spoke often of his hitch in the US Air Corp during WWII. He instilled in his family a great sense of patriotism. At the age of eighteen, Bill not only enlisted and signed up to be a Huey helicopter crew chief, but when asked in Basic Training for his first and second choice of assignment, he said, "Vietnam." The sergeant asking the question was very surprised, but said that would be guaranteed. After watching helicopters in action on the nightly news, he wanted a part of it.

After 36 Air Medals (2 with Valor), 3 Purple Hearts, Vietnamese Cross of Galantry, Presidential Unit Citation and numerous other awards, he got more than he had hoped for.

Missions of Fire and Mercy is the story of his unit in Vietnam, C/227th Assault Helicopter Battalion, 1st Air Cavalry. His unit was responsible for supporting our US Army, Special Forces, ARVN, Korean ROK troops, Australian and other Allied troops. Charlie Company flew a potpourri of missions including, but not limited to: combat assault and recovery, support for troops in every way (including ammo, food, water supply, convoy protection, medivac missions, and aerial surveillance of battlegrounds, before, during and after the fight), BDA consisting of surveying what was left after B52 strikes, and counting enemy bodies. These horrific incidents took place between An Khe, the Central Highlands, Camp Evans in I Corp, the Ashau Valley and Laos.

The goal of this story is to reach out to families and loved ones who never understood why their *warrior* has been so quiet about Vietnam. Hopefully, this will help you to have a better understanding of those men and women, and what they went through. The author also hopes this will bring healing to those of you who served in combat and will help you realize that your memories are not faulty. These things did happen, and you can and should be proud to have served so honorably and bravely.

The author is currently a home inspector and resides in Piney Flats, TN, with his wonderful wife, Cindi.

Bill is a member of The National Purple Heart Hall of Fame.

Made in the USA
Middletown, DE
11 November 2018